Practical Drug Enforcement

Second Edition

CRC SERIES IN
PRACTICAL ASPECTS OF CRIMINAL AND FORENSIC INVESTIGATIONS

VERNON J. GEBERTH, BBA, MPS, FBINA *Series Editor*

Practical Homicide Investigation: Tactics, Procedures, and Forensic Techniques, Third Edition
Vernon J. Geberth

The Counterterrorism Handbook: Tactics, Procedures, and Techniques, Second Edition
Frank Bolz, Jr., Kenneth J. Dudonis, and David P. Schulz

Forensic Pathology, Second Edition
Dominick J. Di Maio and Vincent J. M. Di Maio

Interpretation of Bloodstain Evidence at Crime Scenes, Second Edition
William G. Eckert and Stuart H. James

Tire Imprint Evidence
Peter McDonald

Practical Drug Enforcement, Second Edition
Michael D. Lyman

Practical Aspects of Rape Investigation: A Multidisciplinary Approach, Third Edition
Robert R. Hazelwood and Ann Wolbert Burgess

The Sexual Exploitation of Children: A Practical Guide to Assessment, Investigation, and Intervention, Second Edition
Seth L. Goldstein

Gunshot Wounds: Practical Aspects of Firearms, Ballistics, and Forensic Techniques, Second Edition
Vincent J. M. Di Maio

Friction Ridge Skin: Comparison and Identification of Fingerprints
James F. Cowger

Footwear Impression Evidence, Second Edition
William J. Bodziak

Principles of Kinesic Interview and Interrogation
Stan Walters

Practical Fire and Arson Investigation, Second Edition
David R. Redsicker and John J. O'Connor

The Practical Methodology of Forensic Photography, Second Edition
David R. Redsicker

Practical Aspects of Interview and Interrogation, Second Edition
David E. Zulawski and Douglas E. Wicklander

Investigating Computer Crime
Franklin Clark and Ken Diliberto

Practical Homicide Investigation Checklist and Field Guide
Vernon J. Geberth

Bloodstain Pattern Analysis: With an Introduction to Crime Scene Reconstruction, Second Edition
Tom Bevel and Ross M. Gardner

Practical Aspects of Munchausen by Proxy and Munchausen Syndrome Investigation
Kathryn Artingstall

Quantitative-Qualitative Friction Ridge Analysis: An Introduction to Basic and Advanced Ridgeology
David R. Ashbaugh

Practical Drug Enforcement

Second Edition

Michael D. Lyman

CRC PRESS

Boca Raton London New York Washington, D.C.

Library of Congress Cataloging-in-Publication Data

Lyman, Michael D.
Practical drug enforcement / Michael D. Lyman.—2nd ed.
p. cm.— (CRC series in practical aspects of criminal and forensic investigations)
Includes bibliographical references and index.
ISBN 0-8493-0920-4 (alk. paper)
1. Drug traffic—Investigation—United States. 2. Criminal investigation—United States.
3. Undercover operations—United States. 4. Narcotic enforcement agents—United States.
I. Title. II. Series.

HV8079.N3 L96 2001
363.45′0973—dc22 2001037435

Direct all inquiries to CRC Press LLC, 2000 N.W. Corporate Blvd., Boca Raton, Florida 33431.

Visit the CRC Press Web site at www.crcpress.com

International Standard Book Number 0-8493-0920-4
Library of Congress Card Number 2001037435
Printed in the United States of America 1 2 3 4 5 6 7 8 9 0
Printed on acid-free paper

Series Editor's Note

This textbook is part of the CRC Series entitled "Practical Aspects of Criminal and Forensic Investigation." This series was created by Vernon J. Geberth, a retired New York City Police Department Lieutenant Commander, who is an author, educator, and consultant to homicide and forensic investigations.

This series has been designed by authors who are nationally recognized experts in their respective fields to provide contemporary, comprehensive, and pragmatic information to the practitioner involved in criminal and forensic investigations.

Foreword

For several decades the public has been inundated with statistics and horror stories about the war against drugs and drug abuse. Drugs saturate all levels of society, and stories involving drugs and drug busts constantly prevail in both electronic and print media. No one group seems to be immune from the perils of abuse.

It is well known that drug trafficking is a lucrative criminal activity. It is worth an estimated $30 billion annually when costs such as law enforcement, drug treatment, prevention, corrections, drug-related crime, loss of productivity on the job, and accidents are considered. Illicit drug consumption is now so widespread that it touches most families, neighborhoods, businesses, and many other corners of our society. Crimes committed by professional criminals also reflect the severity of the problem. For instance, in 1999 the National Institute of Justice revealed that two out of three inmates serving time in state correctional institutions admitted that they were under the influence of drugs when they committed the crimes for which they were later convicted.

Adding to the frustration is the fact that drug-related homicides continue to be a problem in our major cities. Police officers across the country are targeted for murder every year by drug dealers who are becoming increasingly reluctant to use deadly weapons. Many drug dealers are superbly organized and have hundreds of thousands of dollars at their disposal for sophisticated equipment, high-priced attorneys, bribes for corrupt judges and cops, and bail to keep them out of prison and on the streets.

The problem is exacerbated by the fact that entry into the market is relatively easy, thereby making the drug trade an equal opportunity employer. Members of the law enforcement community are constantly faced with the challenge of change within their own arena. Perennial problems such as rising officer attrition rates, ongoing training needs, and inadequate funding for drug enforcement projects and equipment still haunt most concerned government agencies. Other problems perpetuated by influences outside the law enforcement area are the overabundance of drug cases burdening our state and federal court systems and the placement of convicted offenders within an already grossly overcrowded penal system.

Despite this, however, federal and local governments have realized that their first responsibility is the apprehension and prosecution of those responsible for the manufacturing and distribution of illicit substances. Drug enforcement policy continues to be shaped by well-established beliefs. First is that the control of those drugs that pose the greatest danger to the public should receive the most attention from drug enforcement personnel. Second is the belief that drug abuse by even casual users contributes to the demand for drugs and constitutes a significant role in the criminal drug scene. Therefore, in an effort to break the supply and demand cycle, drug enforcement officers must eliminate the demand for drugs by the apprehension and prosecution of all known drug offenders, and maintain concurrent initiatives against sources of supply on both a local and national level.

Practical Drug Enforcement, Second Edition is a resource text that discusses drug crime investigative techniques. The drug enforcement initiative is only one segment of the overall solution, which also includes programs aimed at public education, prevention, and treatment. Although it is unlikely that drug enforcement efforts alone will ever abolish the existing drug abuse and trafficking problem in the United States, it is clear that ongoing knowledge of sound drug enforcement practices is essential.

Preface

Police work deals with human nature, which is always changing and, therefore, constantly poses new challenges for the law enforcement officer. The skills learned in basic police training are just that — basic. Officers must seek continual training to keep up with their criminal counterparts.

The investigation of crimes such as burglary, homicide, and rape has undergone changes over the years, but not to the extent that drug enforcement has. Enforcing drug violations is proactive and can require the use of undercover operatives, which makes it unique and casts this mode of investigation into a class of its own. Drug enforcement therefore requires extensive and ongoing training.

When I first began my 11-year career in drug enforcement, all I had to base my decision on was the portrayal of undercover police agents in the movies and on television. The realization came quickly that the actual duties of a drug enforcement agent are much different from those portrayed by Hollywood and the entertainment industry.

For me, the initial learning process was somewhat slow, because the only actual investigative training I received was by accompanying more experienced agents on drug buys, surveillances, and raids. Investigative skills were learned through trial and error. In those early days many drug-buy techniques were untried and untested, and often they were attempted by drug agents working alone.

One does not have to be a narcotics agent to see the impact of drug use and trafficking on society. Law enforcement officers working in all aspects of police work witness, on a daily basis, an array of crimes directly associated with the illicit use of dangerous drugs. Many lose their lives. A basic understanding is therefore necessary in combatting the drug problem, which involves all law enforcement officers in all jurisdictions.

It has been no easy task preparing a text that would be of wide interest to law enforcement officers operating in many different jurisdictions. For example, while researching this book, I spoke with a narcotics agent in Florida who advised me that the only cocaine cases his agency would authorize him to work on were those involving quantities of 10 kilograms or more. I later spoke with a narcotics agent in Kansas who said that a one-ounce cocaine dealer in his jurisdiction is considered a significant violator.

No text can give every investigator all the answers regarding problems encountered in drug enforcement. Any text addressing this subject, however, should offer law enforcement officers from all jurisdictions a suitable guide for the general management of drug investigations and of drug enforcement units as a whole. *Practical Drug Enforcement, Second Edition* is such a text. It addresses contemporary aspects of covert criminal investigation and provides the reader with a look at the management of the drug enforcement unit itself. The goal of the text is to promote thought toward different methods of detecting and capturing drug traffickers while identifying those methods commonly used to avoid detection. This text is offered as a guide to law enforcement officers in their criminal investigations.

The Author

Michael D. Lyman is an Associate Professor of Criminal Justice at Columbia College in Columbia, Missouri. Formerly employed as a generalist police trainer, Mr. Lyman accumulated 11 years of practical experience as a narcotics agent with both the Kansas Bureau of Investigation and the Oklahoma Bureau of Narcotics and Dangerous Drugs Control. In his duties as drug enforcement agent, Mr. Lyman was personally involved in the investigation of hundreds of illicit drug cases. He served as an undercover agent and worked in the intelligence and air smuggling units as well as serving as the public information officer for the Oklahoma Bureau of Narcotics and Dangerous Drugs Control.

Mr. Lyman's academic background includes a Bachelor of Science degree and a Master of Science degree from Wichita State University, as well as a Ph.D. in higher and adult education from the University of Missouri. He has authored seven textbooks in the area of drug enforcement, organized crime, and criminal investigation and policing.

Acknowledgment

It would be impossible to attempt a project of this nature without the collective expertise of many qualified and dedicated law enforcement professionals. This text is therefore a tribute to all who helped in its preparation, and proper recognition is in order for the following law enforcement agencies who provided assistance in its final preparation: the U.S. Drug Enforcement Administration, the U.S. Marshal Service, the Federal Bureau of Investigation; the U.S. Bureau of Alcohol, Tobacco and Firearms, the U.S. Customs Service, the National Institute of Drug Abuse, the International Narcotic Enforcement Officers Association, the National Institute of Justice, the Bureau of Justice Assistance, the Oklahoma Bureau of Narcotics and Dangerous Drugs Control, the Arkansas State Police, the Kansas Bureau of Investigation, the Missouri Bureau of Narcotics and Dangerous Drugs, the Missouri Highway Patrol, the Missouri Task Force on the Abuse, Misuse and Diversion of Prescription Drugs, the Florida Department of Law Enforcement, the Kansas City, Missouri, Police Department, the Columbia, Missouri, Police Department, the Oklahoma City Police Department, the New York City Police Department, the Dallas Police Department, the Oklahoma County District Attorney's Office, and the LaClede County Sheriff's Department (Lebanon, Missouri).

Those individuals who specifically lent a hand in the production of this text are gratefully acknowledged:

Special Agent Dave True of the U.S. Bureau of Alcohol, Tobacco and Firearms; Former Director Tom Heggy and former Senior Agent Dave Dagg of the Oklahoma Bureau of Narcotics and Dangerous Drugs Control; Ernest L. Sjoblom, Former Director of the Missouri Bureau of Narcotics and Dangerous Drugs; Sergeant Rod Combs of the the Arkansas State Police; Bureau Chief Lewis Wilson and Special Agent Ralph Garcia of the Florida Department of Law Enforcement; Assistant District Attorney Richard Wintory of the Oklahoma County District Attorney's Office; Joe Moseley, former Prosecutor of the Boone County, Missouri, Prosecuting Attorney's Office; Detective Mike Himmel of the Columbia, Missouri, Police Department; Chris Egbert of the State of Missouri Peace Officer's Standards and Training, and Rita Walther for her artwork and illustrations. I would also like to extend a special thanks to Series Editor Vernon Geberth for his support and assistance in making this text a part of the CRC Series in Practical Aspects of Criminal and Forensic Investigations.

Table of Contents

Introduction: America's Drug-Abuse Profile

While the drug enforcement agent may not need to know all of the subtleties of the nation's drug problem, having a general background will give investigators a feel for why society asks them to do what they do. This introduction will give you a survey of the nation's drug-abuse profile and then move on to other related topics of interest to the investigator, which include an overview of criminal organizations and the problem of money laundering. These topics are all interrelated and in one way or another are encountered by drug enforcement personnel in the course of their duties.

This introduction addresses the extent to which Americans are using drugs. The National Household Survey on Drug Abuse, an annual survey conducted by the Substance Abuse and Mental Health Services Administration, estimates the prevalence of illicit drug use in the United States and monitors the trends over time. It is based on a representative sample of 25,500 persons from the U.S. population aged 12 and older. The following are some important statistics from this study, published in 2000:

- An estimated 14.8 million Americans were current users of illicit drugs in 1999, meaning they used an illicit drug at least once during the 30 days prior to being interviewed. By comparison, the number of current illicit drug users was at its highest level in 1979, when the estimate was 25.4 million.
- More than 1 in 10 (10.9%) youths aged 12 to 17 were current users of illicit drugs in 1999. The rate was highest in 1979 (16.3%), declined to 5.3% in 1992, then increased to 10.9% in 1995. The percentage of youth reporting current use of illicit drugs has fluctuated since 1995 (9% in 1996 and 11.4% in 1997).
- The survey found that 17.1% of young adults aged 18 to 25 were current users of illicit drugs in 1999. This rate has been gradually rising, from 13.3% in 1994.

- In 1999, an estimated 208,000 Americans were current users of heroin, more than tripling the number in 1993 (68,000). The average age of heroin users is rapidly dropping. In 1998, the typical heroin user was 21.3 years old the first time he/she tried the drug, down from 25 years old in 1990.
- There were an estimated 991,000 new inhalant users in 1998. This number is up 154% from 1990, when it was 390,000. Of first-time inhalant users in 1998, 62% were between the ages of 12 and 17.

Numerous states have experienced increases in drug-related deaths. Heroin-related deaths, in particular, are rising as a result of the increasing purity and decreasing price of that drug. In New Mexico, the Office of the Medical Investigator reported that drug-related deaths increased by nearly 100% over the past 9 years. Viewed in 3-year increments, deaths rose from 205 during 1989–1991, to 317 during 1992–1994, to 401 during 1995–1997. In Florida, the Medical Examiner's Commission reported that heroin-related deaths skyrocketed from 28 in 1993 to 206 in 1998, an increase of more than 600%. In California, the Department of Alcohol and Drug Programs reported an increase in drug-related deaths for the 2-year period 1996–1997 (5407 deaths) compared to the previous period, 1994–1995 (5335 deaths).

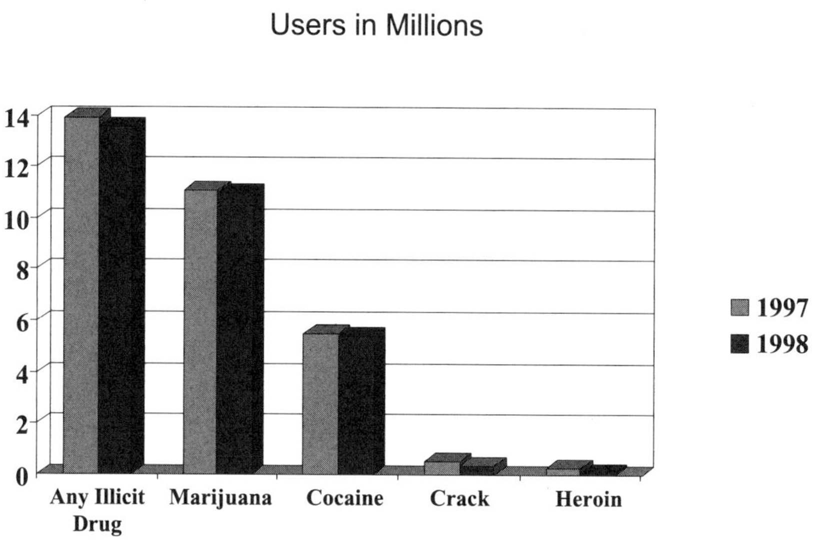

Figure I-1 In 1998 there were 13.6 million users of illicit drugs. Source: Office of National Drug Control Policy, May 2000.

1 Technical Procedures for Drug Investigations

A common problem encountered in criminal investigation is being able to recall not just a particular technique for investigation, but also different investigative techniques. All police officers undergo training in many areas of law enforcement, and in time learn to adapt certain techniques to their particular personalities, abilities, and so forth. It is likely, however, that investigations are not unsuccessful because an officer was unable to apply learned techniques, but because he or she was unable to remember the right one at the right time. The training process must be continuous, and all officers must update their training with new techniques as well as periodically refresh their memories in already learned techniques.

Case Initiation

Much of the literature regarding drug investigations labels drug dealing as a "victimless crime." While it cannot be generalized that all crimes have victims, drug manufacturing and trafficking does in fact have many victims. We must remember that the victims of narcotics transactions are frequently removed from the act itself. This can be illustrated by the following examples of active and passive victims:

1. People who experience drug overdoses or contaminants in impure drugs or diseases related to drug use
2. Victims of crimes against persons (such as assault, robbery, rape, and murder) or crimes against property (such as burglary and auto theft)
3. Taxpayers who must foot the bill for the increased police protection, court costs, and penitentiary facilities necessitated by increased drug-related crime
4. Citizens whose insurance rates rise because of drug-related crimes (auto theft, burglary, larceny, robbery, insurance fraud) and drug-related medical costs (accidents, illnesses, long-term disabilities)
5. Employers who must deal with on-the-job, drug-related accidents, their effects on consumer and employee safety, and their overall effects on costs and productivity

In proactive investigations (such as drug trafficking and other vice crimes), the actual crime has not yet been committed, so there is usually no victim or complainant identified. At times cases are seemingly handed over to agents on the proverbial "silver platter" because of reliable informant information or timely investigative leads provided by other law enforcement agencies. Frequently, however, drug enforcement agents must initiate their own cases with few initial leads. Investigators must therefore be creative when focusing on a particular suspect or criminal organization.

Selecting the Target

Due to the immensity of the drug abuse problem, it is logical to assume that just about anybody can be suspected as a drug user or dealer in any given community. Moreover, restrictions in manpower and money make it impossible for law enforcement agencies to investigate all suspected drug dealers in a particular area. It is therefore the responsibility of the investigating officer to make a determination as to the specific type of investigation. It should be emphasized that the target, regardless of what or who it is, should be a specific one. Such a determination is based on several factors, including: (1) the size of the drug enforcement unit, (2) the availability of equipment and money, (3) agency jurisdiction, and (4) target input from the community (public pressure, informants, anonymous tips, etc.).

Priorities for target selection should also include the type of drug being trafficked, the weight of drugs (grams, ounces, or kilos), and the level of violator (street dealer, wholesaler, etc.).

The initiation phase of drug investigation involves locating and identifying leads that the investigator can follow up. The key word is *information*. Information about people, places, and organizations provides leads that help identify patterns of illicit drug activity. The making of a drug case involves several distinct stages within the initiation phase, each of which might supply the investigator with dependable investigative leads at the onset. Some of these methods include interviewing informants, conducting covert surveillance, and collecting intelligence on criminals. In addition to these techniques, investigators should consider other methods of case initiation, as discussed next.

Receiving Information

Many sources can provide information to the investigator about illegal drug activity. One of the most useful is the *confidential informant* (CI). An informant may be a person facing criminal charges who wishes to provide information in exchange for a lesser sentence or a reduction in criminal

CITY POLICE DEPARTMENT

INFORMATION REQUEST

File:

Date:

AGENT OR AGENCY REQUESTING INFO:

Name and any identifying numbers RACE SEX

ADDRESS DOB PHONE

ANY OTHER INFORMATION

AIRCRAFT # TAG #

TELEPHONE # PRESCRIBER INFORMATION TOLLS

S.D.E.A. ☐	CRIMINAL RECORD IN-STATE ☐	ADDRESS CHECK ONLY ☐
N.C.I.C. ☐	CRIMINAL RECORD OUT-STATE ☐	UTILITY CHECK ONLY ☐
N.I.N.A ☐	DRIVERS LICENSE IN-STATE ☐	CHATTEL MORTGAGE ☐
C.N.I.N. ☐	DRIVERS LECENSE OUT-STATE ☐	CORPORATION COMM ☐
R.I.S.S. ☐	N.A.D.D.I.S. CHECK ☐	F.A.A. CHECK ☐
E.P.I.C. ☐		OTHER ☐

AGENT OR AGENCY REQUESTING INFO:

INFORMATION RETURNED:

SEARCHED BY:

Figure 1.1 Information Request form to be submitted to dispatcher, records clerk, personnel, etc.

charges, or a concerned citizen who offers information to the police out of a sense of civic duty.

Additional valuable sources of information include leads from other law enforcement officers and agencies. These sources include officers in the investigator's own department and in other jurisdictions who have knowledge about criminal activity in a given area (see Figure 1.1).

It is the investigator's responsibility to evaluate the usefulness of any information received. The investigator must be able to judge the probable truthfulness and reliability of the information, because it may be based on guesswork or exaggeration. Moreover, the investigator must always remain cognizant of the motives of those who furnish information.

Verifying Information

Once information is received and its source is evaluated, the verification phase begins. Independent verification of information must be conducted separately from the source itself in order to ensure its accuracy. Three investigative methods are usually considered for this task:

1. **Surveillance**: Monitoring narcotics suspects through observation can be an effective verification tool. When actual criminal acts are not likely to be observed through surveillance, any corroboration of existing data may help substantiate suspected criminal activity.
2. **Use of informants**: Even though the officer's initial information might have been received from an informant, the use of a second informant can be beneficial in verification if the second informant is in a position to acquire information where undercover officers cannot be utilized.
3. **Other sources**: Internal departmental sources may provide much-needed information for investigators. These include arrest records, intelligence files, drug-buy reports, and other reports and files within the investigator's department.

Case Preparation

Because of the complexity of criminal organizations, the wide variety of suspects, and conflicting jurisdictional considerations that arise in drug cases, a thoroughly prepared case is imperative for successful prosecution. Drug investigations are commonly distinguished by the unconventional (but effective) practice of police undercover work, as well as other specialized techniques that have been adapted by investigators. Despite the unusual methodology sometimes practiced by drug investigators, a protocol must be developed to eliminate "trial and error" investigative tactics.

For the most part, drug investigations focus on targets. Targets can be individuals, establishments, or organizations with suspected links to illicit drug activity. Different targets will call for different investigative measures. For example, if the target of an investigation is a nightclub, the investigator should ask him- or herself the following questions: What drugs are allegedly sold at the establishment? Who are the owners and do they have a criminal history that might support suspicions of drug trafficking? Can the establishment be penetrated by informants or undercover officers for gathering intelligence and making criminal contacts? Answers to these questions may give the investigator ideas on how best to approach the investigation.

If, on the other hand, the target is a suspected drug dealer, other questions should be asked: Is the suspect a dealer or user? If the suspect is a dealer, on what level does he or she operate (i.e., street level, mid-level, higher)? Is the suspect considered dangerous, and if so why? Might the suspect be willing to become an informer? Again, answers to these questions will give the investigator an indication as to how to approach the investigation in terms of equipment, manpower, and funds for drug purchases.

Budgeting Resources

At this stage in case preparation a determination must be made as to whether a drug purchase from a suspect would result in an immediate arrest (buy–bust). This will dictate whether surveillance officers, uniformed officers, or special tactics will be necessary.

When budgeting available resources for the drug case, various items must be considered. It is a good idea to create a checklist of resources. The checklist should include:

1. **Financial resources:** Drug investigations are expensive regardless of how they are administered: the costs are built into agent and staff salaries, office administration (i.e., typing and filing), and the purchase of investigative equipment. Unit managers will concern themselves with most of this, but the case officer should consider other possible expenses: cash for drug purchases or informant payments, rent for a house or apartment used for observation, use of a specialty vehicle, or the need for a "flash-roll."
2. **Manpower:** It should be acknowledged from the beginning that additional manpower will be required for cases involving extensive surveillance. This is an area that requires close supervision: much valuable time can be wasted on ineffective investigations, and agents brought in to assist in unproductive surveillances may be forced to "back-bum" their own case loads. In addition, adequate manpower should be accounted for in the event that an informer or undercover agent makes any undercover contacts. A minimum of three cover or surveillance agents should be deployed to assist in every undercover contact.

3. **Investigative equipment:** Unit managers should have responsibility for acquiring equipment to be used in the investigation. During the case preparation phase, however, case officers should make an assessment of the unit's available equipment and determine whether other specialized equipment should also be considered: body transmitters, receivers, tape recorders, video recorders, body armor, weapons, listening devices, etc. In the event that a conspiracy investigation is anticipated, binoculars, night viewing devices, pin registers, cameras, and radio scramblers might also be considered.

Other Information Sources

Traditionally, local police agencies possess more valuable criminal intelligence than any other outside law enforcement agency. This information, however, is generated from a variety of sources that may or may not be reliable. In the early phase of an investigation, the drug unit's own department is the most likely starting point for the collection of a criminal intelligence base. When looking at a particular suspect, establishment, criminal organization, or area, the following sources of information should be queried:

1. *Police intelligence reports*: These reports might be indexed by several methods: suspect name, address, geographical location, or type of suspected criminal activity.
2. *Incident reports*: These are case reports containing records of offenses and minor incidents, most likely filed in a general record section.
3. *National Crime Information Center (NCIC) records*: This source should not be overlooked. It contains valuable information on an individual's criminal history: types of offenses for which he or she has been arrested, convictions, locations of arrests and/or convictions, aliases, and other special information.
4. *Field interview (FI) cards*: These cards are commonly filled out by patrol officers while investigating suspect activity in their districts. If filed and indexed properly, this information may prove beneficial in future investigations.
5. *Traffic citations*: The traffic ticket, although a record of a minor offense, may be helpful when attempting to locate identifiers of a particular suspect. Not only does it provide the suspect's name, address, and date of birth, but it also gives the suspect's physical description, vehicle description, and the location and time of the citation.
6. *Fingerprint files*: These files should contain physical descriptions and the criminal histories of previously arrested suspects.

7. *Arrest records*: These records will contain valuable personal information on previously arrested suspects. Specifically, the information will include name, address, associates, employers, relatives, and former addresses.
8. *Warrant file*: This file will help investigators locate specific identifiers of a suspected offender. Because specific information is required for the issuance of arrest warrants, the warrant file is a valuable resource for investigators.

Outside Law Enforcement Agencies

After examining police records within the investigator's own department, other police agencies should also be queried. In this process, investigators should not only check agencies within their own jurisdictions but identify outside police jurisdictions where the suspect might have lived or worked. If the suspect has ever been processed by law enforcement in these areas, those agencies will also provide valuable arrest and conviction information (criminal history). To aid in locating these jurisdictions, an investigator can examine the suspect's former arrest records, relatives' names and addresses, military service duty stations, etc.

Federal agencies should also be contacted in this phase of the investigation. There are 32 federal agencies involved in drug enforcement. The six agencies listed below, however, are the most likely to have local criminal information.

The Drug Enforcement Administration (DEA)

The DEA is the primary federal drug enforcement agency in the United States. With 121 district offices across the country and 61 offices abroad, the DEA possesses criminal and intelligence information on thousands of convicted and suspected drug traffickers. Especially helpful are the DEA's massive computer systems. The El Paso Intelligence Center (EPIC), for example, furnishes information on smuggling, drug production, and trafficking trends. Additional information is compiled about top-level traffickers and organizations operating in the United States and abroad. EPIC is accessible 24 hours a day and is staffed by agents from the DEA, FBI, IRS, U.S. Marshal Service, Bureau of Alcohol, Tobacco and Firearms (ATF), and the U.S. Customs Service.

The Federal Bureau of Investigation (FBI)

In January 1982 the FBI was granted concurrent jurisdiction with the DEA to conduct drug investigations. Additional expertise offered by the FBI is the investigation of organized crime organizations, financial investigations, and white-collar crime, all of which is useful in the investigation of drug offenses.

The Internal Revenue Service (IRS)

The IRS is part of the Department of the Treasury. Large-scale drug traffickers and money-laundering activities are targeted by the IRS Financial Investigative Task Force, which focuses on reports of financial transactions filed by banks and other institutions.

The Bureau of Alcohol, Tobacco and Firearms (ATF)

The ATF is very active in investigating drug-related criminal activity such as gun running and arson.

The U.S. Customs Service

The Customs Service is most active in interdiction investigation activities involving international drug smuggling.

The U.S. Marshal Service

The U.S. Marshal Service, operating under the Department of Justice, conducts full criminal investigations and is heavily involved in the investigation of outlaw motorcycle gangs and forfeiture of property.

Other Criminal Justice Agencies

The next step is to identify sources of information within the criminal justice system other than law enforcement agencies. These agencies include the following:

Probation and Parole Offices

Because the corrections function of probation and parole requires strict supervision of convicted suspects' activities, it is also an excellent source for current information regarding the associates, residences, and employment of suspected offenders.

Court Records

Criminal proceedings are a matter of public record, and examining these may provide new information to the investigator. Court records include criminal, civil, and juvenile proceedings with which the suspect may have been involved, as well as records pertaining to real estate deeds, grants, mortgages, or powers of attorney. Information on certificates of marriage (which include names of bride and groom), divorce decrees (which include the names of the plaintiff and the defendant, the date of separation, and the names of children), wills, births and deaths, bankruptcy papers, etc.

Prosecutor's Records

At times these records may be of value because they provide a compilation of a suspect's encounters with local police. They will also provide the names of law enforcement agencies that have dealt with the suspect in the past.

Public Service Agencies

Once criminal justice agencies have been checked by the investigator, an examination of other government agencies may be advantageous. These agencies may also give information about the suspect's previous whereabouts and background.

State Departments of Motor Vehicles

The name of this agency varies from state to state, but it can provide extremely valuable information. Again, specific information regarding the type of vehicle registered, number of vehicles, and their descriptions should be available.

Social Service Agencies

Social service agencies are good sources of information about a suspect's current residence and employer. Obtaining information may require a court order, depending on the individual regulations of each agency.

Medical Examiner's Office

The medical examiner's office records will give next-of-kin information for deceased individuals. Although not a common source of information, this could prove beneficial in some circumstances.

City or State Licensing Departments

If the suspect is employed at a liquor-serving establishment, city or state regulations may require him or her to be on record as possessing a license to operate a liquor-serving establishment or to serve liquor. Other types of licenses may be obtained for a variety of purposes.

Tax Departments

Tax departments will have the names of payers of property taxes, legal descriptions of property, and the names of former owners of property.

Departments of Highways or Roads

Maps of cities showing correct street numbers, alleys, rights of way, locations of drains, sewers, or utility conduits.

Health Departments

Local health departments will have birth certificates, records of communicable diseases, and immunization records.

Sanitation Departments

The sanitation department should have landlords' names or subscribers to service.

Boards of Education

Board of education records will contain teachers' biographies, personal background information, education (location), and students' records.

Private Sector Sources

Finally, in the private business sector of the community, there exist many sources of information that can offer the investigator countless leads. Their cooperation is strictly voluntary, so the willingness (or lack of willingness) of these organizations to cooperate with the police may be a stumbling block for the investigator. The professional manner in which the officer conducts the investigation may have a direct bearing on the degree of cooperation received. Frequently, a particular officer within the unit or department will, over time, develop a close working relationship with employees in certain companies, such as the telephone or electric company. This relationship should be taken advantage of, because many of these companies will not provide information without a subpoena or court order. Although the acquisition of these legal instruments is not a difficult task, it could still bog down the overall progress of an investigation. Some of the most helpful private organizations are discussed below.

Telephone/Cellular Phone Companies

If the suspect's phone number is acquired, subscriber information may be obtained to help determine to whom the phone is registered. Conversely, a suspect's phone number can also be found if only a name is known, thereby revealing an associated address. Additional leads may develop from a suspect's phone tolls (a list of outgoing long-distance phone calls). Acquiring this list usually requires a subpoena, but it enables investigators to order past long-distance phone tolls which will reveal the numbers called, dates placed, cities called, as well as the time and length of each call.

In addition to acquiring a suspect's long-distance toll calls, local numbers called can also be documented with the use of a device called a pen register. This looks much like an office adding machine and is affixed to the suspect's telephone line. The pen register records (on a tape readout) information such as the date and time of outgoing calls, the number called, the length of call, the times of incoming calls, and off-hook times.

The use of a pen register will probably require a court order, which should include a clause requesting "technical assistance" from the phone company to show the officers how to set up the machine properly. This process involves identifying specific wires within the phone system which are color coded (binders and pairs) and ascertaining where both the suspect's phone lines and the lines of the investigating agency are located (the appearance) so a bridge can be made.

The pen register may sometimes be located in an undercover apartment or even in the police department. This device requires little supervision or maintenance on the part of investigators, and only has to be occasionally monitored to retrieve the tape readout, which shows each day's telephone activity. Some expense is required to lease a line from the telephone company for the period the investigation is under way.

Public Utility Companies

These are beneficial sources for identifying suspected offenders whose residences are known. Information from the public utility company will show who is on record as responsible for paying the bill. It is common for a suspect to live at a certain location, but the utility bills are registered to a different party (perhaps an associate or live-in girl- or boyfriend). It is also possible for the water, gas, and electric bills to be registered to several different people at the same residence, thereby identifying numerous possible associates.

Banks

It may be difficult to identify a particular bank used by the offender. If this can be accomplished, however, much useful information can be acquired: checking accounts, savings accounts, auto loans, personal loans, IRAs, or certificates of deposit. A subpoena is usually required.

Credit Agencies

Many people make purchases with credit cards. A check of the major credit card companies should be undertaken to establish a suspect's credit holdings. Personal information such as address, employer, relatives, and personal references can be obtained as well as a list of items purchased and from where. In addition, a credit bureau will be aware of many of the suspects' sources of credit. Again, this will require a court order or subpoena, but it is well worth the time.

Telegraph Companies

It is common for drug dealers to use wire services to transport funds and messages to associates. If the use of wire services can be identified through informants or surveillance, the telegraph company might have information needed by the investigator regarding times and amounts of transactions.

Other Sources

Other techniques also may be used to find information regarding suspected drug trafficking activity; they are limited only by the agency's legal restraints and the officer's imagination. Included in these options follow:

Undercover Intelligence

Officers may choose to develop investigative leads by working undercover. If the drug enforcement section has an intelligence unit, this function could be performed by them; however, any undercover officer can accomplish the task. The objective is to collect intelligence covertly without effecting any arrests or in any other way becoming identified.

Trashing

In the case-initiation phase, the suspect's discarded trash may produce possible investigative leads. Although a tedious undertaking, trashing can produce evidence of crimes (through discarded materials such as glassware and chemicals), or information about associates (through discarded phone bills or mail).

The U.S. Supreme Court has held that trashing is a lawful technique provided no laws are broken to acquire the trash. The courts have held that a suspect has no reasonable expectation of privacy in his or her trash (abandoned property), and therefore no warrant is required. Officers are also protected under the Open Fields Doctrine (*Oliver v. United States, 1984*).

Summary

The case initiation phase of an investigation plays a significant role in determining the manner in which the investigation will proceed. There are numerous sources of information on suspects who have criminal records (as well as those who do not), ranging from law enforcement agencies to public utility services. With proper identification of various information sources, drug violations can be documented without the use of undercover techniques or informants. A suspect's close association with other convicted drug dealers, traffic to and from his residence (including descriptions of persons and vehicles), or other factors will give probable indication of a suspect's involvement in the illicit drug trade.

It must be determined at the onset of every investigation whether sufficient funding and other necessary resources will be available to support a lengthy undercover investigation and whether prompt arrests in the investigation are to be expected. Other considerations are whether informants will be used and to what extent.

Investigators must also be cognizant of information sources that will provide continuing information on the locations of suspects as well as personal background and criminal history. Officer safety should be kept in mind through all phases of case initiation, since covert duty is sometimes required. Undercover contacts with suspects should only be attempted after every target suspect has been identified and thoroughly investigated. Often these goals can be achieved through the examination of records and through personal contacts with other law enforcement agencies that might have independent knowledge of the suspect.

Suggested Readings

Abadinsky, H., *Organized Crime,* 4th ed., Nelson Hall, Chicago, IL, 1996.

Dintino, J.J., *Police Intelligence Systems in Crime Control,* Charles C Thomas, Springfield, IL, 1983.

Harney, M.L., *The Narcotic Officer's Handbook,* 2nd ed., Charles C Thomas, Springfield, IL, 1975.

Lyman, M. and Potter, G., *Drugs in Society: Causes, Concepts and Control,* Anderson Publishing, Cincinnati, 1998.

Schultz, D.O., *Police Operational Intelligence,* 3rd. ed., Charles C Thomas, Springfield, IL, 1973.

Ware, M., *Operational Handbook for Narcotic Law Enforcement Officers,* Charles C Thomas, Springfield, IL, 1975.

2 Undercover Operations

Working undercover is one of the best ways for police to learn what is happening on the street. Simply put, the undercover officer's job is to watch and listen. Doing so will enable him or her to obtain, first hand, essential information for prosecuting drug offenders. While effective, working undercover is one of the most dangerous police undertakings. Officers must be aware, alert, and ready for the unexpected.

Selling controlled substances without a license is a criminal violation in all 50 states. Other laws govern the distribution, transfer, possession, and possession with intent to distribute or by any other means conduct business involving illegal or controlled drugs. These laws have been passed in an effort to reduce drug consumption and thereby reduce drug-related crime (see Figure 2.1).

As with other crimes, the investigation of illicit drug offenses may be conducted by techniques that range from the traditional to the unconventional. The technique of using undercover agents to infiltrate criminal groups has been an investigative staple for many years, and its success as one of the most effective methods of obtaining credible, first-hand criminal intelligence. However, even in the law enforcement community, the duties of undercover personnel are probably the least understood of any criminal investigation procedure.

The use of undercover agents poses critical problems for police agencies, police managers, and prosecutors with regard to manpower, training, funding, specialized equipment, and other resources. In some agencies, procedures for undercover work may be clearly and explicitly documented; in others, procedures may be unique to each case, creative, and untried. In either case, undercover investigations must be carried out in strict compliance with agency policy and with local legal restrictions.

In this chapter we consider the undercover assignment and what is required and expected of both the drug enforcement unit as a whole and individual unit agents. It is impossible to recommend one procedure that would be appropriate to all units and jurisdictions. In drug enforcement, there are vast differences in the procedures, restrictions, and requirements

Figure 2.1 Photos depicting (A) a rural Florida homicide crime scene and (B) the remains of the three drug suspects who were murdered, covered with lime, and buried in a pit. (Photo courtesy of the Florida Department of Law Enforcement.)

that govern federal, state, county, and municipal agencies. In addition, drastic operational differences exist between large and small agencies. Because of these disparities, it is only possible to present a general outline for the use and management of undercover personnel. The systems and procedures discussed here should be modified to meet the individual needs of each law enforcement agency or unit.

Preparing for Undercover Assignments

Undercover work can be defined as assuming a fictitious identity and associating with known or suspected criminals for the purpose of collecting information about or evidence of criminal activity. Make no mistake: all undercover work is dangerous! It requires that officers establish a cover story (which may or may not be "blown" at any time during the investigation) and that they associate closely with individuals who may be armed, unpredictable, under the influence of drugs, or mentally unstable.

Personnel

Given the inherent dangers of undercover work, the selection and training of personnel must be meticulous. Consideration must be given to the particular goals (and resources) of the unit, the officers' personalities, their professional backgrounds, and their physical and mental conditions. In addition, an officer's proficiency with firearms, good reporting skills, and ability to keep a cool head and use common sense under stressful conditions must be carefully weighed. Because of concern for officer safety and the increasing potential for agency liability, the days of undercover officers working the streets "deep cover" and under minimal supervision are over.

Those being considered for undercover assignments should be disabused of television and movie stereotypes. Undercover work is not a glamorous job providing the agent with endless expensive meals, luxurious sports cars, and unheard-of electronic gadgetry. Conversely, it is also not a duty that requires the officer to isolate him- or herself from family and friends and become a drug-using martyr.

Most undercover work consists of a brief meeting between the agent and a suspect, an exchange of dialogue, and a transaction — usually a drug purchase. "Deep-cover assignments" — assignments that require agents to operate with minimal protection over much longer periods of time — are not as widely used and require specialized training.

Although required to work one-on-one with a suspected drug dealer, the undercover officer must also realize that both his or her safety and the overall success of the investigation require equal participation by all unit members. All roles for unit personnel (undercover contact, surveillance, raid, and arrest) are of equal importance. Even though every officer within the unit must maintain his or her own caseload, each officer should regard the overall mission of the unit as the effort of a team rather than one individual.

The Roles of the Officers

There are two general roles for officers to perform within a drug enforcement unit. The *undercover officer* contacts individuals or infiltrates establishments or organizations suspected of illicit drug trafficking or other criminal activities. Usually, such contacts are possible because the officer's appearance, mannerisms, dress, and overall demeanor are similar to those of the suspect. Much time and money are spent in carefully cultivating the officer's ability to function effectively in this capacity; the true identity of the undercover officer should be protected at all times.

The *support officer* (sometimes called an intelligence, cover, or tactical officer) is a plain-clothed officer who works with the drug unit, but not in an undercover capacity. Support officers assist undercover officers by observing drug transactions in which they (or informers) are involved. Support officers also participate in drug raids at the culmination of an investigation, interview arrestees, and perform other functions within the unit that would otherwise jeopardize or expose the identity of the undercover agent.

Drug enforcement organizations differ in their resources, methods, procedures, and philosophies. The operational distinctions between undercover and support officers may not be feasible in some agencies. In such circumstances, officers may be required at different times to perform both functions.

Equipment

To approach any covert investigation effectively, the first order of business is to determine what equipment is necessary and issue it to each agent as soon as he or she is assigned to the unit. The choice of equipment will, of course, vary according to the agency's financial resources, the size of the unit, and the type of assignment. However, when considering an equipment purchase, careful thought should be given to its purpose and user, its usefulness, and its durability.

Undercover investigators require equipment different from that given to support officers. Also, equipment assigned to an agent might be regularly carried with him or her in an assigned vehicle. Therefore, it may experience much wear and tear from being bounced around in the trunk of a car or in the back of a van, or it may suffer from drastic changes in weather conditions (especially in older vehicles, which may leak).

Vehicles

Generally, each vehicle owned by the agency should be assigned a separate number; a maintenance and repair file should be kept on each vehicle. The kinds of vehicles the agency should own and the equipment the vehicles should contain depend upon how they are used.

Support Officer Vehicles. Unit vehicles for support officers should be generally nondescript: two-door sedans in plain colors such as tan, white, gray, or dark blue. (Exotic or expensive sports cars might be advantageous in short-term undercover assignments, but they will also be easily remembered or "burned" by nervous or attentive suspects during any moving surveillance.) Unit commanders should consider using vehicles other than standard passenger cars: foreign cars, pickup trucks, vans, campers, or older cars.

Vehicles should also be assigned to match the driver. For example, a more expensive car should be assigned to an appropriately dressed agent; a sports car should be assigned to an agent who fits the role of someone who would typically drive one. If local laws permit it, seized vehicles (if in good condition) are a great asset and can provide a constant source of plausible vehicles for the unit. Undercover personnel should not use vehicles assigned to support officers. Support officers' vehicles need to be outfitted differently than those assigned to undercover officers. These vehicles should have more standard "police-type" gadgetry, which benefits them — but which would "burn" an undercover agent. All support officer vehicles should be equipped with a set of "kill-switches." These are standard toggle switches (usually mounted in the glove box) that are wired so that a single headlight, the tail lights, or brake lights can be turned off. This is beneficial in night-time surveillances to change the appearance of a vehicle when suspects view it through the rear-view mirror.

Undercover Officer Vehicles. Vehicles used by undercover agents should not contain the same kinds of equipment used by support officers. Undercover vehicles must be kept "clean." Drug dealers will frequently be inside the vehicle while negotiating with the undercover officer. It is common for a suspect to examine the agent's vehicle for possible radio wires or hidden microphones, to check the vehicle registration, or to search for personal effects. *Anything* the suspect finds in the vehicle should be placed there purposely (e.g., a checkbook, mail) to support the officer's cover story.

Again, many agencies use seized vehicles — especially for undercover work. Others purchase or rent cars for undercover agents. The obvious benefit of a borrowed or rented vehicle is that it can be returned to the lender after the investigation is over, thus enabling officers to have different vehicles for each assignment.

Radios

A police radio, if installed in a vehicle, should be hidden from view. Many agencies place the radio in the trunk and the radio head where it can be concealed from inquisitive suspects (e.g., in the glove box). The radio antenna should also be nondescript. Antennas resembling those for standard AM-FM radios ("Dick Tracy antennas") should be considered. A portable two-way radio, which can be plugged into a cigarette lighter, can also be used. Even cellular phones have distinct advantages. They permit an officer to possess communication that is readily acceptable to drug dealers, because they use them as well.

Hand-held radios are another essential piece of equipment for the support officer. They are useful during surveillances conducted away from the car and during raids and arrests. They are also expensive, however, and may not be available to every agent. If it is necessary to check walkie-talkies in and out, or to assign them to particular agents, procedures should be established to ensure that they will be returned, serviced, and available whenever needed.

Regardless of what radio system is used, a frequency scrambler (encoder) should be installed on every radio. This device literally scrambles the transmitted voice of the officer, and only other radios with scramblers (and the correct scrambler code) can decipher the transmission. This is important because of the increasing number of drug traffickers who use programmable police scanners to monitor law enforcement activities.

Tape Recorders

The use of tape recorders is essential in most covert operations. A recorder can be used to tape field notes, undercover contacts, or telephone conversations (with a suction-type induction coil). Ideally, the tape recorder should be small and be equipped with a remote control or an extended microphone lead. These features can be found in many mid-sized recorders. Be sure, however, that the record selected does not have a "warning beep" to indicate the end of a tape.

Because many drug traffickers now use RF (radio frequency) detectors to identify hidden tape recorders used by undercover officers (see Figure 2.2), the drug unit should consider removing the erase head (which emits an RF signal) from the recorder. Even though tapes cannot be re-recorded after the head is removed, its removal greatly reduces the chance of detection. The cost of this procedure is usually less than $100 per recorder and is money well spent.

Before tape recorders are purchased, unit managers should note what kind of transcription machines the unit's secretarial staff has. The advantages of using compatible equipment (i.e., tape recorders and transcription machines that use the same size tape) are obvious, and this is easily guaranteed if all unit equipment is purchased at the same time. All drug enforcement units should require that every taped undercover and telephone contact be transcribed for later use in court proceedings.

Undercover Identification

Another essential piece of "equipment" is adequate undercover identification. The undercover name chosen by the officer should be one he or she will respond to instinctively. In order to avoid confusion under stressful conditions, it is often a good idea for an undercover agent to use his or her given first name with a fictitious last name.

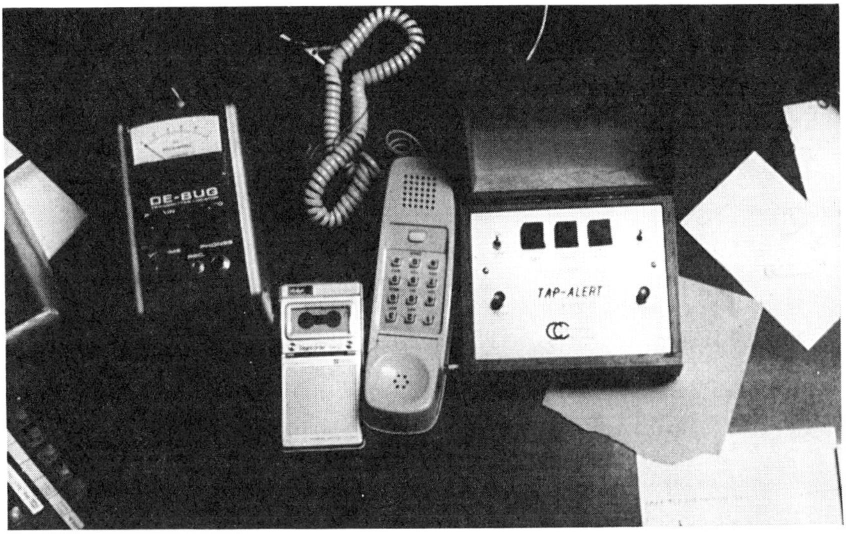

Figure 2.2 Devices found in a drug trafficker's residence to detect wiretaps or "RF" signals from concealed transmitters. (Photo courtesy of the Florida Department of Law Enforcement.)

The first piece of identification to obtain is a driver's license. This is usually acquired through the state department of motor vehicles; most often it requires a letter from the agency's chief executive officer addressed to the head of the department of motor vehicles.

Second, gasoline credit cards should be issued to the undercover agent in the same name as is on the driver's license. If this is not feasible, the credit cards should bear the name of a fictitious company. (Note: If a company name is used, it should be worked into the agent's cover story.) Some agency supervisors may require agents to purchase gasoline at a particular gas or service station in order to avoid accounting nightmares or other unforeseen complications later.

Third, it is imperative that unit managers obtain fictitious social security numbers for all undercover personnel in case agents seek undercover employment. The process may take two or three weeks, so unit commanders should plan ahead. The application criteria for state and local agencies is as follows:

1. The Social Security Administration (SSA) can only provide fictitious (cover) social security numbers in instances in which there is specific legal authority (e.g., state law, a standing court decision, agency regulations) that permit the agency to engage in undercover law enforcement activities and to use false identification in furtherance of their lawful functions.

2. All requests from an agency for cover identity social security numbers should be channeled through a designated agency liaison office for approval and control.
3. Social security numbers issued under these arrangements must only be used in connection with the undercover officer's official duties and only to the extent necessary to carry out the agency's lawful functions.
4. Any social security cards issued for undercover law enforcement activity must be returned to the Office of Assessment at the end of the undercover assignment. A cover letter explaining whether the social security number was used in an employment situation should accompany the returned card. If the card was so used, the cover letter should contain sufficient detail about the employment (name, address, gross salary, period of employment) so that the SSA may adjust its records.
5. Although earnings may be reported for the undercover agent during the operation, these earnings would generally not be covered for social security purposes inasmuch as a valid employer-employee relationship would not exist in most cases. When the operation is completed, the SSA will delete any existing records.

Weapons

The type of personal handgun carried by an agent is usually an individual choice. Most law enforcement agencies, however, require officers who carry weapons in addition to those issued by the department to qualify with the weapons individually before being permitted to carry them in service. Both revolvers and semiautomatic handguns have distinct advantages, which should be weighed by each agent. The usual considerations are those of concealability, comfort, and topping power.

In the event that an investigation results in a shooting, unit officers should request the assistance of tactical officers who are trained in SWAT-type maneuvers. (This option may not be available to officers in emergency situations, and in some jurisdictions such assistance may not be available.) Depending on the structure of the department, a tactical assault team should also be used when a raid or other tactical situation is anticipated. Use of such a unit, trained in the use of assault weaponry, may reduce the likelihood of an agency's liability in the event of a shooting.

If a department does not have a tactical unit, each officer must be adequately trained in the use of both handguns and long guns. Two long guns in particular should be considered for use by support officers in the unit: a 12-gauge shotgun and a rifle (.30–.30, .223 caliber, etc.). Depending on the circumstances in which support officers find themselves, they may need to be experienced with both types of weapons. In the case of raids on residences or buildings, shotguns might offer maximum protection. In raids on marijuana fields, clandestine laboratories, or other rural operations, however, rifles might be necessary in the event of an ambush. These two weapons may be carried in the support officer's assigned vehicle on an as-needed basis. Fully automatic weapons, concussion grenades, tear gas, and other weaponry might also be necessary in different circumstances; each requires specialized training.

Officers must be properly qualified for the use of each weapon issued. Such qualification should take place throughout the year on a regularly scheduled, "in-service" training basis. Weapons training should prepare the agent for all street circumstances including day and night shooting, strong/weak hand shooting, shoot-don't-shoot techniques, and barricade and prone qualifications from 5–25 yards. It is also recommended that agencies train officers regularly in "red-handle" shooting exercises. This is a practical and realistic type of training in which special training weapons are loaded with special ammunition that shoots cotton projectiles.

Standard-Issue Police Equipment

The issuance of basic police equipment is also necessary for arrest, raid, and tactical situations. This equipment should include:

- Body armor (lightweight and heavy-duty)
- Raid jackets and hats (marked with the word "POLICE")
- Sam Brown belt with holster, speed loaders, and handcuff case
- Flashlight with auto-charger
- Handcuffs (both metal and plastic flex-cuffs)
- First aid kit
- City and state maps
- Binoculars

Special Equipment

Some specialized equipment is also necessary for special circumstances. Because much of this equipment is rare and may be extremely expensive, it may not actually be issued to each support officer but may instead be available through an equipment checkout procedure. If the latter is adopted by the drug unit, a log should be maintained showing dates, times of equipment use, the names of officers using the equipment, and the maintenance schedule (dates and types of service performed). Depending on the assignment, other types of equipment are commonly used to ensure an agent's cover (Figure 2.3). This equipment includes:

- A 35-mm camera with special lenses (e.g., 500-mm telephoto, wide-angle, and zoom), special film (e.g., infrared), and flash attachments
- A Polaroid® camera with a light bar and extra film

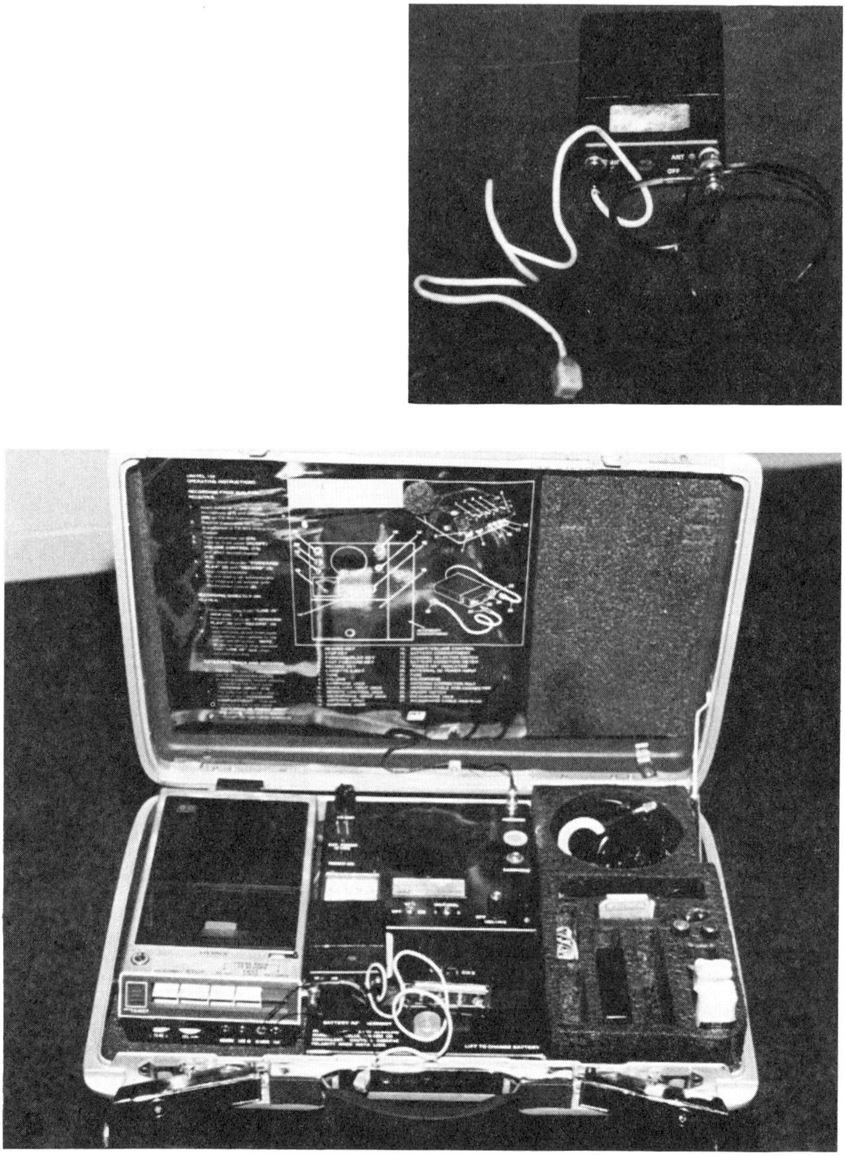

Figure 2.3 (A) The concealable voice transmitter is commonly used by undercover officers in conjunction with (B) the receiver and briefcase cassette recorder.

- Night viewing devices
- Video cameras with attachments
- Concealed body transmitter with receivers (plus extra batteries if required)
- Hard-line room transmitters ("spike-mikes")

- Vehicle tracking devices ("bumper beepers")
- Battering ram (for tactical units)
- Bolt cutters
- Teargas guns (for tactical units)
- A bullhorn

Other equipment to be kept in the support officer's vehicle should include:

- Evidence bags
- Evidence tape, duct tape, or masking tape
- Drug field test kit (Note: evidence bags, tape, and testers should also be kept in undercover officers' vehicles in a bolted, locked strongbox to prevent tampering or theft)
- Blank forms: consent to search, informant statement, *Miranda* warning cards (rights waiver), suspect statement, evidence submittal forms, prisoner personal history form
- Extra undercover license plates (in and out of state)
- Portable scales for weighing small quantities of drugs
- A three-day change of clothes

Working Undercover

Working undercover has unique benefits as well as a serious downside. It is the one investigative method by which the officer can see firsthand the inner workings of criminal organizations. Officers can also converse and strategize with their criminal targets and learn the ways in which criminal minds think. On the down side, the close interaction may place the officer in jeopardy, as he or she might reveal something inconsistent with his or her cover story. Furthermore, exposure to criminal elements in a close, undercover capacity for extended periods of time might cause the undercover agent to act and speak in a manner unlike they are accustomed — even when off duty, reflecting poorly on the officer's credibility.

The Cover Story

A prerequisite for assuming an undercover role is to establish a cover story. Simply defined, the cover story is a fictitious story that the agent will convey to suspects concerning his or her background: name, address, hometown (or area), and employment. Other details may be included, but it is a good idea to keep the cover story simple in case the agent must deal with inquisitive drug dealers.

The cover story should fit with the area and people involved with the investigation. When an officer chooses to associate him- or herself with a particular town or area, it should be one with which the officer is already familiar in case he or she later meets someone from that area. Officers should remember: a partial truth makes the best lie. When claiming a place of employment, the officer should choose one that cannot be easily checked out by suspects. (This is more of a problem in rural areas because people are more likely to know each other in small communities.) It may be desirable to choose an out-of-town place of employment that requires a lot of travel, or to present a fictitious job in which the officer is self-employed (and therefore more difficult to verify). Whatever story is chosen, the officer should be provided with business cards, customized stationery, credit cards, checking and savings account books, and other supporting credentials to corroborate it. Moreover, the officer should be familiar with the profession chosen for the cover story for the same reasons he or she should be familiar with a purported hometown.

The officer's appearance and mannerisms should also fit the cover story. If the officer claims to be an oil-field worker, it might be out of character for the officer to be seen after hours in an expensive business suit. Conversely, if the officer's cover story is that of a financier for a big-money drug deal, then expensive clothing might be more appropriate. It might also be necessary for an undercover officer to wear expensive jewelry to help convince sellers of the cover story. (Jewelry can sometimes be borrowed from local stores for short periods; however, the safety and security of the jewelry are the responsibility of the undercover officer.)

Protecting the Undercover Officer's Cover

Once the cover story has been established, the undercover officer is committed to it. Certainly the basics — name, hometown, and vocation — cannot easily be changed without jeopardizing the officer's safety and the integrity of the investigation. Even if changes are not necessary, however, the undercover officer must be able to detect and withstand attempts by suspects or their associates to test and invalidate the officer's cover story.

Typically, suspects will barrage the officer with questions in an attempt to catch a lie or inconsistency in the cover story. If they are successful (or think they are), suspects will usually attempt to frighten or intimidate the officer into admitting he or she is an undercover agent or abandoning the investigation out of fear for personal safety — sometimes banding together to do so.

Panic is the undercover officer's worst enemy. Officers must realize two important things: (a) paranoia is common among drug dealers, and (b) no matter what suspects say they know about the agent, many times they are just attempting to bluff the officer into an admission for which they have no proof. If the officer keeps the cover story general, most questioning and suspicion should be easily overcome. Moreover, if the officer has been properly trained and responds to the suspects according to his or her training, a bond of trust may develop between the officer and suspects, which can pave the way to a successful investigation.

Drug traffickers use a variety of methods to expose undercover police agents. Even though good field training should prepare undercover personnel for most of them, not every confrontation can be anticipated. Undercover personnel should remember that most questions about the cover story are bluffs, and they should remain calm and confident, discounting the challenges presented without appearing scared, intimidated, or timid.

Case History

A state narcotics agent was assigned to investigate drugs in a small military town. The first night he worked undercover, he decided to go play pool at a local night spot where Detective Clark, the agent's contact on the local police department, had told him there was a lot of drug activity, and where the agent could probably make some drug contacts. The agent arrived at the club and immediately walked toward the pool table area of the tavern. While waiting his turn at the pool table a young black GI sat next to the agent and said, "Hey man I need to talk to ya about your assignment. I know you don't know me but there's a problem, Clark sent me." The agent, not knowing the man, denied knowing anything about an assignment or anyone named Clark. The GI persisted in trying to convince the agent that the detective sent him to deliver an important message, but the agent did not give in. Finally, the man said, "Sorry man, I was just checking you out to see if you were cool. I've got some dynamite coke for sale if you're interested."

Officers should also be aware that traffickers can be quite tricky and cunning when trying to expose possible police infiltration. They may, for example:

- Attempt to intoxicate the officer in the hope that he or she will say something inconsistent with the cover story while under the influence of alcohol
- Use prostitutes, girlfriends or boyfriends, or associates to attempt to seduce the officer; in so doing, the upper torso will be felt for body mikes, the waist area for weapons, and pockets for police credentials or anything else indicating an association with police work
- Ask the officer questions about the cover story when the suspects already know the answers; the suspects hope to observe nervousness on the part of the officer
- Ask the officer to furnish drugs to a friend or associate

- Ask the officer to consume drugs furnished by the suspect
- Attempt to learn information about the officer's family (spouse, children, other relatives, friends) so that the officer's story can be more easily verified
- Ask the officers to perform various illegal acts
- Attempt to rummage through the officer's car or personal belongings in order to locate police-related material or information showing that the officer was lying about the cover story
- Ask the undercover officer excessive questions to see how many he or she is willing to answer before becoming suspicious

Infiltration

Once a cover story is established, a methodical process of infiltration must take place. During infiltration a relationship is established between the officer and the suspect. Frequently, an officer finds it difficult to meet or establish any rapport with the suspect without the help of an informant. In some cases, however, informants may cause more trouble for the officer and the investigation than they are worth; therefore, their use should be carefully considered. Infiltration requires inventiveness and originality on the agent's part because he or she might have to create his or her own opportunity to speak with the suspect. The following case history provides an example of this.

Case History

> A suspected drug dealer was living alone in a trailer court. Surveillance had shown that he was somewhat of a recluse and did not go out to taverns at night where agents could possibly meet him. In the front of his trailer, however, there was a vintage 1963 Chevrolet Corvair with a for-sale sign. A quick-thinking undercover officer noticed the vehicle and did some homework on the value and history of the Corvair, knowing that it was a collector's item. The agent then approached the suspect in his home under the pretense of purchasing the vehicle. This was a good lead-in to meet the suspect: it created an environment of social interaction and an acquaintanceship was formed. After a half hour of car talk, the agent was invited inside the suspect's house to inspect some additional paperwork on the vehicle. Once inside, the agent observed scales and a water pipe on the coffee table. The conversation then turned to drugs, and a subsequent purchase was made.

Once contact is made between the officer and the suspect, the suspect's confidence must be gained as soon as possible. An officer can best accomplish this by learning of an interest of the suspect's which the officer can then discuss: jobs, the opposite sex, local bars, motorcycles, cars, drugs, and so on. Contacts must be regularly attempted throughout the investigation to maintain a rapport with the suspect. When working without an informant, it might be necessary to canvas a target area. The undercover officer can expedite the investigation by reviewing intelligence on targeted suspects and locations; concentrating on areas with high incidences of drug traffic might provide investigative leads. Typical starting places might be bars, nightclubs, or taverns, which can be excellent sources of intelligence for undercover officers. A lot can be learned by just being present; generally people do not have a reasonable expectation of privacy when "openly" conversing in public places such as a bar. The undercover agent can simply overhear otherwise private or guarded information about suspects: their names, types of criminal activity, places of employment, and their vehicles. Once the officer learns such information and if it appears that the information might be useful in showing criminal activity, it should be promptly documented in intelligence reports. The lack of such properly generated intelligence reports accounts for the loss of much valuable criminal information to the unit.

It should be noted that although bars, nightclubs, and taverns can be lucrative sources of information, officer safety is greatly reduced in these settings. If two undercover officers are available, it is a good idea to assign both of them to a particular tavern, working independently of each other. This accomplishes two things: it gives both officers additional backup, and it provides each officer the chance to identify different suspects and criminal groups operating in the tavern.

If a tavern is to be infiltrated, the undercover officer has several potentially good targets to consider. The initial people contacted may not be offenders but might know those who are. Without being too aggressive, the undercover officer might consider befriending one of the following people in the bar:

- *Bartender*: Bartenders may or may not be involved in criminal activity, but they will most likely know of any criminal activity occurring and who is responsible.
- *Waitresses*: Waitresses, too, are frequently aware of dealers and users operating in the bar.
- *Bar regulars*: Regular customers in a tavern might be good players to befriend; they, too, often know who might be involved in criminal activity.

Sometimes an informant will arrange a drug transaction and a "first-time" meeting between a dealer and the undercover officer. In this case, the seller will have some degree of suspicion about the officer, and some initial questioning should be anticipated. At this point in the investigation the officer should remember a few significant guidelines.

First, the officer should not let the suspect question him any more than if the roles were reversed. Some questioning is understandable, but it can become excessive. If this occurs, the officer should deal with it the best way possible, perhaps by acting angry and advising the seller that he's asking too many questions — that the deal is either on or it is not. This should help convince the seller that the officer is aware of what the suspect is attempting and is not willing to be manipulated. Undercover officers will find that subsequent transactions are usually much easier because the dealer feels confident in that he has not been arrested as a result of dealing with the officer.

Second, while working a bar, an officer might purchase drinks or pay for pool or video games in order to start a conversation with a suspect. However, officers must carefully abide by established policy regarding the consumption of alcoholic beverages while on duty. Most law enforcement agencies permit officers to consume liquor while working undercover, but because an officer's judgment may be impaired and because he or she might become less likely to remember necessary facts, this must be done with discretion. In addition, in case it becomes an issue in court later, the officer should drink as little as possible in order to avoid attacks on the officer's credibility by defense attorneys.

Third, if the undercover assignment takes the officer to the suspect's house, in addition to taking additional safety precautions, officers must recognize that this is a good opportunity to learn new information about the suspect. The officer should mentally map out all entrances, exits, and windows which the suspect may use for escape during a raid. The officer should mentally note the number on the telephone, which might furnish a lead to the name of a new associate later. Discretely observing mail laying out in the open may also reveal the names of associates. Last, noting the presence of controlled substances and their hiding places may be useful later when obtaining a search warrant or conducting a raid. (See Figure 2.4.)

Fourth, officers should remember that the practice of lying and deceiving is common for drug dealers. If the officer gets caught in a lie, he or she should never become prematurely paranoid and fearful that his or her cover has been blown. The officer should react with disinterest, or perhaps even laugh it off for the suspect's benefit. It is best to try to justify the lie by claiming that he or she doesn't "want too many people knowing too much about my personal business." The suspect will most likely identify with and respect such an explanation.

Drug Buy Operations

Although there are many methods of accumulating evidence on drug traffickers, the drug buy is one of the most reliable. Because drug enforcement is proactive rather than reactive and because the undercover officer is personally involved with the suspect, opportunities to purchase drugs as evidence frequently present themselves in undercover investigations. The purchase of

Figure 2.4 An automatic weapon cased with bullets, a scope, and a silencer, found on a drug raid. (Photo courtesy of the Florida Department of Law Enforcement.)

drugs by the law enforcement officer is unique because the officer actually participates in the crime. Such participation in criminal acts is lawful provided prosecutors can show that the suspect was predetermined to commit the act without the participation of the officer. Documenting a suspect's "criminal intent" through recorded conversations and the actions of the suspect can accomplish this.

Preparations

For all drug purchases, the unit should have an established policy requiring officers to completely identify the suspect before the buy operation. If the officer fails to do this, subsequent meetings between the officer and suspect may never take place, resulting in an open case showing an expenditure of funds with no leads to make an arrest. Suspect identification should include:

1. Full legal name
2. Identifiers (date and place of birth, Social Security number)
3. Address
4. Criminal history
5. Known associates (including friends, partners, ex-wives, and girlfriends)
6. Full vehicle description

The drug buy should be strategically planned to serve a particular purpose in the investigation. For example, an investigator may first wish to learn more about the seller's supplier, and additional purchases may be required to accomplish this. Conspiracy investigations necessitate multiple purchases. In other circumstances, however, a straightforward "buy–bust" operation may be best. Multiple purchases from suspects without a specific need will only lengthen the investigation, waste agency funds, and expose officers to unnecessary risks. Moreover, if the suspect is later convicted, the sentences incurred from several different purchases may end up being served concurrently rather than consecutively.

The narcotics buy operation involves an "agent" — either an undercover police officer or an informant — who makes the buy or purchase from the dealer. Though this may sound quite basic or simple, it is not. The narcotics buy operation is the most potentially dangerous, "tricky," and unpredictable of any police investigative technique. Many variables are involved, any one of which might create a new complication during the delicate and dangerous interplay between police agent and dealer:

1. The behavior and personalities of both the agent and dealer are unpredictable.
2. The conditions of the "set" (the location where the sales are taking place) are unpredictable.
3. The required movements of the police backup team trying to maintain surveillance and react to actions of the dealer and/or the undercover agent cannot be planned.
4. Both vehicular and pedestrian traffic can affect both observation and movement of the backup team.
5. Weather conditions can affect observation and movement.
6. The conditions given by the dealer to the undercover agent under which he or she will complete the deal are never fully controllable (although they are somewhat negotiable). The undercover agent must have options available and these options must be realistic.
7. There may be mechanical breakdowns or equipment failures: backup autos may break down, transmitting difficulties may occur, or batteries may go dead. In addition, certain areas are "radio dead zones," where transmission is impossible.
8. Erratic actions by the dealer and/or evasive methods taken by the suspect to avoid surveillance may make the "tail" or effective observation impossible.
9. Third-party situations may arise unpredictably: (a) The dealer's connection or supply runs out. (b) Someone fouls up on the proposed meeting time. (c) An unexpected police action by other police officers unaware of the "buy" operation can occur against the suspect, the undercover officer, or both.

10. The dealer or his people may rob the undercover officer (the "rip-off"). This is the most dangerous situation that can occur during a drug-buy operation, and only the undercover officer can decide how to handle it. Even with a predetermined trouble signal, the first few seconds of the crisis fall upon the undercover agent. Another situation under this category, although not as dangerous, is the "beat" package, whereby the undercover is sold a phony or "dummy" bag. Short of examining the contents, which is nearly impossible to do effectively in front of the suspect, there is little the undercover officer can do. However, immediately after discovering the "beat," the undercover officer (with a backup team) should make it his or her business to get back to the dealer and make his "beef"; the same goes for a "short" package (one that weighs less than the agreed-upon amount). This is what a dope dealer would do, and the undercover agent should do the same.

Hazards

Dangerous circumstances may arise at any time during drug buy operations. Many of these circumstances can be avoided; many are unforeseeable. A strict time limit must be given to each arranged drug deal. This way, support officers will know when to check on the safety of the undercover officer. If this is necessary, support officers may have to use inventive ways to check on the status of a drug deal without actually identifying themselves (prior planning is necessary for this tactic). However, on those occasions when the officer is not out of the residence within the predetermined time, it might be necessary for backup officers to storm the residence and make any necessary arrests.

The Buy–Walk Procedure

The buy–walk is a drug purchase for which an immediate arrest is not planned and the suspect keeps the money. There are good reasons why this is considered both a productive and a nonproductive investigative practice. An agency conducting a lengthy undercover investigation will soon find that if an arrest is made immediately after each drug purchase, the undercover officer's identity will rapidly become known. In order to protect the cover of the officer and enable the investigation to net numerous suspects at its culmination, the buy–walk method can be used. The agency then sets a specific date to conduct a coordinated raid during which suspects can be arrested through the use of "buy–busts." At the same time, arrest warrants are served on other suspects who have been identified earlier in the investigation, and search warrants are served on residences containing known stashes of drugs.

The chief advantage of the buy–walk practice is that many investigative leads can be developed when buying drugs from suspects: places of residence and employment may be observed, associates may be identified and observed, and the existence of organizations can be documented by investigators. Other benefits of the buy–walk method are that *small* drug purchases enable investigators to have the drugs analyzed for *purity*, and with each drug purchase, larger quantities can be negotiated to help identify suppliers farther up the distribution ladder.

The biggest drawback to the buy–walk investigation method is that it is expensive. The cost of continuous drug purchases may become quite substantial over an extended period of time. Additional investigative expenses include the officers' salaries (including overtime), and incidental expenses, such as expense for working the street and taverns (food, drinks, bar cover charges), gasoline, and vehicle expenses. To help defray these expenses, many agencies pursue restitution from the defendant to recover the expenditures made during the investigation (drug-buy money, laboratory fees, overtime, etc.).

Another major problem associated with a buy–walk investigation is the suspects' transience. Over a period of time, suspects may relocate several times and be difficult to find at the end of the investigation. In a buy–walk investigation, one of the support officer's duties is to keep track of suspects as they may move from place to place so that they can be quickly located when the investigation is concluded and warrants are finally issued. The record keeping in buy–walk investigations may be time-consuming and tedious, and in investigations involving several suspects can be almost overwhelming. This is why the length of a buy–walk investigation should be carefully considered; it may even be determined by a support officer's ability to keep track of the suspects during the investigation.

The Buy–Bust Procedure

The buy–bust procedure is to purchase drugs from a suspect and immediately place him or her under arrest. Because of the necessary physical proximity between the suspect and officer, this is considered one of the most hazardous duties performed by drug enforcement officers. It is because of this eminent danger that all "busts" must be meticulously planned and arrangements should be made in anticipation of any possible problems. It is not uncommon in buy–bust situations for a suspect to be armed and attempt to kill the undercover agent at the time of the arrest. When the suspect resorts to violence in a drug arrest situation, he or she will sometimes claim the action was self-defense — that he or she was not aware that the agent was a police officer and that the killing was an attempt to protect his or her own life. This is why undercover and support officers should be prepared to properly document every buy–bust operation to show that the arrest was properly conducted and that the officer did, in fact, properly identify him- or herself.

In buy–bust operations, it is also necessary for the undercover officer to make early arrangements with backup officers regarding when the arrest will take place. In most drug buys, an actual delivery of the drugs might be required to successfully prosecute the suspect, so backup officers might need to time their arrival on the scene just after the undercover officer gives the signal. This will give the undercover officer time to follow through with the needed elements of the transaction. Once the transaction is complete, the signal is given. This can either be a visual signal (such as taking off hat) or an audio signal (such as using a specific word in conversation). Using this system, the length of time between the backup officer's arrival on the scene and the time the signal is given can be predetermined.

Case History

On the evening of a drug raid, a narcotics agent arrested an individual, who then agreed to become an informant and introduce the agent to his cocaine supplier. After a series of telephone calls, a cocaine deal was arranged: 4 ounces for $8000. The supplier agreed to come to the informant's house to meet with the undercover agent.

The supplier soon arrived at the informant's house and said he would have to go to a second location and get the cocaine. The agent argued with the supplier and was able to convince the supplier to let the agent ride along with him to meet the individuals who were furnishing the cocaine. The agent was thinking that he could arrest all of the players at the same time (and seize numerous vehicles), all from one transaction. The agent asked the supplier the location of where they were going, but the supplier would not say. The agent felt confident, however, that the four surveillance vehicles observing and monitoring him would have no trouble following him in the supplier's car.

The informant, the agent, and the supplier all left in the supplier's vehicle. Unbeknownst to the agent, the surveillance vehicles lost sight of him and, because of a recent snowfall, were unable to track the vehicle. The backup team could hear the conversations of the agent through the body mike the agent was wearing, but they could not visually locate him. After about 15 minutes, the backup team could hear the agent meeting with the dealers inside a residence. The agent, still believing that the backup team was just outside the door, drew his weapon and placed the suspects under arrest. A scuffle then ensued between the agent and his four arrestees, and the agent was knocked to the floor. The surveillance officers, by luck, recognized the supplier's vehicle parked on a side street. By observing the footprints in the snow from the vehicle to a house, the officers stormed the house and probably saved the agent from being killed. *Lesson*: Don't change locations in the middle of the deal!

The buy–bust is also considered an extremely useful tool for investigators because it is much more cost effective for departments operating on modest budgets. Actually, the undercover officer needs only to display cash to the suspected drug dealer and receive drugs from him to complete the commission of the crime.

Location of the Buy

There is no ideal location for all undercover drug transactions because every drug deal is different and all drug deals are dangerous. Many factors may affect the outcome of the transaction. For each drug buy operation, however, basic questions should be asked:

1. Can surveillance adequately cover the undercover officer?
2. Does the location offer the officer maximum safety?
3. Was the location chosen by the officer, the informant, or the suspect?
4. In case of a violent altercation, is it likely that innocent bystanders will be hurt?
5. In case of trouble, how soon can support officers arrive on the scene?

The first priority in any undercover drug transaction is *officer safety.* This variable will often be the determining factor in deciding the location of the transaction. Another important consideration is whether the transaction is a buy–walk or a buy–bust, since both have unique considerations when determining the location of the drug deal. Here we will examine the different types of locations for the drug transaction.

Outdoor Locations

If the purchase is a buy–walk, the degree of danger associated with it is greatly minimized. This is especially true if it is the second or third buy: the suspect will feel more comfortable dealing with the officer.

Good outdoor locations are shopping center parking lots or crowded city parks. In these locations surveillance officers can get closer to the officer and blend in with the surroundings. An officer should never agree to meet at a location suggested by the suspect: the suspect may employ counter surveillance to look for police, or the suspect may be planning a rip-off. In contrast, a poor outdoor location might be a shopping center parking lot in the middle of the night: surveillance officers would have a difficult time staying near the agent because the stores are not open and little public activity is taking place.

When an immediate arrest is the planned result of the drug purchase (buy–bust), officers should consider some crucial factors. Unlike a buy–walk operation, a public place is not a good idea. There will be armed officers (and perhaps armed suspects), and the possibility of gunplay should be taken into account. A busy parking lot would increase the likelihood of an innocent bystander getting shot during the arrest.

An isolated location, however, is not the best solution either, as it will be difficult for surveillance officers to get near enough to cover the undercover officer. A good compromise might be a location adjacent to a shopping center parking lot where there is minimal traffic. The location should have good visibility and access from the street to allow backup officers easy access.

Indoor Locations

Indoor locations pose different problems. Once an officer enters the residence of a suspect, the officer's level of protection is considerably reduced. Suspects feel more at ease on their own turf, and they will be more inclined to ask the undercover officer more questions. In addition, suspects might require agents to consume some quantity of drugs before the transaction can be completed. The officer must bluff his or her way out of this predicament: such behavior is usually against policy, and will reflect poorly on the case, the officer, and the agency. Exceptions would be, of course, situations in which the officer is facing immediate danger to his or her life by not taking the drugs. Proper field training is the key to best dealing with these circumstances. Below is an illustration of how indoor and outdoor transactions can interface with one another.

Case History

A rookie narcotics agent was assigned to investigate drug dealing by juveniles at a local video arcade. After a week or so, the agent began purchasing small quantities of heroin from a 15-year-old dealer. A surveillance team was observing one particular transaction with the boy when an older white male entered the arcade and appeared to deliver something to the boy. Surveillance then followed the visitor to an apartment complex which, as it turned out, he managed. After subsequent investigation into the man's background it was learned that the man was the boy's father. A major conspiracy case was then developed, resulting in the seizure of a large quantity of heroin and a huge cache of stolen property.

Another problem associated with an officer conducting a transaction in the suspect's residence is that the suspect may have others present to check out the officer, or possibly assist in a rip-off. However, an advantage to the deal occurring at the suspect's residence is that probable cause for a search warrant can usually be obtained. In addition, the officer will have an opportunity to observe locations of drugs and entrances and exits within the residence. Basically, the indoor buy–walk is a good method for criminal intelligence but risky for the undercover officer.

Indoor buy–busts are extremely dangerous. Being in the suspect's residence and away from visual contact with surveillance officers minimizes the safety level of the undercover officer. Undercover agents should attempt to draw the suspect out into the open, in most circumstances, so surveillance officers can better observe the actions of the undercover officer.

Precautions

Even though drug transactions will differ according to their locations, the amounts of drugs and money involved, and the suspects, certain general precautions should be observed in all circumstances. It is easy for undercover officers to get "caught up in the moment" when negotiating for a major deal and forget safety considerations. However, every undercover officer should expect the unexpected and observe the following precautions:

- Never let the suspect establish the location for the transaction: it could be a setup for a rip-off.
- Never let an informant establish the location for the transaction without the prior knowledge and approval of the informer's control officer.
- Never change locations for a drug transaction during a drug deal. If a change of location is necessary, the undercover officer should call off the transaction and arrange it for a later time after support officers have been informed.
- Beware of drug transactions at the suspect's residence. In case of an altercation, support officers may have a difficult time entering the residence to assist the undercover officer.
- Never agree to conduct a transaction where more suspects than undercover officers are present. If this occurs, the deal should be called off and arranged at a later time.
- Always be aware of innocent bystanders. In case of an altercation with the suspect, have a plan!
- Always be cautious during big-money drug transactions.

Planning the Drug Buy

Finally, when planning the drug purchase, it should be remembered that many criminals operate in an organized and regimented fashion in much the same manner as the police. This is evident in cases where there are multiple suspects, each with a specific duty during the transaction; i.e., counter surveillance, guarding the suspect's residence, etc. To counter these situations, officers should consider pre-buy and post-buy planning.

Pre-Buy Planning

Much preparation should be undertaken in the planning phase of the drug transaction. Initially, when the buy is being arranged, all conversations between the undercover officers or informers and drug suspects must be recorded. Frequently, a drug deal might be arranged in the early conversations between players, but when the deal finally transpires, the seller might make little conversation. Practicing the "record-when-you-can" philosophy will aid the investigator in properly documenting all pertinent conversations.

On the day of the transaction, the operative should make a "pretext" telephone call to the suspect for three purposes:

1. To record the voice of the suspect outlining the specifics of the drug transaction: the price of the drugs, what quantity is being sold, and what quality (purity) is being sold.
2. To verify that the drugs are still available at the designated time.
3. To determine (if possible) whether the supplier is expected to meet with the dealer prior to the deal.

It is always a good idea for officers to set up surveillance around the location of the arranged drug buy because frequently the dealer will say that he has possession of the drugs when he is actually expecting an associate to deliver them just prior to the deal. If the dealer does not have possession of the drugs at the time of the negotiations, the supplier will likely give ("front") the drugs to the dealer just prior to the transaction (and remain close by). If officers are watching, they can document the delivery of the drugs to the dealer and then follow the supplier to other locations, such as a residence or place of employment.

Another important element in pre-buy planning is the location and documentation of possible countersurveillance (by associates) on the part of the dealer. Countersurveillance is covert observation by criminals to locate police observers in the area of the drug buy, or to assist suspects in a related criminal activity (a rip-off or getaway).

Post-Buy Planning

Just as the supplier may have delivered drugs to the dealer before the transaction, he might also be returning after the transaction to pick up his share of the profits. In another circumstance, the dealer might leave his residence shortly after the transaction to meet with the supplier and deliver the money owed. Either of these circumstances will make it worthwhile to continue surveillance on the location of the transaction to document new associates.

The tactical plan is only a tool or guide to be used in the planning process. It should not become a biblical or administrative panacea for the "paper tiger" type commanders who are neither "streetwise" nor adaptable to split-second change and are usually more concerned with "form" and "control" of personnel than with the specific objectives of the investigation. This type of supervisor has been known to use such forms as "cover" in the event that something goes wrong during the investigation, and should not be assigned to "operational-type" commands. A more realistic approach should be to appreciate the different variables available to the supervisor, choose among alternative actions, develop a "game plan," and then remember: the only thing that you can be sure of in a narcotics buy is that you cannot be sure about anything.

From Vernon J. Geberth
Narcotic Buy Operations
***Law and Order,* 1979**

The Flash-Roll

A primary goal of the drug enforcement unit is to identify the largest traffickers within a community. Therefore, it is common for undercover agents to work their way up the trafficking ladder to the point where a big-money transaction is necessary to identify a top supplier. In this case, the investigating law enforcement agency must acquire a "flash-roll" to demonstrate to the traffickers that they can afford the drugs. The flash-roll is simply a large sum of money used in undercover drug transactions to show to the dealers (flash) without permitting them to actually take possession of the money. The size of the flash-roll may range anywhere from $5000 to $100,000; it therefore creates a potentially violent atmosphere because some suspects might consider robbing the agent of the currency.

The sources of flash-rolls will vary from jurisdiction to jurisdiction, but if the investigating agency has no specific fund designated for a flash-roll, funds may be borrowed from the city or state treasury, or from local financial institutions willing to loan the money, interest free, on the signature of police officers; sometimes more than one source is pooled to generate enough money for a flash-roll. The law enforcement agency having possession of the roll is totally accountable and responsible for its protection.

Large money transactions may result in violence; undercover agents have been murdered for a flash-roll. The following is a checklist of considerations essential before undertaking any transaction using a flash-roll:

1. Complete identifiers and criminal history information should be obtained on all known suspects involved in the transaction.
2. Note whether the suspect has previously been observed with a weapon.

3. If the suspect is claiming to deliver large quantities of a drug that is relatively scarce in the area, a rip-off might be planned.
4. Officers must choose the location for the transaction and conduct it on their "turf."
5. Notice any other conditions that might be conducive to a rip-off (including the officer's "gut" feelings about the deal).

At some time during the transaction, the officers will be required to show the flash-roll to the suspects. This is necessary to convince the suspects that the officers can afford the drugs. This is the point in the transaction where the situation could become violent, and the officers should have a contingency plan. The location for the transaction is one of the most significant considerations, and should focus on the following areas of concern:

1. Support officers should have easy access to the undercover agent in the event a rip-off occurs.
2. Support officers should be located so that they have a good vantage point to observe suspects entering and exiting the area, or suspects conducting countersurveillance on the transaction.
3. The area should have adequate lighting.
4. In the event of an altercation, any exit points should be easily blocked by the support officers.
5. If a motel room is used as a neutral ground for the transaction, the officers (rather than the suspects) should choose the room, and it should have an adjoining room with a common door for easy access by support officers.
6. All currency in the flash-roll should have its serial numbers recorded prior to the transaction in the event the roll is stolen.
7. In all cases, the undercover officer in possession of the flash-roll should be equipped with a concealed body mike, or any device enabling surveillance officers to listen to the transaction (hard wire, RF room monitor, etc.), so the surveillance team officers can monitor the progress of the transaction.

Sometimes it might be advisable to show the flash-roll to one of the main suspects without advance notice. This will catch the suspect off guard and give the agent the edge because (a) the flash can be conducted at a protected location of the agent's choosing, (b) the agent can have sufficient backup at his disposal, and (c) the suspects should not need to see the money a second time before the transaction; once is enough. In this case, the officer has upheld his or her end of the deal by demonstrating the ability to produce the money. It is then up to the suspects to produce the drugs.

Another method of showing the money is to advise the suspect that the buyer will telephone him when the money is available to show. This will require the suspect to stay home and wait for the agent's telephone call. Officers can then establish surveillance on the suspect's residence and watch for associates coming and going. When the call is made by the undercover agent, the suspect is advised that he will be picked up in ten minutes or so. This short notice will reduce the suspect's time to arrange a rip-off. A second undercover officer then arrives at the suspect's residence (without the flash-roll), and picks up only the suspect. The suspect is then driven to a predetermined location, unknown to the suspect, where agents have established stationary surveillance. The agent driving the vehicle should always be careful to observe mobile countersurveillance. When the suspect arrives, he or she is shown the money and is permitted to count it. In the event the suspect insists that his or her supplier would also have to see the money, a Polaroid picture should be taken with the current day's newspaper in the picture showing the date. The photo can then be taken by the suspect to the supplier.

In any transaction where the officers suspect anything indicating a possible rip-off, the transaction should be called off. The momentum of the case in this phase may create an "ostrich" effect on the part of the undercover agents, causing them to become overly anxious for the buy, and possibly causing careless mistakes.

Entrapment

A common defense for drug cases is entrapment. In this defense, the suspect claims that he was tricked into commission of the act. The term entrapment is defined as "the procurement of one to commit a crime that he did not contemplate or would not have committed, for the sole purpose of prosecuting him."

When the defendant claims entrapment, he or she must first admit that he committed the crime before he or she can complain about police misconduct. This requirement alone usually deters a defendant from claiming this defense. Additionally, if the prosecution can show that the suspect was predetermined to commit the crime, this defense cannot be used.

An example of entrapment might be an officer claiming to be physically addicted and who needs another quantity of drugs immediately in order to avoid withdrawal. The suspect, in this example, could claim to have procured drugs for the officer out of compassion for the alleged addiction rather than for profit. A good method for avoiding the entrapment defense is to make more than one drug purchase from the suspect (and possibly purchasing different types of drugs). This helps establish the suspect's criminal intent to commit the act by establishing that he or she is conducting a business.

Many suspects mistakenly believe that if an undercover officer lies to them about being a police officer, it constitutes entrapment. In addition, some suspects also believe it is entrapment when officers record conversations, mark drug purchase money, or use paid informers. All these acts have, however, been upheld as lawful investigative techniques.

Conspiracy Investigations

The undercover drug purchase is an excellent investigative technique allowing an undercover officer the opportunity to observe the violation as it occurs. In such a case the officer's testimony is generally considered the best evidence in the prosecution of the case (especially when backed up with surveillance photos, videotapes of meetings, and phone records). High-level offenders and leaders of criminal organizations, however, are usually not receptive to meeting new people (which would allow informers or undercover officers access to them). In these cases, drug enforcement units should consider undertaking a conspiracy investigation.

A conspiracy is defined as when two or more persons enter into an agreement to violate the law and there is a commission of one or more overt acts in furtherance of the agreement. Conspiracy investigations enable law enforcement agencies the means to get to the leaders of criminal organizations who no longer personally handle drug transactions and would otherwise be too well insulated by associates operating on the lower levels of their organization. The law of conspiracy makes each conspirator liable for the actions of others, thus permitting the arrest, prosecution, and conviction of "kingpins" for drug sales they did not personally conduct. Investigation of these individuals through conventional investigative channels may prove to be a waste of time, thereby creating the need for a conspiracy investigation.

An enormous amount of overtime and manpower must be invested in a conspiracy investigation. Evidence and documentation must be obtained to link each member. It is not necessary to show that all conspirators are personally acquainted with each other, but investigators must establish some form of direct or indirect cooperation between suspects. Investigators may, for example, document noncriminal associations between suspects who are also involved with a criminal conspiracy. This noncriminal association can be used to show an acquaintanceship that will aid in proving the overall conspiracy.

The irony of conspiracy prosecutions is that a criminal act does not have to be completed. Additionally, drug trafficking conspiracies might take months to put together because most drug traffickers have more than one customer, thus requiring investigators to take long periods of time to properly document all essential players in the conspiracy.

Element One: The Agreement

The first element of a conspiracy investigation is that the agreement between the suspects must be shown. The agreement may take place in many different forms; for example, it could be in writing (not common), through telephone conversations, or through verbal agreements made in person. More commonly, the agreement is inferred from evidence showing that the conspirators acted in concert toward an unlawful purpose, or is confirmed through the testimony of a cooperating coconspirator.

The initial agreement is usually made between two persons. Others, however, may later join the conspiracy as it progresses. In most cases newcomers to the conspiracy need not know all of the details of the original agreement, only their particular roles. An example would be a smuggling operation, which is planned by two parties. One of the parties later decides to hire a pilot to fly to Mexico, pick up drugs, and return to the United States. In this case the pilot has knowledge of a criminal plan but only has personal knowledge of a portion of it. The pilot in this case is still liable as a coconspirator because he or she voluntarily joined the original agreement.

Element Two: The Overt Act

The second step in a conspiracy investigation is to document an overt act on the part of one or more of the conspirators. In the absence of an overt act, even though the agreement to commit the crime has been established, the suspects still have a chance to back out of it. Once an overt act has been completed, however, the offense (the conspiracy) is complete. The overt act must be something done by at least one of the coconspirators to help achieve the objective of the conspiracy. It may be making a telephone call, purchasing a weapon, or driving to another conspirator's residence; it could also be an actual criminal act. Basically, the overt act depends to a great extent on the agreement and the type of crime being planned.

Once a conspiracy investigation is under way, many smaller conspiracies may develop. These will frequently be interrelated, but officers must differentiate between each coconspirator and the specific conspiracy to which he is associated. The following general guidelines should help illustrate how to link conspirators:

- When large scale distributors sell drugs to middlemen, knowing that they are middlemen, all may then become members of a conspiracy.
- A single sale of drugs does not constitute grounds for a conspiracy between the buyer and seller.
- For a drug buyer to become a conspirator, he or she must know the conditions of the agreement and be a part of the original agreement.

- In order for a vendor of supplies or equipment to be considered a conspirator, he or she must have knowledge of the unlawful objective of the conspiracy; however, it is not necessary for his or her act to be unlawful.

Types of Conspiracies

A conspiracy may be shown in three different ways, each with its own peculiarities. The following ia a hypothetical case history that illustrates this.

Case History

At 3:00 PM John contacts Steve and advises that he has an ounce of cocaine for sale for $1800. Steve says he wants to purchase it, but first he needs to go to the bank to get the money. If the investigators can document this agreement, the first step in proving the conspiracy has been accomplished. If Steve then goes to the bank, this action will suffice as the overt act in furtherance of the agreement. In this case, Steve and John can both be arrested and charged with conspiracy. (*Note*: A charge of conspiracy cannot be alleged or substantiated if an undercover agent [or informer] is one of two parties making the agreement.)

The Chain Conspiracy

When substantiating a chain conspiracy, the investigator must show that the goal of the suspect individuals is dependent on the successful participation of each member. In addition, each member of the conspiracy must realize that the success of the scheme is dependent on every other member of the conspiracy. Generally speaking, the chain conspiracy is relatively easy to prosecute, provided investigators can show that the members of the scheme have one common goal (e.g., drug trafficking). Difficulties arise when the members are engaged in a variety of criminal endeavors and it becomes difficult to show each member's participation in one common goal.

The Wheel Conspiracy

A wheel conspiracy is one in which the primary conspirator, called the "hub," makes an agreement with others, called the "spokes." In substantiating this type of conspiracy, each of the spokes must be shown to be aware of each other and to know of the others' roles in the scheme. The "rim" of the wheel is the agreement that ties each member to the scheme, and must be demonstrated by the prosecutor. As one can see, this is a difficult method of investigation because a common agreement among all members is difficult to prove. The typical result of a wheel conspiracy prosecution is that the hub is charged with the crimes of the organization based on his individual association with each spoke, and each spoke escapes responsibility for the criminal actions of the other spokes.

The Enterprise Conspiracy

Under federal statutes, an enterprise conspiracy is considered a separate offense, thereby making it a separate crime to agree to participate in an enterprise by engaging in a "pattern of racketeering activity." The enterprise may have numerous criminal activities, so showing a chain is not necessary. The members of an enterprise may not be aware of each other's role in the schemes, and all that needs to be shown is each member's agreement to participate in the organization (enterprise). In this type of conspiracy, at least two acts of racketeering need to be shown. Federal law defines the term racketeering as any of the following activities:

- Drug violations
- Hobbs Act violations
- Loan-sharking
- Mail fraud
- Bankruptcy fraud
- Mann Act violations (white slavery)
- Bribery
- Counterfeiting
- Embezzlement of union funds
- Obstruction of justice
- Wire fraud

Prosecution of an enterprise conspiracy can result in massive trials in which everyone charged in the case is present for one criminal proceeding. Juries sometimes have difficulty isolating each defendant and his or her particular charges from the others on trial because an atmosphere of "guilt by association" prevails. As a consequence, convictions obtained at these trials run the risk of being overturned on appeal because of the inability of the prosecution to distinguish between one large conspiracy and numerous smaller ones.

Forfeiture Sanctions

Because drug dealing has created enormous profits for drug dealers, many have accepted the risk of arrest and a long prison term as merely "a cost of doing business." Only by stripping the perpetrator of his or her profits can law enforcement pose a significant deterrent for drug trafficking.

In recent years, laws enabling law enforcement officers to seize personal property of suspected drug traffickers has accounted for much of the overall success in drug suppression. The 1984 Federal Comprehensive Forfeiture Act has provided increased authority to seize a suspect's property based on the presumption that:

> ...any property of a person convicted of a drug felony is subject to forfeiture if the government establishes probable cause that the defendant acquired the property during the period of violation, or within a reasonably short period thereafter, and there was no likely source for the property other than the violation.

The Comprehensive Forfeiture Act (and similar state laws) enables officers to seize automobiles, aircraft, vessels, bank accounts, securities, real estate holdings, and privately owned businesses. Moreover, it enhanced the penalties of the 1970 Controlled Substances Act (CSA), specifically providing for a 20-year prison term and fines up to $250,000. The CSA contains many valuable provisions for seizing a violator's property. The types of property subject to seizure under the CSA include

1. All controlled substances
2. Raw materials and equipment
3. Any property use as a container for controlled substances
4. Any vehicles, boats, and aircraft used to transport controlled substances
5. Business records, books, computers, and other materials used in violation of the CSA
6. All money or negotiable instruments used for exchange for controlled substances
7. Real property or improvements used to facilitate the commission of violations of the CSA

Under the CSA, for example, if a drug dealer uses his automobile to drive to a location where he is to sell drugs, his car then becomes the conveyance which the dealer uses to facilitate the crime. The car is, therefore, seizeable under the law. Additionally, if investigators can show that a suspect purchased an automobile with illegal drug revenues, then the vehicle is subject to seizure. The process of property seizures under federal and most state laws is a civil process rather than a criminal proceeding. In many instances it is possible for a defendant to be acquitted on a felony drug charge and still lose his property.

Sharing Provisions of Federal Forfeiture Laws

Since the passing of the 1984 Comprehensive Crime Control Act, the U.S. Attorney General was given authority to make an "equitable" transfer of the forfeited property. Basically, this divides any property seized in a joint federal and local operation and allows both parties to benefit from seizures. After seizure of the property, a determination is made assessing the percentage of involvement of each participating agency, and a proportionate distribution of the assets is then made between the agencies. Listed below are two ways state or local law enforcement agencies may participate in seizure and subsequent forfeiture of property:

1. The state or local agency can join forces with a U.S. Department of Justice agency (FBI, DEA, INS, etc.) in a federal investigation and share any property forfeited as a result of its participation.
2. The state or local agency can request that one of the federal investigative bureaus adopt a seizure it has made and request an equitable share of that property once it is forfeited. This is beneficial when a state forfeiture is not feasible or when a federal seizure would be more advantageous.

Case History

A city narcotics agent and two agents from the Drug Enforcement Administration proceeded to the $250,000 home of a prominent doctor for the purpose of seizing his 1984 Ferrari automobile, from which he bad been selling cocaine. At the time of the seizure, the physician had already been indicted on drug charges and was out on bail. The agents served the proper paper work on the doctor, and as they were backing the Ferrari out of the driveway, the unthinking but enraged physician screamed, "You have no right to do this to me. Hell, if you can take my car from me just because I sold dope out of it then why don't you just take my whole goddamn house, too? That's where I had my coke parties." The agents thought about it and based on the doctor's statement … they did!

When considering the seizure of property, the FBI and DEA apply two general conditions in the acceptance of a seizure for adoption:

1. There must be a valid prosecutorial purpose in requesting the adoption. Officers should remember that while many state laws require proof "beyond a reasonable doubt" in seizure cases, federal forfeiture laws require only "probable cause."
2. Property referred for adoption must meet the following minimum monetary requirements:

Conveyances:	
Vehicles:	$2500
Aircraft:	$5000
Vessels:	$5000
Non-conveyances:	
Real property:	$10,000
All other property:	$1000

The Vehicle Indemnity Form

A frequent problem encountered in seizing a suspect's vehicle is when the seized vehicle is registered to someone other than the suspect. In some cases it might be registered to a friend or relative who may not realize that the vehicle was used for the purpose of dealing drugs. In this case, the vehicle must be returned to the lawful owner unless the police can show that the lawful owner had knowledge of the unlawful use of the vehicle. The same applies when a bank, credit union, or other financial institution is financing the vehicle. Once seized, it must be turned back to the institution (or the seizing agency must pay off the existing loan in order to lawfully keep the vehicle).

To combat this problem, it is a good practice for investigating officers to use a Vehicle Indemnity form (Figure 2.5) when returning seized vehicles to the lawful owners, banks, or other financial institutions. The Vehicle Indemnity form is used basically to notify the owner that the vehicle was seized during a narcotics investigation and that it is being returned. It also advises the owner that if the same vehicle is loaned out again to the same individual who used it for trafficking drugs, it will be seized and forfeited if the individual is caught a second time. Once advised in this fashion, vehicle owners, especially banking institutions, will seldom return the seized vehicle to the lien holder.

Similarly, with the widespread use of residential property by drug traffickers, a Real Estate Indemnity form should be considered. This form could be structured basically like the vehicle indemnity form but address the use of property for drug trafficking. A model vehicle indemnity form is shown here and can be modified to meet the needs of each jurisdiction.

Summary

Working undercover is a valuable investigative tool, but it should be approached with caution. Undercover work is costly, time consuming, and dangerous. The deeper under cover one gets, the less safety he is afforded. Consequently, many precautions must be observed.

CITY POLICE DEPARTMENT
VEHICLE INDEMNITY AGREEMENT

This agreement is made between ______________________________
(Name) (Title)

____
(Firm Name) (Address)

and the City Police Department.

The agreement is made in consideration of the return of a ______________________________

____
(Description of Property)

registered to ______________________________
(Name and Address)

used in violation of the Controlled Substances Act, and for the consideration, the receipt of which is hereby acknowledged:

______________________ being the ______________________
(Firm or Person Involved) (Type of Interest)

Of the property as evidenced by a:

______________________ dated ______________
(Title, Registration, Contract, Note, etc.)

It is hereby agreed to unconditionally release and hold harmless the City Police Department, its officers, employees and agents from any and all claims, demands, damages, causes of actions or suits, of whatever kind and description, and wheresoever situated, that might now exist or hereafter exist by reason of or growing out of or affecting, directly or indirectly, the seizure of the return of the above described property.

It is further incumbent upon the individual and/or firm to whom the above described property is being released to be aware of the provisions of state law (statute no.). This section of the state law provides that a claimant of any right of a seized vehicle may be called upon to prove that such "right, title, or interest was created without any knowledge or reason to believe that the vehicle, airplane, or vessel was being, or was to be, used for the purpose charged." In the event you and/or firm choose to authorize the future control of the above described property or any other vehicle, airplane, or vessel to the individual or individuals causing the seizure addressed in this agreement, such vehicle, airplane, or vessel may be subject to forfeiture to any violation under state law regardless of your and/or your firm's right, title, or interest.

Executed in triplicate this ______ day of ______________ 20____ .

____
(Police Case Number)

____
(Signature & Date of Person Executing)

____
(Signature & Date of Police Dept. Employee)

____
(Title of Police Dept. Employee)

IN WITNESS HEREOF, the above signed parties have read and understand fully the terms of this VEHICLE INDEMNITY AGREEMENT and so state by subscribing their names thereto.

Subscribed and sworn before me this ______day of ______________, 20____ .

____
Notary Public

My commission expires: ______________________

Figure 2.5 Vehicle Indemnity Agreement form.

To accomplish undercover work most effectively, the proper investigative equipment is required. This includes equipment to assist the officer in observing and documenting his case as well as equipment to help protect the officer while dealing with criminals. The list of investigative equipment for undercover agents should include properly equipped vehicles, appropriate weaponry, undercover identification, and recording equipment such as cameras, videotape recorders, and cassette recorders.

When working undercover, officers must decide what type of investigation is best suited for the department and the community. A lengthy investigation will be more expensive because in buy–walk situations money spent for drugs is usually not recovered. If a lengthy investigation is not feasible, then conducting buy–busts might be considered. This is an inexpensive way to arrest violators, but the undercover agent's identity is revealed and officers will not be able to work up the drug trafficking ladder much higher than the street level.

Regardless of which method of investigation is pursued, critical attention should be given toward planning the location of the buy. Determining whether the buy is to take place at an indoor or outdoor location may have a direct bearing on the degree of safety available to the undercover officer. Additionally, the status of the drug deal as a small money or big money deal may also be an indicator of the degree of danger facing undercover personnel.

Those who operate in an undercover capacity may find that they are limited as to how far up the trafficking ladder they can maneuver. If progress is limited in the undercover investigation, other more inventive ways of collecting evidence might be considered. One such method is the use of the conspiracy investigation that enables investigators to target leaders of an organization who would otherwise use associates to insulate them from law enforcement intervention.

Another investigative technique that should be considered in all drug investigations is the effective use of federal (and state) forfeiture laws. These laws make it possible for law enforcement officers to seize any currency or property that might have been acquired either through the illicit dealing of drugs or from profits made from drug trafficking.

Suggested Readings

Abadinsky, H., *Organized Crime,* 2nd ed. Nelson Hall, Chicago, IL, 1986.

Bennett, W.W. and Hess, K. M., *Criminal Investigation,* 2nd ed., West Publishing, St. Paul, MN, 1987.

Fisher, B.A.J., *Techniques of Crime Scene Investigation,* 4th ed., Elsevier, New York, 1987.

Geberth, V.J., *Practical Homicide Investigation,* Elsevier, New York, 1983.

Harney, M.L. and Cross, J.C., *The Narcotic Officer's Notebook,* 2nd ed., Charles C. Thomas, Springfield, IL, 1975.

Hicks, R.D., II, *Undercover Operations and Persuasion.* Charles C. Thomas, Springfield, IL, 1973.

Macdonald, J.M., *Criminal Investigation of Drug Offenses.* Charles C. Thomas, Springfield, IL, 1983.

America's Habit, Report to the President and the Attorney General, President's Commission on Organized Crime, U.S. Government Printing Office, 1986.

The Impact, Report to the President and the Attorney General, President's Commission on Organized Crime, U.S. Government Printing Office, 1986.

Drug Identification

3

Drug investigators need to know about the effects of drugs. Such knowledge helps them understand not only the drugs they will be purchasing and seizing but the drug abusers that they will come into contact with.

The literature on drug identification and pharmacology is rich with research findings, which suggest that different drugs affect different people in different ways. For example, drugs such as alcohol and cocaine often have varying effects on users. Not only do the user's moods differ from one drug to another, but the development of tolerance and addiction differ from one user to the next.

In this chapter, we examine drugs that are currently popular and potentially hazardous in today's society. We also study legal distinctions and categories of drugs as well as the effects those drugs have on those who use them.

Drugs and the Brain

We know generally the ways many drugs affect the user. However, the pharmacological mechanisms through which some drugs exert their effects are only partially understood. Researchers have identified locations and substances in the brain that are closely associated with the effects of drugs and their reinforcement properties. Although the process is complex, the neurotransmitter dopamine appears to play an important role in determining the effects of drugs such as cocaine and heroin. Cocaine acts on the pleasure center of the brain to the extent that in some people, particularly those with personality disorders already in place, cocaine becomes more important and pleasurable than some of the most basic human needs such as food, sex, or exercise. Normally, dopamine is released by nerve centers and is then withdrawn. In the case of cocaine, dopamine continues to be transmitted, significantly raising the blood pressure and increasing the heart rate.

How central is dopamine's role in the brain? Scientists are still trying to find an answer to that question, but they do know that it is no accident that people are attracted to drugs. The major drugs of abuse, e.g., narcotics such as heroin or stimulants such as cocaine, mimic the structure of neurotransmitters, the most powerful mind-altering drugs the human body creates. Neurotransmitters underlie every thought, emotion, memory, and learning process.

They carry the signals between all the nerve cells (neurons) in the brain. Among some 50 neurotransmitters discovered to date, at least 6, including dopamine, are known to play a role in addiction.[1]

At a purely chemical level, every experience people find enjoyable, whether listening to music, embracing a lover, or savoring chocolate, amounts to little more than an explosion of dopamine. Dopamine, though, like most biologically important molecules, must be kept in strict bounds. Too little dopamine in certain areas of the brain triggers the tremors and paralysis of Parkinson's disease. Too much causes the hallucinations and bizarre thoughts of schizophrenia.[1] Probably the most significant breakthrough in addiction came in 1975 when psychologists Roy Wise and Robert Yokel at Concordia University in Montreal reported on the behavior of drug-addicted rats. One day they were placidly dispensing cocaine and amphetamines to themselves by pressing levers attached to their cages, and the next they were banging at the levers with frantic persistence. The reason was that the scientists had injected the rats with a drug that blocked the action of dopamine. In the years following, evidence has mounted regarding dopamine's role in drug addiction.

We also know that drug abuse may be a symptom of a larger problem. For example, people with certain psychiatric disorders may be prone to drug abuse. Drug and alcohol problems often occur along with other psychiatric disorders. People with drug problems frequently have affective, anxiety, or personality disorders. Sometimes, however, the reverse is also true. One example of this is the self-medication hypothesis. In this case, a person who is depressed may use drugs to elevate his or her mood, or a person who is suffering severe anxiety may seek relief through the relaxing effects of certain drugs. In other cases, people who are addicted to one drug may seek to counter that drug's effects by taking another drug with opposite effects. This poly-drug use may result in overdose or death, depending on the mixture of drugs.

Side Effects

Adding to the dangers of substance abuse is the fact that drugs alter people's behavior. Psychoactive drugs alter moods, perceptions, attitudes, and emotions. As a result, drug use has an impact on work, family, and social relations. Many drugs also provide the user with unintended side effects. Although some of these side effects may be short term and relatively harmless in nature, some have the opposite effects. Heroin users, for example, take the drug initially for its euphoric effects, but they soon discover that nausea, constricted pupils, and respiratory depression also accompany euphoria.

Cannabis products such as marijuana and hashish can result in memory loss and disorientation. Users of hallucinogens such as LSD may experience bad hallucinations and imagined flashbacks. Exactly what constitutes the effects of any particular drug depends on a number of factors, such as the mood of the user and how the drugs are taken. A good example is cocaine, a drug that usually elevates one's mood. In users who are depressed prior to drug consumption, however, a deeper depression may result. In addition, after the initial effects of the drug wear off, cocaine users experience anxiety, depression, fatigue, and an urge for more cocaine.

Drug users often look to drugs such as those in the stimulant family to enhance their intellectual or physical performance. Because these drugs increase alertness, there is a perception of improved performance, but in reality the user experiences severe fatigue and a reduced capacity for learning, which can offset any physical improvements caused by the drugs.

Outcomes of Drug Abuse

To best understand the many different drugs abused on our streets, we should first consider some clinical terms commonly associated with drug abuse. These terms define the predominant effects of drugs and are generally associated with the most dangerous drugs of abuse.

- *Physical dependence* (or physiological dependence) is characterized by a growing tolerance to a drug's effects so that increased amounts of the drug are necessary in order to prevent withdrawal symptoms.
- *Psychological dependence* is a controversial term that generally means the craving for or compulsive need to use drugs because they provide the user with a feeling of well being and satisfaction. However, attempts to equate physical dependence or addiction with psychological dependence are highly questionable because psychological dependence may be developed for any activity from listening to rock music to enjoying sex.
- *Tolerance* is a situation in which the user continues regular use of a drug and must administer progressively larger doses to attain the desired effect, thereby reinforcing the compulsive behavior known as drug dependence.
- *Withdrawal syndrome* is the physical reaction of bodily functions that, when a body is deprived of an addictive drug, causes increased excitability of the bodily functions that have been depressed by the drug's habitual use.

We should note that psychological dependence is subjective and difficult to define but is characterized by a person's compulsive need to use drugs. The extent to which drugs produce physical dependence will vary. Heroin, for instance, has an extremely high potential for physical dependence. In comparison, cocaine is not addictive in the same way as heroin, but its potential for psychological dependence is high in some people, particularly those with obsessive personality traits and especially when the cocaine is in the form of crack, because of the intense initial dose in the vapor. This variation in the potential for physical dependence is one reason for the scheduling of drugs under federal and state laws.

Dependence vs. Abuse

When addressing the task of understanding the many different drugs that have been popularized on the street, we should first consider certain clinical terms and definitions commonly associated with drugs and drug use. These terms define certain predominant effects of drugs and are generally associated with those drugs that are considered the most dangerous.

Drug abuse can be described in many different ways. Generally, however, the pathological use of substances that affect the central nervous system falls into two main categories: substance dependence and substance abuse. Let us look closer at these two terms. *The Diagnostic and Statistical Manual of Mental Disorders (DSM-IV)*, endorsed by the American Psychiatric Association, outlines the criteria for substance dependence as the presence of 3 or more of the following symptoms occurring at any time in the same 12-month period:[2]

1. Tolerance, as defined by either of the following:
   a. A need for markedly increased amounts of the substance to achieve intoxication or desired effect
   b. Markedly diminished effect with continued use of the same amount of the substance
2. Withdrawal, as manifested by either of the following:
   a. The characteristic withdrawal syndrome for the substance
   b. The same, or closely related, substance is taken to relieve or avoid withdrawal symptoms
3. The substance is often taken in larger amounts, or over a longer period than was intended
4. There is a persistent desire or unsuccessful efforts to cut down or control substance use
5. A great deal of time is spent in activities necessary to obtain the substance (e.g., visiting multiple doctors or driving long distances), use the substance (e.g., chain smoking), or recover from its effects
6. Important social, occupational, or recreational activities are given up or reduced because of substance use

7. The substance use is continued despite knowledge of having a persistent or recurrent physical or psychological problem that is likely to have been caused or exacerbated by the substance (e.g., current cocaine use despite recognition of cocaine-induced depression, or continued drinking despite recognition that an ulcer was made worse by alcohol consumption)

Substance abuse is another term commonly used in both conversation and the literature of drug abuse. It has also been defined by the DSM-IV.[2] Substance abuse differs from substance dependence in that it is a less severe version of dependence.[2] In short, "abuse" is diagnosed when the person's use of a substance is maladaptive but not severe enough to meet the diagnostic criteria for dependence. Understanding these terms helps us not only categorize drugs but also recognize abnormal behavior that often accompanies drug use.

Drug Categories

To better understand the various types of drugs and their effects, a system of categories has been generally recognized. Each of these six categories (stimulants, depressants, hallucinogens, narcotics, cannabis, and inhalants) may contain both legal and controlled substances. Each substance possesses unique characteristics. They are discussed next.

Stimulants

Stimulants are a category of drugs that literally stimulate or excite the user's central nervous system (Figures 3.1, 3.2). The two most common stimulants are nicotine, found in tobacco products, and caffeine, commonly found in soft drinks, coffee, and tea. These substances are an accepted part of our culture and are widely used. Generally speaking, these products are consumed not only for recreation, but when used in moderation, they may be taken to relieve minor fatigue.

Although health problems are commonly associated with the regular use of nicotine and caffeine, other stimulants such as cocaine and methamphetamine can produce a more powerful physical and psychological dependence. Stimulants are popular because they make the user feel stronger, more alert, and decisive. As stated earlier, excessive use of stimulants ("uppers") may evolve into a pattern in which they are taken regularly and countered in the evening with depressants ("downers").

Stimulants are used by an array of people including dieters, people involved in boring, repetitive work, and those working extra jobs and in need of additional energy for a longer period of time than the average workday.

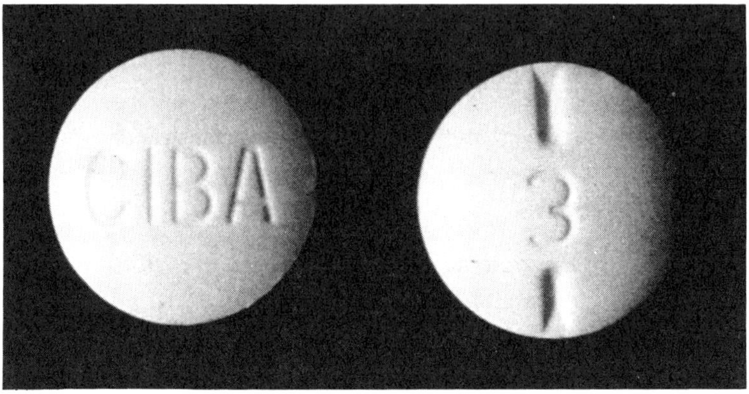

Figure 3.1 Close-up photo of Ritalin Hydrochloride (methylphenidate hydrochloride), a commonly abused synthetic stimulant. (Photo courtesy of the U.S. Drug Enforcement Administration.)

Figure 3.2 Close-up photo of Preludin (phenmetazine hydrochloride), a commonly abused and powerfully addictive amphetamine. (Photo courtesy of the U.S. Drug Enforcement Administration.)

Accompanying a temporary sense of exhilaration is irritability and loss of appetite. When the effects of the stimulant wear off, the body experiences a "crashing," or sudden exhaustion. Depending on the stimulant in question, the "crash" is sometimes experienced in tandem with chest pains, headaches, and even bouts of paranoia. We will now consider some of the primary drugs of abuse that the drug investigator will be encountering on the street.

Cocaine

Cocaine has advanced in popularity to become one of the most commonly abused drugs in the United States (Figure 3.3). Cocaine, considered the most

Figure 3.3 Packets of crack cocaine ready for distribution on the street.

potent natural stimulant, is extracted from the South American coca plant. In the late 1980s and early 1990s, cocaine became an illicit drug of great popularity on the streets, generating considerable wealth for criminal organizations in the U.S. and South America. In fact, cocaine and its freebase form, crack, have grown into a multibillion-dollar industry that sustains the emerging entrepreneurial drug gangs such as the Crips, the Bloods, and the Jamaican posses, as well as a number of well-established criminal organizations.

Cocaine was hailed in the nineteenth century as a wonder drug for addiction and other ailments. Like the opiates, it was controlled by such legislation as the 1914 Harrison Narcotics Act. Now, because it is one of the most available and inexpensive drugs on the black market, there is an increasing demand for the drug. Cocaine, a white crystalline powder, is commonly diluted through the use of other white powders such as baking soda, lactose, mannitol, and even some local anesthetics like lidocaine. It traditionally has been snorted and then absorbed through the linings of the nose into the brain. Since the mid-1980s, smokeable "freebase" cocaine called "crack" has become popular in many U.S. cities.

Cocaine's limited legitimate use is in nose and eye surgery. It is considered invaluable because of its ability to anesthetize tissue while simultaneously constricting blood vessels and limiting the amount of bleeding. Most other applications of cocaine have become obsolete due to the synthesis of other drugs that have similar characteristics. For many years, cocaine was thought to be relatively safe, unlike other drugs such as LSD and PCP. Studies have shown, however, that side effects from cocaine use are common. They include anxiety, restlessness, extreme irritability, and paranoia. In the early 1970s, studies of cocaine-related deaths indicated that between 1971 and 1976 only 111 deaths had been reported. However, with the advent of freebasing, those statistics increased markedly, with the number of cocaine-related deaths quadrupling between 1979 and 1981, the years when freebasing came into popularity. Current estimates are that those who inject or freebase cocaine (as opposed to snorting it) account for the majority of all cocaine-related deaths. In any case, the risk of death prevails in the form of heart attack or stroke from excessive use.

Because of its pleasurable effects, cocaine has the potential for dependency. In recent years there has been much debate as to whether cocaine users can become physically addicted to the drug. Little doubt exists that cocaine has a strong potential for reinforcing compulsive use, but its use results in different symptoms than those resulting from heroin use. Scientific evidence suggests that the powerful neuropsychologic reinforcing property of cocaine is responsible for individual use, despite harmful physical and social consequences.[3] Recurrent users may resort to larger doses at shorter intervals in order to maintain their highs. The danger of psychological dependence may be directly related to the amount and frequency of use. For years it appeared that the high cost of cocaine would serve to limit use and to control many of the dysfunctional attributes of users of the drug. However, with the advent of crack cocaine, the drug has become more affordable and more commonly available.

The intensity of psychological effects of cocaine, as with many psychoactive drugs, depends on the rate of entry into the blood. Intravenous injection or freebasing produces an almost immediate and intense high. Conversion of cocaine hydrochloride into cocaine base yields a substance that becomes volatile when heated and produces crack, which is discussed below.

Excessive doses of cocaine may cause seizures and even death from respiratory failure, stroke, cerebral hemorrhage, or heart failure, most likely in individuals with pre-existing respiratory, circulatory, and heart ailments. There is no specific treatment for cocaine overdose. Because tolerance for the drug may not develop, users may never be able to gauge how much cocaine they can ingest safely. In fact, it is thought by some that repeated use lowers the dose at which toxicity occurs, so that there is no known safe dose.

On the other hand, it is commonly accepted that the lethal dose of cocaine is one and one-half grams of pure cocaine hydrochloride. In terms of "street" cocaine, this means that ingesting about 10 grams at a single sitting would be lethal. This is a very unlikely prospect for even the most robust cocaine users.

How Cocaine Works. The exact effects of cocaine on the human body are not clear. However, according to an article appearing in the January 1989 issue of *National Geographic*, the physical cyclical effects of cocaine are as follows:[4]

> Upon ingestion, cocaine first enhances then later interferes with the transmission of the pleasure signals of the brain. A message is carried across the synapse between the axon of one nerve cell and the body of another by chemicals called neurotransmitters.
>
> Of the neurotransmitters released by cocaine, the most important is dopamine. Dopamine fills receptors on the body of the next cell and sparks a continuation of the message.
>
> Normally, pumps reclaim the dopamine but, according to a leading theory, cocaine blocks this process. Dopamine remains in the receptors, sending an enhanced message before breaking down. Prolonged cocaine use may also deplete dopamine, rendering the sensation of pleasure impossible for the user.

Crack. Since the mid-1980s, the practice of smoking, or freebasing, cocaine has become increasingly popular. Freebasing can be accomplished either through traditional methods (explained below) or through the smoking of crack cocaine. Traditional freebasing, the method used before the advent of crack, is accomplished by mixing cocaine hydrochloride with ether or some other volatile liquid, adding water, and heating it. The fumes are then inhaled. The drug is absorbed by the lining of the lungs and delivered within 15 seconds to the brain.

The method of smoking crack is less complicated than the traditional freebase method. It is also safer from a logistical point of view, because crack is not a volatile material. All the user has to do is heat a chunk of crack with the use of a small glass pipe (Figure 3.4). The crack vaporizes, and the fumes are inhaled. The freebase high only lasts from 8–11 minutes, requiring the user to smoke more and more of the drug to prolong its effects. Crack is made from a cocaine hydrochloride solution that is heated in a pan together with baking soda. This yields a solid chunk of cocaine product, which is subsequently cut up into hundreds of tiny chunks resembling soap chips. The chips are then placed into small vials or plastic packets and sold at anywhere from $5–$50 per container.

Methamphetamine

Methamphetamine, or "meth," is a dangerous, sometimes lethal and unpredictable drug. Meth is also known as speed, ice, and crystal. Like cocaine, meth is a potent central nervous system stimulant. Meth represents the fastest growing drug threat in America today.

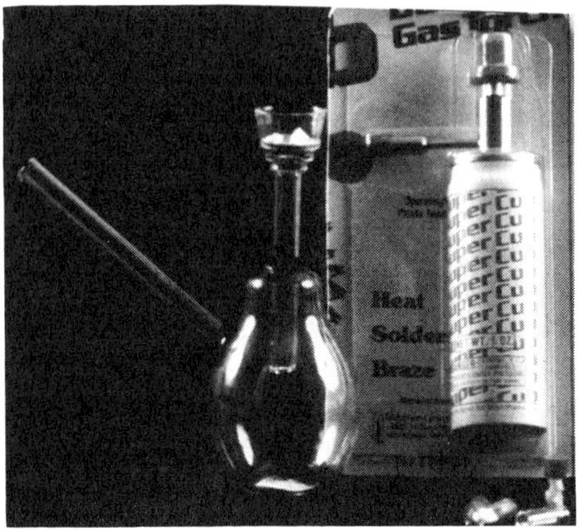

Figure 3.4 A water pipe and small butane torch commonly used to smoke "crack," an inexpensive, ready-made freebase form of cocaine. (Photo courtesy of the U.S. Drug Enforcement Administration.)

Meth can be smoked, snorted, injected, or taken orally, and its appearance varies depending on how it is used. Typically, it is a white, odorless, bitter-tasting powder that easily dissolves in water. Another common form of the drug is crystal meth, or "ice," named for its appearance (that of clear, large chunky crystals resembling rock candy). Crystal meth is smoked in a manner similar to crack cocaine and about 10–15 "hits" can be obtained from a single gram of the substance. Users have referred to smoking ice as a "cool" smoke, while smoking crack is a "hot" smoke. The euphoric effect of smoking ice lasts longer than that of smoking crack.

Methamphetamine use increases the heart rate, blood pressure, body temperature, and rate of breathing, and it frequently results in violent behavior. Meth also dilates the pupils and produces temporary hyperactivity, euphoria, a sense of increased energy, and tremors. High doses or chronic use have been associated with increased nervousness, irritability, and paranoia. Withdrawal from high doses produces severe depression.

Chronic abuse produces a psychosis similar to schizophrenia characterized by paranoia, picking at the skin, self-absorption, and auditory and visual hallucinations. Violent and erratic behavior is frequently seen among chronic, high-dose methamphetamine abusers. The most dangerous stage of the binge cycle is known as "tweaking." Typically, during this stage, the abuser has not slept in 3–15 days and is irritable and paranoid. The tweaker has an intense craving for more meth; however, no dosage will help recreate the euphoric high. This causes frustration and leads to unpredictability and a potential for violence.

The 1999 *National Household Survey on Drug Abuse* estimated that 9.4 million Americans tried methamphetamine in their lifetime.[5] This figure shows a marked increase from the 1994 estimate of 3.8 million. According to the *Drug Abuse Warning Network* (DAWN), methamphetamine-related emergency department episodes more than tripled between 1991 and 1994, rising from roughly 4900–17,700. Possibly due to a shortage of methamphetamine between 1995 and 1996, there was a decrease in incidents between those years before rising to 17,154 in 1997. Between 1993 and 1995, episodes increased in 9 of the 21 metropolitan areas surveyed by DAWN. The number of methamphetamine-related episodes more than doubled in Atlanta, Dallas, Denver, Minneapolis, and St. Louis. Likewise, treatment providers in California, Oregon, Georgia, Arizona, and North Carolina reported significant increases in the number of clients entering treatment with methamphetamine problems. The director of one clinic in Arizona reported that 70–80% of its clients are meth abusers.

Sources. Historically, suppliers of methamphetamine in the United States were outlaw motorcycle gangs and other independent trafficking groups. Although motorcycle gangs continue to produce meth and control a share of the market, Mexico-based trafficking groups entered the illicit methamphetamine market in 1995 and now dominate the trade. With their ability to obtain wholesale (multi-ton) quantities of precursor chemicals on the international market, their access to already established smuggling and distribution networks, and their control over laboratories capable of large-scale production and distribution of methamphetamine, these criminal groups from Mexico now dominate wholesale meth trafficking in the United States.

Over the past few years, these groups revolutionized the production and distribution of methamphetamine by operating "super labs" that can produce unprecedented quantities of high-purity methamphetamine. Each such lab is capable of producing 10 pounds or more per manufacturing cycle.

The majority of the methamphetamine made and distributed by Mexico-based organizations is produced within the United States, particularly in California and other Western states. Recently, there has been a dramatic increase in the number of methamphetamine laboratories operating in other states such as Kansas, Missouri, Oklahoma, and Arkansas. The rise in laboratory seizures in these states does not reflect a concerted effort by major traffickers to shift production from sites in California. Rather, it reflects the increasing effort by independent entrepreneurs who operate on the periphery of the methamphetamine market to exploit the expanding demand for the drug by producing smaller amounts of the drug in less complex laboratories. (See Figure 3.5.)

Ice. The 1980s introduced the specter of a new drug epidemic. The new drug was a freebase form of methamphetamine known as "ice." Primarily

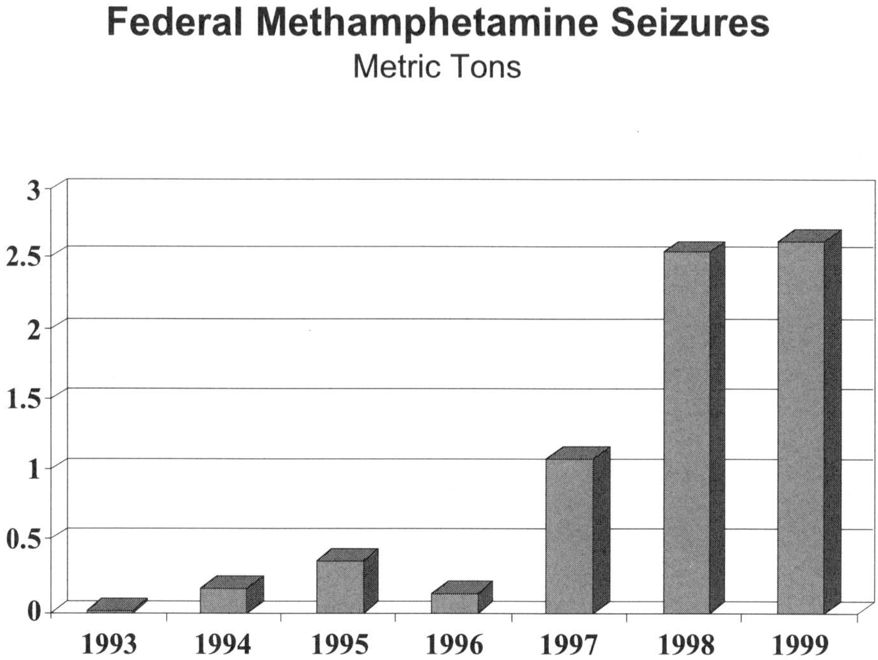

Figure 3.5 Graph showing the rise of federal methamphetamine seizures in metric tons from 1993 through 1999. (Source: Office of National Drug Control Policy, May 2000.)

seen in Hawaii and along the West Coast, in 1996 ice sold on the street for about \$200–450 per gram.[6] It was first developed by traffickers out of reconstructed methamphetamine, a popular recreational stimulant. Ice, whose popularity has had particularly serious impact in Japan, is also called *shabu* or *hiroppon* in the Orient. It consists of tiny, ice-like crystals designed to be smoked (freebased) by the user. The expected high reported by the typical ice user lasts anywhere from 8–16 hours, compared to the 8- to 10-minute high offered by its close cousin, crack, which is also a stimulant.

Side effects of ice include fatal lung and kidney disorders in addition to long-lasting psychological damage. As mentioned, ice is not a new drug; it is a converted drug, as crack was converted from cocaine. It has appealed both to recreational users as well as those who desire a supercharged type of speed for alertness and physical strength.

The emergence of ice in the United States is also distinguishable from the mid-1980s emergence of crack in that the host drug of ice, methamphetamine, can easily be manufactured domestically. This is obviously an advantage for local traffickers who are proficient in the manufacturing and distribution of methamphetamine powder. The popularity of ice in the United States began in Hawaii in the mid-1980s. During a brief four-year

Figure 3.6 Close-up photo of a Valium (diazepam) tablet, a widely abused hypnotic sedative and a commonly diverted pharmaceutical drug. (Photo courtesy of the U.S. Drug Enforcement Administration.)

period, police estimate that it surpassed the popularity of marijuana and cocaine there. The genesis of ice in Hawaii can be traced back to Korea, which, along with Taiwan, leads the world in manufacture and export of the drug. Koreans learned of the drug methamphetamine from the Japanese, who developed it in 1873.

Khat

For centuries, Khat (the fresh young leaves of the *Catha edulis* shrub) has been consumed where the plant is cultivated, primarily in East Africa and the Arabian peninsula. There, chewing khat predates the use of coffee and is used in a similar context. When chewed in moderation, khat alleviates fatigue and reduces appetite. Compulsive use, though, can result in manic behavior along with paranoid delusions. In recent years khat has been brought to the United States for use by emigrants from the source countries. The plant contains a number of controlled substances, including cathinone (Schedule I) and cathine (Schedule II).

Depressants

Opposite to stimulants are depressants. Drugs falling into the depressant category also have a potential for abuse due to their physical and psychological characteristics (Figure 3.6). Like many dangerous substances, if taken under the supervision of a physician, drugs in this category may be beneficial, usually in treating conditions such as anxiety, irritability, tension, and insomnia. When abused, depressants produce a state of intoxication closely resembling that of alcohol.

As with stimulants, drugs falling in this category are not all controlled or unlawful. That is, even compounds that can be purchased over the counter can have dangerous effects on the user. One such substance is alcohol, which, when taken in moderation, will produce mild sedation. The name "depressant" does not literally mean that the user becomes depressed but refers to the depression of his or her central nervous system. Initially, in heavier doses some depressants may give the user an uplifting feeling similar to that produced by stimulants. After prolonged use, however, the user tends to become sluggish, with impaired judgment, slurred speech, and loss of motor coordination.

Tolerance to depressants (as with stimulants and narcotics) develops rapidly with regular use, which adds to the likelihood of overdose or even death. Some depressant users who fail to follow their physicians' dosage recommendations may find that their daily doses will increase 10–20 times the recommended therapeutic dose.

Stimulant users will frequently use a depressant to help them calm down at the end of the day. The level of danger rises when the user chooses to mix depressants with alcohol, creating a synergistic effect. This effect occurs when two or more drugs are taken together and the combined action increases the normal effect of each drug. Because of this action, a drug that can normally be taken safely can have a devastating effect if taken with a drug that acts synergistically with it. Perhaps one of the most important dangers of depressant use is the abrupt cessation of high-dose depressant intake, which results in the characteristic withdrawal syndrome. Such a condition manifests itself by feelings of anxiety, vomiting, loss of appetite, increased heart rate, profuse sweating, and possibly convulsions similar to those occurring in grand mal epilepsy. The latter symptom will usually peak in approximately the third to seventh day of abstinence, depending on the type of depressant used, and is considered to be life threatening unless conducted under medical supervision.

Barbiturates

The most frequently prescribed depressants are barbiturates, which are commonly prescribed to induce sleep. About 15 derivatives of barbituric acid are currently in medical use. These are used to induce sleep or calm nervousness and usually take about one hour to take effect. Barbiturates are classified as ultra-short, short, intermediate, and long-lasting, with the duration of effect lasting from 6–16 hours. These include such drugs as hexobarbital (Sombulex), pentobarbital (Nembutal), secobarbital (Seconal), and phenobarbital (Luminal).

Quaaludes

A widely abused depressant of the late 1970s and early 1980s was Quaalude, or methaqualone. Although now outlawed, quaalude (in counterfeit version) is still manufactured clandestinely in foreign markets, smuggled into this country, and sold on American streets. Quaalude is chemically unrelated to the barbiturate but has been responsible for many cases of poisoning and overdoses. It is sold in a tablet form, which is ingested through the gastrointestinal tract, and is commonly stamped with the name "Lemon 714" or "Rorer 714." In large doses, it can cause coma and convulsions. Methaqualone also has been marketed under other names, such as Parest, Mequin, Optimil, Somnafac, and Sopor.

Hallucinogens

Although hallucinogens have been in existence in one form or another for hundreds of years, they first gained widespread, popular appeal during the 1960s. Hallucinogenic drugs are both natural (organic) and synthetic (human made) and act on the central nervous system by distorting auditory, tactile, and visual perceptions. Although the use of some hallucinogens has been known to sharpen the user's senses, some experiences, particularly when "coming down," are of a negative and depressive nature. Tolerance is another trait of hallucinogen use. Users frequently require more and more of the drug to feel the original effects.

Hallucinogen users experience the ability to "hear sights" and "see sounds." Colors are amplified into a kaleidoscopic prism within the mind. Occasionally, depression accompanies a negative or "bad trip" and may manifest in the form of suicidal tendencies. Another negative side to the use of hallucinogens is the possibility of "flashbacks," which are fragmentary or recurring (probably imagined) hallucinations that may occur many months or even years after the last dose of the drug has been taken.

LSD (Lysergic Acid Diethylamide)

LSD is produced from lysergic acid and is a clear, odorless liquid substance derived from the ergot fungus that grows on rye. Because of the extremely high potency of LSD and its structural relationship to a chemical already found in the human brain, its effects were originally studied as treatment for some types of mental illness. LSD is clandestinely manufactured and comes in several street forms:

- *Window Pane*: this form consists of thin squares of gelatin, each containing approximately one drop of LSD.
- *Blotter Acid*: this form is impregnated on paper, often with numerous miniature cartoons printed in rows (Figures 3.7 and 3.8). Each cartoon contains approximately one drop of LSD.
- *Micro Dot*: these are tiny multicolored tablets, which are so small that they can be concealed under a thumbnail. They are called such names as Purple Haze, Orange Barrels, and Strawberry Sunshine.

Figure 3.7 Blotter LSD — each square contains one drop of liquid LSD.

The average effective oral dose is from 30–50 micrograms, but the amount per dose varies greatly. The effects of higher doses will persist for 10–12 hours.

PCP (Phencyclidine)

Phencyclidine (PCP) is a hallucinogen originally developed in 1957 as a general anesthetic (DEA, 1996). Because of negative side effects such as convulsions and delirium, its use for human patients was rapidly discontinued. In the 1960s, PCP became commercially available for use as a veterinary medicine under the trade name Sernylan. In 1978, PCP was transferred from a Schedule III to a Schedule II drug under the *Controlled Substances Act*. Because of this legislation, most (if not all) of the PCP encountered on the street is manufactured in clandestine laboratories rather than diverted from legal channels.

PCP has been sold under numerous other names that reflect its bizarre and unpredictable effects (e.g., Jet Fuel, Angel Dust, Supergrass, Rocket Fuel, etc.). Other names include Wac, Water, Shirms, Dips, and Shirm Sticks (names for liquid PCP or cigarettes dipped in liquid PCP). PCP is available in two forms: powder and liquid. The powdered form achieved most of its popularity during the early 1970s and through the mid-1980s but has been replaced in many areas with liquid PCP. The liquid form of the drug is yellowish-tan in color, much easier to manufacture than the powdered form,

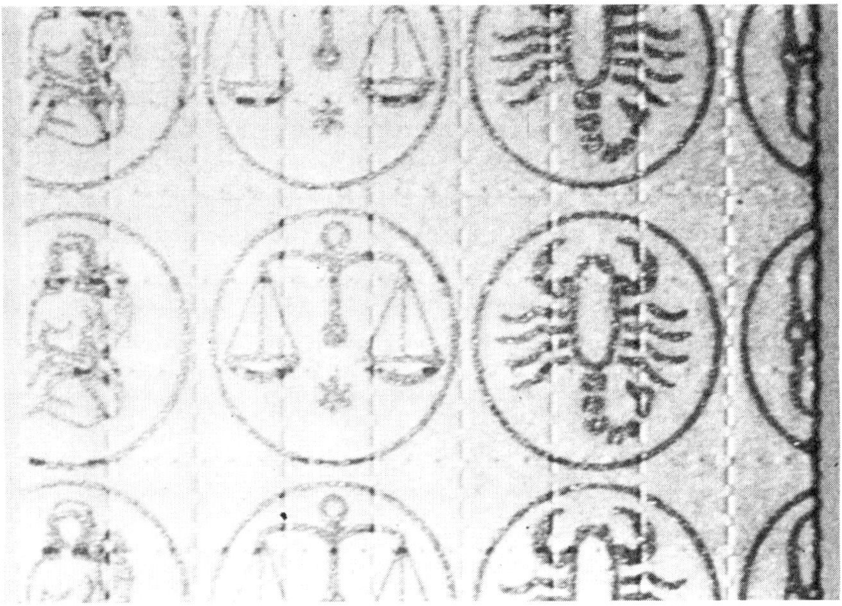

Figure 3.8 Example of "blotter" LSD, usually a cartoon picture containing one drop of liquid LSD in each square. (Photo courtesy of the U.S. Drug Enforcement Administration.)

and able to retain a high volatility due to a higher concentration of ether in its chemical makeup.

Along with the rescheduling of the drug in 1978, the respective penalties for manufacture, sale, and possession of PCP were increased to serve as a deterrent. Since the early 1980s, however, the proliferation of clandestine PCP laboratories has become evident in numerous states across the country.

Peyote and Mescaline

While PCP is a synthetic hallucinogen, the peyote cactus and its psychoactive ingredient mescaline are of an organic origin. Mescaline affects the user much like LSD. Peyote is derived from the so-called "buttons" of the peyote cactus. The use of the peyote cactus by Indians in northern Mexico has been common since the earliest recorded history. The religious use of peyote by the Native American Church has been exempted from certain provisions of the 1970 Controlled Substances Act. Peyote is usually removed from the cactus, allowed to dry, ground up into a powder, and taken orally.

Psilocybin Mushrooms

Another organic hallucinogen is the psilocybin or "magic" mushroom (also called "shrooms"), which has seen some traditional use by Native Americans and is also relatively popular among recreational hallucinogenics users. The active ingredient is psilocybin, which can also be manufactured synthetically. When taken orally, psilocybin is one of the most rapidly acting hallucinogens. Its effects can usually be felt in 10–15 minutes, and reactions will last for about 90 minutes to 4 hours. Physical effects include dilated pupils, increased heart rate, and a rise in blood pressure. Psychological effects include difficulty in thinking, mental relaxation, detachment from surroundings, and feelings of anxiety. Tolerance to psilocybin has been well documented over the years.

Ecstasy

Adding to the list of popular hallucinogens is the relatively new drug MDMA (3,4-methylenedioxymethamphetamine), which is also known on the street as Ecstasy, XTC, Eve, and Essence. This drug, which gained much popularity during the mid-1980s, had the misleading reputation of creating a strong euphoria for the user while being a relatively harmless drug. MDMA was developed in 1914 by the German pharmaceutical company, Merck, as a diet pill, but was never commercially manufactured. Its possession or use was not prohibited until 1985. The popularity of the drug saw a brief upsurge during the 1970s as a substitute for the popular hallucinogen MDA (methylenedioxyamphetamine), which was illegal. Nevertheless, its popularity was overshadowed by the prevalent recreational use of LSD. (Figure 3.9.)

MDMA was finally outlawed in 1985 and classified as a Schedule I drug. Strong opposition to this measure came from the psychiatric community, which claimed that the drug was beneficial in therapy. Just before that time, MDMA was especially popular in college towns and urban areas; it was thought by some to be an aphrodisiac. The popularity of MDMA during this period was fueled by many newspapers and television stations that carried stories about it. Even the popular comic strip *Doonesbury* featured the drug on occasion.

MDMA is taken orally and is commonly packaged as a white powder contained within a gelatin capsule or as an off-white tablet. Street prices range from \$6–\$30 per dosage unit throughout the country.[7] Chemically, MDMA is similar to mescaline and possesses both hallucinogenic and stimulant properties. At low levels, it is mildly intoxicating, it rarely produces hallucinations typically associated with other more common hallucinogens, and the effects last about 30 minutes.

Although much research is needed on MDMA, the National Institute of Drug Abuse (NIDA) reported in 1989 that MDMA can temporarily destroy brain-cell nerve endings in animals and may be capable of inflicting permanent brain damage in the long term. Because research findings have been inconclusive about MDMA's impact on humans and because there is some indication of therapeutic benefits, MDMA remains a controversial drug.

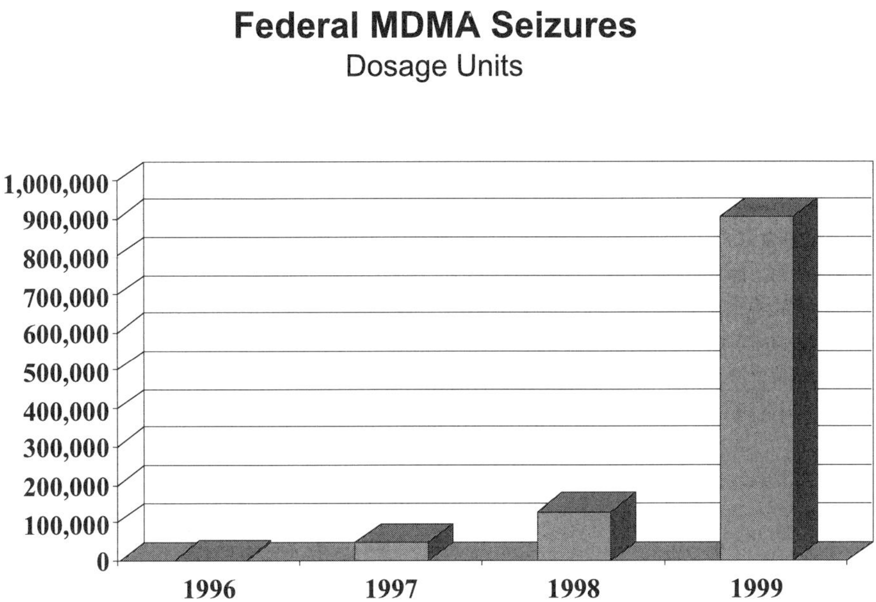

Figure 3.9 Graph showing increase in federal MDMA seizures in dosage units from 1996 through 1999. Source: Office of National Drug Control Policy, May 2000.

Narcotics

The term narcotic signifies a legal category of drugs that refers to opium and opium derivatives or their synthetic substitutes. Generally speaking, these drugs are painkillers that are indispensable in medical treatment but are also very potent and extremely addictive. The initial effects of the drugs may be unpleasant and may include such side effects as nausea, vomiting, drowsiness, apathy, decreased physical activity, and constipation. Strong doses can lead to respiratory depression, loss of motor coordination, and slurred speech. Users who desire the brief euphoric effects of narcotic drugs may develop tolerance and increase their doses of the drug. Repeated use of narcotics will almost certainly manifest itself in both physical addiction and psychological dependence. Usually, narcotics are administered either orally or by injection. Intravenous drug users will commonly use one of two methods of injection:

1. Skin popping: injecting the drug just under the skin and into the muscle
2. Mainlining: injecting the drug directly into the veins

When the physically addicted user is deprived of the drug, the first withdrawal signs are usually noticed shortly before the time of the next

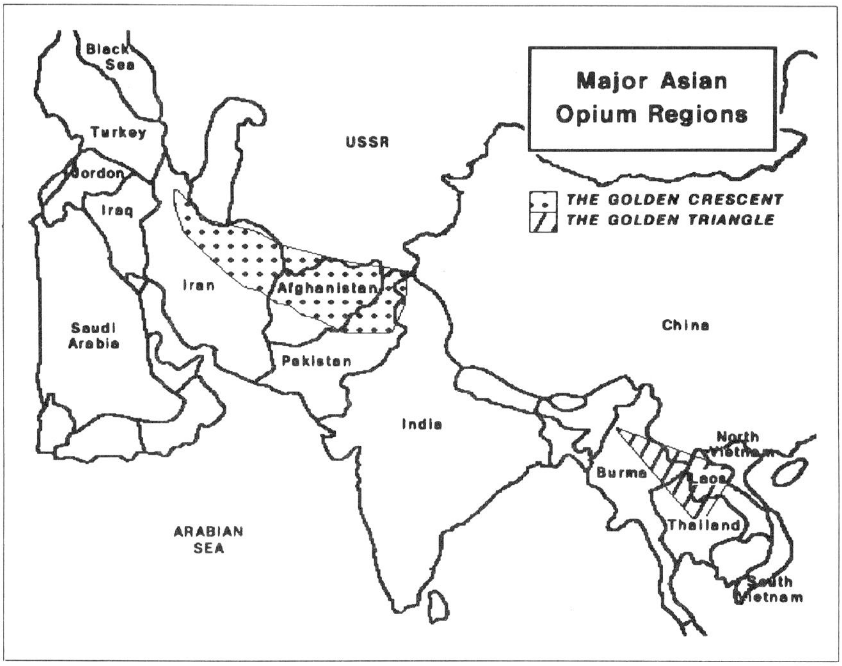

Figure 3.10 The Golden Triangle and the Golden Crescent, opium- and heroin-producing regions.

desired dose, which is anywhere from 36–72 hours after the last dose. Other symptoms (such as watery eyes, runny nose, yawning, and perspiration) will appear about 8–12 hours after the last dose. As the abstinence syndrome progresses, the user will experience loss of appetite, irritability, insomnia, "goose flesh," and tremors accompanied by severe sneezing. When the symptoms reach their peak, the user becomes weak and vomits while experiencing stomach cramps, diarrhea, and an increase in heart rate. These symptoms linger for 5–7 days, then disappear.

Narcotics are of both natural and synthetic origins. Of the natural-origin narcotics, the most common are opium, heroin, and morphine. All of these are derived from the opium poppy plant *papaver somniferum*. This plant only grows in certain parts of the world and is most commonly found today in South America, Southeast Asia, Southwest Asia, and Mexico. (Figures 3.10, 3.11.)

The opium poppy produces a seed pod that when unripe is traditionally lanced with a knife by farmers to obtain a milky liquid that oozes out of the incision. A more modern method, however, is the industrial poppy straw process of extracting alkaloids from the mature dried plant. Through this method of poppy harvesting, more than 400 tons of opium or its equivalent in poppy straw is legally imported annually into the United States.

Figure 3.11 The opium poppy is an attractive flowering plant that produces raw opium, which is harvested and processed into heroin. (Photo courtesy of the U.S. Drug Enforcement Administration.)

The United States Drug Enforcement Administration estimates that at least 25 alkaloids can be extracted from raw opium. These fall into two categories:

1. The phenanthrene alkaloids, which principally produce morphine and codeine and are used as analgesics and cough suppressants.
2. The isoquinoline alkaloids, which are used in the production of intestinal relaxants and cough suppressants. (This category has no effect on the central nervous system and, therefore, is not regulated under the Controlled Substances Act.)

Heroin

Heroin (diacetylmorphine), a narcotic originally synthesized from morphine in 1874, was initially thought to be a cure for morphine addiction. It is a central nervous system depressant that will also relieve pain. Heroin was first controlled by the Harrison Narcotics Act of 1914, a law born out of international concerns about opium use and an increasing problem of addiction among middle-class women who used it as an over-the-counter remedy. Despite legal controls, it took some 20 years before existing stocks of heroin were ultimately removed from store shelves.

Today, heroin is considered the most widely abused drug in the narcotic family and is produced exclusively on a clandestine or illegal basis. In fact, it is considered a top choice of drugs trafficked by traditional Italian organized crime groups, African-American organized crime groups, international Chinese drug cartels, and, more recently, Colombian cartels.

Pure Asian heroin is white (brown heroin comes from Mexico) and has a bitter taste. The differences in brown and white heroin are attributed to the methods of manufacturing, which make use of various refining methods, leaving different impurities (Figure 3.12). In fact, pure heroin is rarely sold on the street. Street heroin is usually only 2–3% pure and may be diluted with lactose, starch, quinine, or even strychnine, the latter of which accounts for many heroin overdoses (see Figure 3.13).

Heroin is usually administered through intravenous injection, but some users inject the drug under the skin or smoke it on the tip of a cigarette. It is also administered orally or intranasally. Because of the physically addictive nature of the drug, addicts may require several injections (or "fixes") daily.

Heroin depresses the central nervous system, but also acts as a pain reliever. Because of the depressant nature of heroin, it tends to severely reduce the potential for aggressive behavior in users. Accompanying effects include a feeling of euphoria or "floating" and a sensation described as orgasmic. Additional effects include constipation and suppression of the cough reflex, followed by sleep or "nodding off."

Black Tar Heroin. A crude form of heroin that appeared on the drug scene in the early 1980s is "black tar" heroin. This type of heroin is thought to be manufactured by Mexican traffickers in the Sonora, Durango, Sinaloa, and Guerrero states of Mexico, smuggled to the United States by illegal aliens and migrant workers, and distributed through extended family connections in the United States. In 1987, according to the DEA, law enforcement authorities found black tar in at least 27 states, with most of the use concentrated in Mexican-American communities.

Black tar is crudely processed heroin that may appear dark brown in color (Figure 3.14). It is either sticky like roofing tar or hard like coal. It is known by such street names as "tootsie roll" and "goma," and its growing acceptance in the street stems from its high purity, low price, and widespread availability. Black tar is typically smoked by the user, and its high level of purity may pose dangers for those who choose to inject it. The purity levels for black tar have been documented to be as high as 93%, with 60–70% considered common. Because of its high purity, a sharp increase in heroin-related injuries has been reported since its emergence in the early 1980s.

Figure 3.12 Asian white and Mexican brown heroin. (Photo courtesy of the U.S. Drug Enforcement Administration.)

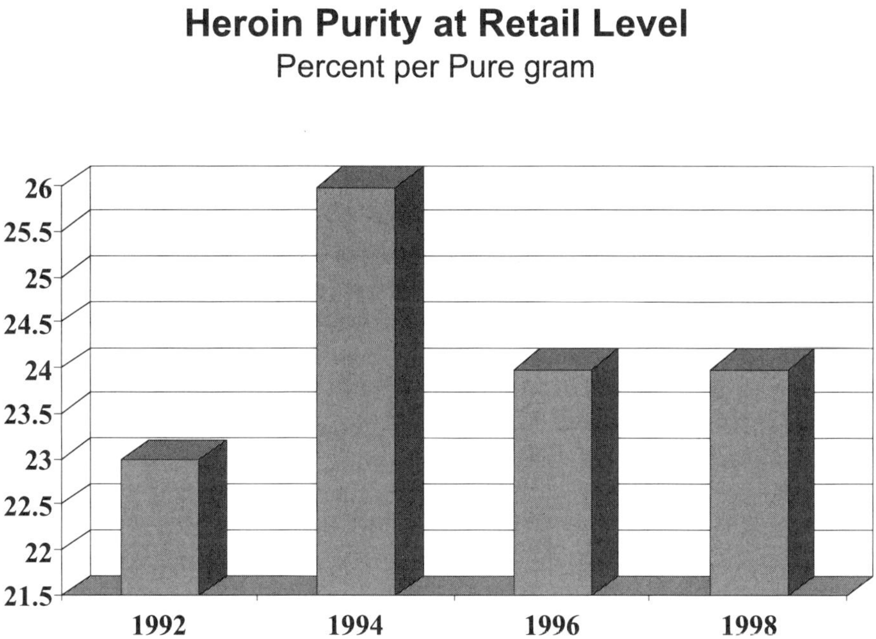

Figure 3.13 Graph showing percent per pure gram of heroin purity at the retail level. (Source: Office of National Drug Control Policy, May 2000.)

Hydromorphone

A commonly abused synthetic narcotic is hydromorphone, which is also known as Dilaudid (Figure 3.15). Marketed in both injectable and tablet form, it is faster acting and has a greater sedating effect than morphine, and it is anywhere from two to eight times as potent. Dilaudid is commonly

Figure 3.14 "Black tar" heroin, a rock type of heroin originating in Mexico. (Photo courtesy of the U.S. Drug Enforcement Administration.)

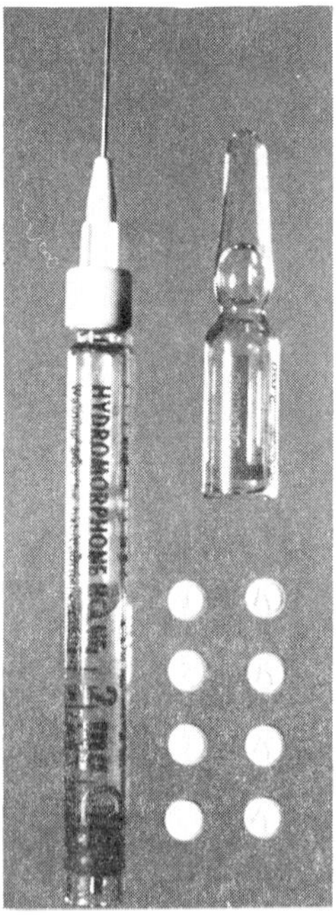

Figure 3.15 Dilaudid in both injectable and tablet form. (Photo courtesy of the U.S. Drug Enforcement Administration.)

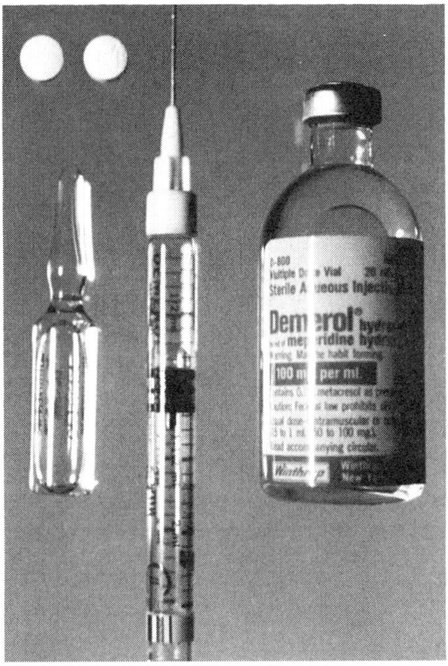

Figure 3.16 Injectable Demerol, a popular and highly addictive drug. (Photo courtesy of the U.S. Drug Enforcement Administration.)

obtained through theft from drug stores, fraudulent prescriptions, and diversion from legitimate manufacturers. The tablet form is normally stronger than the liquid form. The tablet is frequently dissolved and injected by the drug user (Figure 3.16).

Methadone

German scientists synthesized methadone during World War II because of a shortage of morphine. It is chemically unlike morphine but produces the same effects. The methadone maintenance program, introduced in 1964, was designed as a treatment for heroin addicts. Methadone is administered in both oral and injectable form and has a longer duration of effect than morphine or heroin. In fact, its effects may last up to 24 hours, thus making the drug a valuable aid in the treatment of heroin addiction.

Designer Drugs

"Designer" drugs have risen out of a new technology adopted by illicit drug manufacturers. That is, manufacturers produce potent drugs that are not yet covered by criminal codes and, therefore, may be legally possessed. This process involves resynthesizing already-existing drugs to the point at which they have the same basic effects on the user, but the chemical-molecular

Figure 3.17 The marijuana leaf is easily distinguishable by its dark green color and saw-toothed leaves.

structure of the drugs is altered so that they cannot be defined as illegal under the law. Most states today have adopted laws dealing with this problem; many of them have subsequently outlawed the analogs (basic chemicals) with which designer drugs are made.

One of the most dangerous of the designer drugs that emerged during the mid-1980s is "China White" heroin. Designer China White should not be confused with the China White common during the operation of the French Connection, which was actually an opiate derivative. Designer China White is a totally synthetic white powder that has the same general characteristics of heroin but is estimated to be at least 1000 times more potent. Designer China White heroin is actually a compound known as fentanyl (3-methyl fentanyl or 3-alpha fentanyl). Users of this drug have reported dangerous side effects such as Parkinson's disease, which cripples part or all of the body.

Cannabis

Although indexed in this text as a substance in a category all its own, cannabis is classified by the Controlled Substances Act as a Schedule I drug, a mild hallucinogen. *Cannabis sativa,* or the hemp plant (Figure 3.17), grows wild throughout most areas of the world and has long been cultivated for its use in manufacturing rope, textile materials, certain feed mixtures, and as an ingredient in paint. Despite a lengthy history of both use and abuse, marijuana (also spelled marihuana) was outlawed by the 1937 Marijuana Tax Act, and by 1941 it had been deleted from the *U.S. Pharmacopoeia* and the *National Formulary,* the official compendium of drugs. Marijuana, both a domestic and foreign moneymaker for drug traffickers, is produced in large quantities in countries such as Colombia, Mexico, Jamaica, and Panama, as well as in Hawaii, Kentucky, Oregon, and California. Clandestine growers are constantly striving to increase the THC (delta-9-tetrahydrocannabinol) content of the plant, as the THC content gives the user the desired high and reflects a corresponding market price for the drug. Most commercial marijuana ranges from 3–4% THC content. However, advances in the chemistry and horticulture of marijuana cultivation have increased the plant's potency over the years. A rare strain of marijuana, considered the most potent, is sinsemilla (a Spanish word meaning without seeds). Sinsemilla is a hybrid strain of marijuana that is prepared from the unpollinated female cannabis plant and may produce a yield of more than 12% THC content.

Cannabis products are usually smoked by the user. The high from the drug is felt in minutes and usually lasts for 2–3 hours. The effects of the drug vary among users but in mild doses generally include feelings of restlessness, wellbeing, relaxation, and a craving for sweets. Stronger doses will elicit stronger reactions, such as subtle alterations in thought formation, changes in perceptions, rapidly fluctuating emotions, an altered sense of self-identity, and impaired memory.

Research into the medicinal benefits of cannabis during the last 20 years has focused on the development of a cannabis product that will not produce negative side effects. Probably the most active research being performed on cannabis is for the treatment of nausea and vomiting caused by chemotherapeutic agents used in treating cancer patients. In addition, research continues on the use of marijuana in the treatment of glaucoma. Some medical professionals also claim that marijuana's THC content tends to aid in the remission of cancer of the iris.

Marijuana's potential dangers are subject to intense debate, and the issue is far from resolved. One widely embraced but controversial theory opposing the use of marijuana is the "gateway theory," which holds that marijuana users will typically move to harder drugs. Researcher Joseph Califano Jr., president of Columbia University's Center on Addiction and Substance, explains: "A child 12–17 years old who smokes marijuana is 85 times as likely to use cocaine or harder drugs."[8] Other researchers, however, point out that many other substances, even innocuous ones, can be viewed as gateway substances depending on how one interprets statistics. In 1996, the *Journal of the American Medical Association* reported that heavy marijuana users tend to have trouble paying attention and taking in new information for at least one day after using the drug.[9] Finally, a report by George Koob and colleagues at Scripps Research Institute stated that years of marijuana smoking might alter brain chemistry such that when the user is deprived of the drug, a type of withdrawal, usually in the form of anxiety, is likely.[10]

Figure 3.18 Two hundred pounds of Turkish hashish seized in Columbia, Missouri. Hashish is a byproduct of the marijuana plant and has a much higher THC content than marijuana.

Another potent cannabis product is hashish or hash (Figure 3.18). Most of the hashish encountered on American streets originates in the Middle East, where large plantations of the plant flourish. Basically, hashish (and its cousin "hashish oil") is made by a boiling process in which all but the THC resins of the plant are extracted. Although usually smoked, hash can be eaten as well, and contains about 20% THC.

Inhalants

Inhalants are a chemically diverse group of psychoactive substances composed of organic solvents and volatile substances commonly found in more than 1000 common household products such as glues, hair spray, air fresheners, lighter fluid, and paint products. While not regulated under the Controlled Substances Act, many states have placed restrictions on the sale of these products to minors.

Inhalants may be sniffed directly from an open container or "huffed" from a rag soaked in the substance and held to the face. Alternatively, the open container or soaked rag can be placed in a bag where the vapors concentrate before being inhaled. Although inhalant abusers may prefer one particular substance because of the odor or taste, a variety of substances may be used because of their similar effects, availability, and cost. Once inhaled, the extensive capillary surface of the lungs allows rapid absorption of the substance, and blood levels peak rapidly. Entry into the brain is so fast that the effects of inhalation can resemble the intensity of effects produced by intravenous injection of other psychoactive drugs.

The effects of inhalant intoxication resemble those of alcohol inebriation — stimulation and loss of inhibition, followed by depression. Users report distortion in perceptions of time and space. Many users experience headache, nausea or vomiting, slurred speech, loss of motor coordination, and wheezing. A characteristic "glue sniffer's rash" around the nose and mouth may be seen. An odor of paint or solvents on clothes, skin, and breath is sometimes a sign of inhalant abuse.

Sniffing highly concentrated amounts of the chemicals in solvents or aerosol sprays can directly induce heart failure and death. These chemicals also cause death from suffocation by displacing oxygen in the lungs and subsequently in the central nervous system, causing breathing to cease. The chronic use of inhalants has been associated with a number of serious, long-term, and often irreversible health problems. These include hearing loss, brain and central nervous system damage, bone marrow damage, liver and kidney damage, and blood oxygen depletion.

Inhalant abuse is shockingly common among children and adolescents. In a 1998 survey by the *National Parents' Resource Institute for Drug Education,* 2.2% of fourth graders and 2.7% of sixth graders admitted to sniffing glue and other inhalants on a monthly basis. By the time they reach the eighth grade, 5% will be using inhalants monthly, and 19.7% will have used inhalants at least once in the lifetimes, according to statistics from the 1999 *Monitoring the Future* study.

Inhalants are readily available, inexpensive, and easy to conceal. Therefore, they are increasingly popular with young people and are, for many, one of the first substances abused. The extent of the inhalant problem among children and adolescents was at first virtually unrecognized by the general public. However, a tragic event in early 1999 called national attention to this severe problem. Five high school girls were killed in a car accident outside Philadelphia, and the coroner's report showed that four of the five, including the driver, had ingested "significant" amounts of a computer keyboard cleaner. Since this event, there has been an increased awareness of the threat of inhalant abuse.

Other Drugs of Abuse

Steroids

Anabolic steroid abuse has grown to become a national concern. Typically, these drugs are abused by weight lifters, body builders, long distance runners, cyclists, and others who believe that these drugs give them a competitive edge or improve their physical performance. Once thought to be a problem only with professional athletes, one recent report estimates that 5–12% of male high school students and 1% of female students have used anabolic steroids by the time they were seniors.[6] The Controlled Substance Act defines steroids as any drug or hormonal substance chemically and pharmacologically related to testosterone that promotes muscle growth. For the most part, steroids are smuggled into the country, although a limited number of them are approved for medical and veterinary use. The legitimate use of these substances is to replace inadequate levels of testosterone resulting from a reduction of functioning testes. When used in combination with exercise and a high protein diet, anabolic steroids can increase the size and strength of muscles, improve endurance, and decrease recovery time between workouts. Steroids are either injected or taken orally. While the adverse effects of large doses of multiple anabolic steroids are not well established, there is increasing evidence of serious health problems, including cardiovascular and liver damage as well as damage to reproductive organs. Physical side effects include increased blood pressure and cholesterol levels, severe acne, premature balding, and reduced sexual functioning.

Mood Drugs

Since the late 1980s, new forms of drugs have emerged as promising treatments for clinical depression. Of these, Prozac® is the best selling and most visible member of the new class of drugs known as antidepressant drugs or selective serotonin reuptake inhibitors (SSRIs). Since its introduction in 1988, Prozac has been taken by an estimated 11 million people worldwide. Manufactured by Eli Lilly and Co., Prozac (the trade name for the synthetic compound fluoxetine) is one of three SSRIs on the market in the United States. The other two, Paxil® (SmithKline Beecham Pharmaceuticals) and Zoloft® (Pfizer, Inc.) have not achieved nearly the degree of popularity.

Since the introduction of Prozac, controversy over the drug has caused an ongoing debate over the use of psychoactive drugs vs. traditional "talk therapy." Stated simply, Prozac has enjoyed considerable success in treating clinical depression, and its success supports the growing trend in psychology that mental illness might be caused through a biological dysfunction. Modern technological advances have enabled researchers to link physical disturbances in the brain to some mental disorders. Because of such findings, drug manufacturers are now synthesizing new compounds that affect these disturbances. Prozac, for example, offsets imbalances of serotonin, a brain chemical linked to depression. In addition to treatment of depression, it is also approved for treatment of obsessive-compulsive disorder and, more recently, bulimia.

Rohypnol: The "Date Rape" Drug

Date rapes are among the most difficult cases to prove in a court of law. A new type of drug has recently emerged that robs victims of their memories and ability to defend themselves. This has made a tough job tougher. The most common offender is flunitrazipan (Rohypnol®), along with gamma hydroxybutyrate (GHB), a liquid made from ingredients available in health food stores. These are used in bars, clubs, and parties as an inexpensive way to get high and, more often, as "date rape" drugs. In September 1996, a 15-year-old El Paso, Texas, girl died after being given a drink containing Rohypnol, and a 17-year-old girl from La Porte, Texas, died after she drank a soda spiked with GHB.

GHB can be deadly because it depresses breathing and restricts oxygen to the brain. Rohypnol, a benzodiazepine in the same family as Xanax®, Valium®, Librium®, and Halcion®, works by interfering with chemical activity in the brain. Rohypnol is a tasteless, colorless, and odorless substance that dissolves quickly in drinks. It causes intoxication with slurred speech, difficulty walking, and impaired judgment. It also causes deep loss of memory and paralysis of the extremities. Within 12 hours amnesia sets in, along with loss of inhibitions. In combination with alcohol, this drug can kill.

Rohypnol, manufactured by Hoffmann-La Roche, goes by various street names, such as roofies, rope, roaches, etc., and is often smuggled into the United States from Mexico and Colombia. Often called the "lunch money drug," it sells for $1–$2 a pill. In October 1996, President Clinton signed into law penalties of up to 20 years in prison for possession of Rohypnol with intent to commit a crime.

Summary

Perhaps one reason for drug abuse is a misunderstanding about the effects of drugs and their general pharmacology. Frequently, drug users listen to other drug users about the effects of a particular drug; such information is often incorrect. Drugs can be virtually anything that alters the user's physical or psychological makeup; they can be either legal or illegal to possess. Therefore, the word "drug" could rightfully refer to such compounds as heroin, LSD, and marijuana, along with sugar, salt, and caffeine.

All drugs, whether or not they are controlled, fall into one of six categories: stimulants, depressants, hallucinogens, narcotics, cannabis, and inhalants. Drugs in the stimulant category literally stimulate the central nervous system and make the user feel more alert. The most commonly abused illicit drugs in this category are cocaine (including crack), amphetamines, and

Figure 3.19 Mail bags containing kilos of marijuana that were smuggled into Florida and seized by drug agents. (Photo courtesy of the Florida Department of Law Enforcement.)

methamphetamines. The depressant category represents drugs that have a different effect on the user. Although early stages of ingestion of depressants may create a feeling of exhilaration, these drugs actually depress the central nervous system. Alcohol is a lawfully obtainable depressant, while depressants such as barbiturates and sedative hypnotics are usually physically addicting and pose great physical dangers to the drug abuser.

Hallucinogens are a unique category of drug, as they are not physically addicting and their use is not as common as other categories of drugs. Hallucinogens such as LSD, PCP, and MDMA (Ecstasy) are considered dangerous for other reasons. For example, LSD users encounter the possibility of "bad trips" or "flashbacks" resulting from the use of the drug. PCP users frequently become completely detached from reality while experiencing violent hallucinations. Those who use PCP can injure themselves (even breaking bones) unwittingly because PCP also acts as an anesthetic.

The narcotic category refers to drugs such as heroin, morphine, opium, and Dilaudid, which are physically addicting and which emulate the effects of opium. All drugs within this category are controlled, and possession of lawfully manufactured narcotics is permitted only pursuant to a lawful prescription.

Marijuana or cannabis is discussed as an individual category of drug, but the Drug Enforcement Administration considers it a mild hallucinogen. Although cannabis had a legitimate use in the early history of the United States, it is outlawed to one extent or another in all states (Figure 3.19). Its beneficial use in medicine is still under study.

The use of inhalants has become popular (especially among adolescents) because they are both readily available and legal to posses. Breathing the fumes of such household products as glue, paint, and gasoline, however, may pose more risk of physiological damage to the user's brain than other dangerous substances encountered on the street.

Mood drugs, most notably Prozac, have emerged for the treatment of clinical depression, but have been questioned in terms of their side effects. Other drugs, such as flunitrazipan (the "date rape" drug) and "fen-phen" (a dangerous diet drug combination) have also entered the picture.

Suggested Readings

Fields, R., *Drugs and Alcohol in Perspective*, W.C. Brown, Canbury, NJ, 1992.

Abadinsky, H., *Drug Abuse: An Introduction*, Nelson Hall, Chicago, 1997.

Inciardi, J.A. and K. McElrath, *The American Drug Scene*, Roxbury, Los Angeles, CA, 1995.

References

1. Nash, J.M. (1997). Addiction: why do people get hooked? *Time* (May 5): 69–76.
2. *Diagnostic and Statistical Manual of Mental Disorders,* Fourth Edition (1994). Washington, DC: American Psychiatric Press.
3. National Institute on Drug Abuse (1996). *Cocaine Abuse.* Washington, DC: U.S. Government Printing Office.
4. White, P.T. (1989). Coca: an ancient indian herb turns deadly. *National Geographic* 175: 1 (January).
5. Emergency Department data from the Drug Abuse Warning Network Annual, DHHS Publication No. SMA00-3462. Rockville, MD: U.S. Department of Health and Human Services.
6. Drug Enforcement Administration (1996). *Drugs of Abuse,* 1996 Edition. Office of the Attorney General. Washington, DC: U.S. Department of Justice.
7. National Narcotics Intelligence Consumers Committee (1996). *The NNICC Report 1995: The supply of Illicit Drugs to the United States.* Washington, DC: U.S. Government Printing Office.
8. Della Cava, M.R. (1995). Drug czar: it is time to sound the alarm. *USA Today* (February 15): Al.
9. Painter, K. (1996). Heavy marijuana use may impair learning. *USA Today* (August 8): 2A.
10. Sternberg, S. (1997). Marijuana's Active Ingredient May Cause Addiction. *USA Today* (June 17): 1C.

Managing Informants

4

Of the many tools afforded the drug investigator, the informant is probably one of the most important. Informants are people who know the dealers and the users. They can save the investigator an immense amount of time and effort in locating targets and documenting the extent to which those targets are involved in illegal activity.

In 1992, Gambino family mob boss John Gotti was sentenced to life in prison by a federal court in New York City. Probably the most important tool used by the prosecution was testimony from underboss-turned-snitch, Salvatore ("Sammy the Bull") Gravano. Gravano, who himself pled guilty to 19 murders, is a good example of the role that informants can play in the prosecution of high-level people in organized crime cases. Gravano was originally supposed to stand trial along with Gotti, but he struck a deal with prosecutors. In return for a 20-year sentence, which he is currently serving in a high-security cellblock, Gravano agreed to testify in Gotti's trial (and almost 10 others since). Thus he became one of the highest-ranking Mafiosi ever to turn state's evidence since mob soldier Joe Valachi turned on his Genovese family boss in 1963.

The concept of informants in society is nothing new. In fact, both police and civilians from time to time encourage public participation in solving crimes. For example, the well-known program *Crimestoppers* encourages citizens to engage in "anonymous" informing to assist police in developing suspects in crimes or to catch criminals in the act of committing them. Although some people complain that *Crimestoppers* makes "snitches" out of law-abiding citizens, others argue that it is simply a system of public responsibility similar to the old days when all citizens assumed responsibility for public order.

In addition to allowing tipsters to call the police anonymously, cash rewards are sometimes offered for their cooperation. The amount of the reward depends on the "quality of information" provided by the citizen; that is, information that results in an arrest. All communication between the police and the citizen is accomplished by the assignment of a number to the caller. That number is used in lieu of a name for the remainder of the citizen–police relationship, negating the need for the police ever to know the true name of the tipster.

Along similar lines to *Crimestoppers* are efforts by victims of crimes to convince the community to become more involved with identifying known criminals and reporting violators to police. One example of this is the well-known television show *America's Most Wanted.* This show has helped track down over 500 fugitives and 20 missing children.[1] In one case the show spotlighted fugitives who shot and killed two Newark, New Jersey law enforcement officers. Both men were caught within a week of the segments about them due to tips generated from people who watched the show. In recent years, the FBI has issued a public statement commending the show for putting a "human face on crime" and depicting the dangers to law enforcement.[2] Other shows, including *Unsolved Mysteries* and *U.S. Customs*, have taken a similar stance in generating public interest.

Another public forum for locating criminals has been around longer than the television shows discussed above: the FBI's Top Ten Most Wanted list. The FBI has maintained its Most Wanted list since 1950, and although it was once a mainstay in crime fighting, it has lost some of its appeal in today's high-tech age of television, computers, and the Internet. Still, it is designed to encourage citizen participation in sharing information with the police about crime and criminals who are wanted. The Most Wanted list was invented by a wire service reporter and later adopted by the publicity-driven director of the FBI, J. Edgar Hoover. As of 1997, 422 of the 449 fugitives who appeared on the list had been captured, a 94% success rate.[2]

Informants are also sought by private citizens. During August 1997, the parents of murder victim JonBenet Ramsey ran their fourth advertisement in a local newspaper appealing for help from the public. The ad included handwriting samples from the ransom note and commented that "the killer appears to be obsessed with techno-crime movies and phrases from them."[2] In addition, the ad includes quotes from the movies *Dirty Harry* and *Speed* that the family claimed were similar to the statements used in the ransom note.

In any case, whether it is a paid police informant or an anonymous tip, police rely heavily on information from the public to solve crimes. Experience has shown that a primary component of crime control is proactive law enforcement. Proactive investigations typically include cases such as drug trafficking, prostitution, and gambling, in which investigators actually seek out potential crimes and intervene before a crime is committed. Accordingly, the use of informants as sources of criminal information in such crimes has proved to be invaluable. Consequently, law enforcement officers are insistent on protecting the identities of their sources so that the wellbeing of the informants will not be jeopardized, and so they will continue to be of use to the officer in future criminal investigations. (Note: informants are also commonly called informers, confidential informers, and CIs, or cooperating individuals. In this book they are usually referred to as informants.) However, in spite of the usefulness of informants, many misconceptions still exist about the value and utility of the criminal informant.

Some people may think that police officers who are using an informant will be tolerant of that person's criminal lifestyle and might be less willing to report criminal wrongdoing on the part of the informant. Although through the years some improprieties have been documented regarding the use of informants, the value of such people has proved immense in the prosecution of many high-level crime figures and in aiding law enforcement in understanding the inner workings of sophisticated criminal organizations.

In addition, some people believe that in dealing closely with informants, police officers may themselves become tainted and their positions compromised. In this chapter, we consider the role of informants in criminal investigations and how best to manage the information provided by them.

Few investigative tools offer as much value to the criminal investigator as the informant. Historically, it is the hard-to-get information rendered by these civilians that has resulted in the successful conclusion of many major cases. Although there are many types of informants, the United States Drug Enforcement Administration (DEA) offers the following definition:

> Any nonlaw-enforcement person who, by reason of his familiarity or close association with criminals, supplies regular or consistent information about criminal activities to a police officer.[4]

Anyone is a potential candidate to be a police informer. A high percentage of law violators, however, are likely candidates because of their close proximity to crime. Consequently, with proper handling — which must include accurately identifying their motives — quality criminal cases can frequently be made from informant information. This chapter will address the handling of informants by officers, how to identify informant motives, and how to properly manage various informant-officer relationships.

Who Becomes an Informant?

Although the word *informant* has many negative synonyms, such as snitch and stoolie, the term can be defined as "anyone who provides information of an investigative nature to law enforcement."[5] Exclusions to this definition, of course, are victims of crime who have reported specific criminal activity to law enforcement; these people can be categorized as complainants.

Indeed, the informant is most typically used in cases in which there is no complainant, such as drug trafficking cases. Because informants can be virtually anyone in the community, the drug investigator should consider anybody with whom he or she comes in contact as a potential source of criminal information. That is, the premise of locating a knowledgeable informant is to realize that someone somewhere is aware of the commission of various crimes. It is therefore the investigator's responsibility to locate and develop relationships with such people.

Generally, people who become informants can be classified into four general groups.

1. **Average citizens:** Although not necessarily criminal sources, people falling into this group may still be excellent sources of information. Most good investigators have several informants of this type who are contacted periodically for leads. Examples of these informants are waitresses, bartenders, dancers, and private investigators.
2. **Fellow law enforcement officers:** On an average day, investigators will exchange valuable information with other investigators many times. Although much of this information is between "friends" who are investigators, a considerable amount is also exchanged by officers working in other units within the department. In addition, investigators who befriend officers with other local, state, or federal agencies can also benefit from useful information about criminals and criminal activity.
3. **Mentally ill people:** A certain percentage of informants fall into the category of the mentally ill or deranged. The experienced investigator can detect when such individuals are simply fabricating information or passing on news stories or gossip. One should consider that although an informant may be deranged, his or her information might still have some validity.
4. **Criminals or their associates:** Without question, the criminal informant has proved to be most valued in many police investigations. This is a person who is currently, or has been, associated with a particular criminal element and is therefore in an excellent position to supply firsthand information about criminal activity. Informants come from diverse backgrounds and frequently view their role in different ways. For example, one may give information with no reservations about his or her identity becoming known. Conversely, another may have valuable information to render but may do so only with the understanding that his or her identity remain concealed. Those falling into the latter category typically want their identities to be kept secret for two reasons: (1) for their own protection, or (2) because if their true identities become known, their function as informants would be ended.

Types of Informants

Three general classifications of informants should be recognized for better understanding of informant management. They are:

1. **Occasional informants:** This informant is one who is used by officers over long periods of time, and who offers information sporadically. This individual participates only when he or she wants to, and will not testify in cases. Occasional informants are often cultivated as a result of becoming acquainted with an officer through a variety of situations. The reliability of this individual may be questionable, and information rendered will usually have to be verified by investigators.
2. **Regular informants:** Generally considered a productive informant type, the regular informant works frequently with officers over a period of time. This individual is usually a reliable source who has provided past information resulting in arrests and convictions. The regular informants' motives vary, but because of the long-established relationship with the law enforcement officer, his or her information is usually reliable.
3. **Arrested informants:** The arrested or "hammered" informant cooperates with police to escape prosecution for crimes for which he or she has been charged. This individual is typically available for one particular investigation and seldom offers subsequent information after his or her initial relationship with the police has ended. It is common for the arrested informant to testify against others in exchange for a dismissal or reduction of criminal charges.

Informants can be extremely helpful during an investigation, and their usefulness may outweigh any distaste the officer may experience when working with them. The principal purposes for using informants are:

- To gain firsthand knowledge of the prices and types of drugs on the street, who is dealing them, and locations where the drug dealing is taking place
- To furnish information from sources not readily available to the officer
- To make covert observations in localities where strangers would be suspected
- To conduct undercover negotiations with suspects

Before considering the proper procedure for interviewing a prospective informant, his or her motives for involvement should be identified. Without question, this is the first responsibility of the investigator, because an informant's motives could weigh heavily against the officer's safety or the credibility of the investigation.

Reasons for individuals becoming involved with police as informers are offset by their reasons for not wishing to associate with law enforcement. These include dislike of the police, loss of respect from criminal associates, fear of retribution from other suspects, loss of self-respect, or feeling that involvement is not worthwhile.

Psychological Motivations of Informants

The reasons people desire to deal with law enforcement may vary, but in order to avoid any problems in an investigation, the informant's psychological motives should be identified. These include, but are not limited to, the following.

The Fear Motivation

Because the risks are so great and trust is so scarce in the drug trade, potential informers will sometimes assist in an investigation out of fear. This may manifest itself in many different ways. An arrest informant may participate because of his or her fear of punishment for crime. This is generally considered a good "control" motivation for an informant because if he or she fails to perform properly for the officer, the original charges can be filed and the reluctant informant can be prosecuted.

Fear may also stem from a fear of retribution from associates who might be at odds with the informer. In this case, an informant's desire to protect his or her own wellbeing and that of family or friends would also be a strong motivator and could produce good quality information.

The Revenge Motivation

Although a questionable motive, the informant who seeks revenge may prove to be well worth the agent's time and effort. The revenge motive may stem from a sour drug deal, anger toward associates who have reneged on drug transactions, profit-sharing disagreements, or other events. Sometimes, noncriminal acts will motivate the informer: jealousy of associates or disputes involving girlfriends, boyfriends, or spouses.

Officers must identify this motive early on in the investigation. The informant might resort to entrapment (discussed later) to achieve his or her goal, or perhaps heal the breach with the target of the investigation later on, and then refuse to continue working with the officer.

The Perverse Motivation

Perverse is defined as "to turn away from that which is right." An informant with a perverse motivation has an underlying motive other than what has been acknowledged to the officer. For example, the informer may approach the police with seemingly good information, when he or she is actually trying to observe other undercover officers working in the unit. This is a dangerous motive, because this informant is not trustworthy, and his or her true motivation must be discovered by officers as soon as possible.

The Mercenary Motivation

The mercenary informant is one who works for the police for financial gain. This individual is not facing criminal charges and may or may not be considered a criminal, but because of his or her personal lifestyle, the informant is in a good position to be acquainted with violators. The informant may be extremely effective, but he or she may also become a source of aggravation for the control officer. It is common for the mercenary informant to always want more than he or she is getting. It is also common for the mercenary informant to have another motive (such as revenge or fear) while working with the police.

The Repentance Motivation

This informant desires to repay society for personal wrongs he or she has committed in the past. Considered a fairly rare motive, when it presents itself it can be a productive one. However, informers in this class have a tendency to return to criminal behavior after becoming involved as informants in investigation.

The Egotistical Motivation

An egotistical informer is one who enjoys associating with the police and is intrigued by police work. As in the case of the mercenary informer, he or she may not be personally involved criminal activity, but may attempt to infiltrate the criminal element on behalf of the police. Sometimes this individual can be very productive and ask little of control officers, thereby making this motivation a good one for investigators. Caution should be observed, however, because the egotistical informant is not "hammered," and therefore control may be minimal.

The Unwitting Informant

The unwitting informant is probably the most useful and productive of all. Basically, the unwitting informant is an individual whom the undercover agent befriends during the course of an investigation. The informant, of course, does not realize that the undercover officer is a law-enforcement officer; because of this, he or she is willing to provide information and make introductions to other criminal suspects.

Great care must be practiced when working with an unwitting informant. Because he or she is usually in the presence of undercover officers regularly, suspicions may eventually be aroused if the informant notices that the officer never engages in criminal activity. This can sometimes be remedied by staging a fake drug deal between two undercover officers for the informant's benefit.

Informant Interviews

The initial interview of the potential informant is critical (Figure 4.1). It will identify the informant's motives and help the officer determine whether the individual is suitable for a professional working relationship. When dealing with informants, the keyword is "control," since many possess strong personalities and may attempt to dominate the initial conversation (and the investigation, for that matter). Once it is determined that a subject should be interviewed, the following basic guidelines should be adhered to:

- Do not rush the interview, but try to keep the conversation from wandering; be subtle when pressing for details.
- Sympathize with the informant about any problems he or she may be experiencing; try to build rapport.
- Show appreciation for *any* information rendered, in particular information that is of value.
- Never belittle seemingly worthless information.
- Do not try to show the informant how his or her information differs from that of other sources.
- Take notes or document the conversation as soon as possible.
- To verify the informant's information or truthfulness, ask about information you already know.
- Constantly attempt to identify any motives that are causing the informant to render information.
- Avoid questions that might embarrass the informant.
- Avoid unnecessary prying into the informant's private affairs.
- Avoid arguments with the informant.
- Always maintain control of the interview.
- If two officers are involved in the interview, one should do the talking while the other takes notes.

CITY POLICE DEPARTMENT

HISTORY SHEET

Case # ____________ Case File No. ____________
Soc. Sec. # ____________ Date ____________
Driver Lic. # ____________ Time ____________

Name ____________ A.K.A. ____________ Marital Status ____________
Maiden Name ____________ Former Married Names ____________
Address ____________ Previous Address ____________
Telephone ____________ Lives With ____________ How long ____________
City & State of Birth ____________ Date of Birth ____________ Sex ____________
Race ____________ Height ____________ Weight ____________
Scars or Marks ____________ Glasses.......Yes ______ No ______
Drug Used ____________ Armed: Yes ______ No ______ Facial Hair ____________
Education (years) Elementary ______ High School ______ College ______ Vo. Tech ______
Location of Schools ____________
Wife (Maiden Name) ____________ Address ____________

Husband ____________ Address ____________

Father ____________ Address ____________

Mother ____________ Address ____________

Children (Names and Ages) ____________

Brothers and Sisters ____________

Employed ____________ Address ____________

Occupation ____________ Draft Registration No. ____________

Military Service Yes ______ No ______ Branch ____________ Serial No. ____________

Prior Drug Treatment Yes ______ No ______ Dates (years) ____________

Prior Arrest — Place of Incarceration — Dates

Associates ____________

Questioned by ____________

Place of Interview ____________ Arresting officers ____________

Signed Statement of Rights and Waiver Yes ______ No ______

Figure 4.1 Sample of a Personal History Sheet.

Great caution should be exercised when working with informants. Officers should be careful not to give out too much personal information, as this could result in reducing the effectiveness of the officer's control over the informant or even compromising the safety of the officer in the investigation. In addition, officers should be certain the informant understands that any criminal activity on his or her part will not be tolerated and may result in prosecution. This should not only include violations of criminal law, but also lesser infractions such as traffic violations and public intoxication.

Many informants are deeply involved in a criminal lifestyle and this will be reflected in their personal ethics. Control officers must be conscious of this and take care not to adopt a similar lifestyle for the sake of maintaining cover. For example, many informers are prostitutes who may also be topless dancers in nightclubs. To these individuals, sexuality is business and they may attempt to seduce a male officer in order to exert more control over him during the course of the investigation. This predicament will not only jeopardize the integrity of the officer in the investigation, but will also blacken the reputation of the agency.

Contracting an Informant

After an officer has decided to use an informer, basic understandings must be discussed with regard to his or her role and actions while working with the officer.

The Method of Payment

No payments are to be made to an informant unless he or she has first been fingerprinted, photographed, and otherwise properly documented. Payments can be made only on a per diem basis, and only if the informant is providing reliable information or services to the department. The specific amount of per diem should be established by the officer's supervisor at the onset of the relationship, so that any future misunderstandings can be avoided. Any money for relocation of the informant after the investigation is over should first be authorized by the officer's supervisor.

Expenditures of Official Drug Funds

Informants should be advised of the consequences of absconding with money issued to them for drug purchases. Drug-purchase money or "buy money" should only be used for the purchase of drugs, unless otherwise authorized. When issued drug-purchase money, the informant should sign a receipt for the money. This receipt will set forth the responsibility of the informant while in possession of the money. In particular, if the informant steals the money, he or she can be prosecuted for theft. If this happens, the informant should be declared unreliable and he or she should be permanently removed from the files as a cooperating individual.

Criminal Activity by the Informant

There must be no misunderstanding regarding the expected behavior of the informant. It must be made clear that informants are not permitted to engage in any type of illegal activity, either in the presence of the control officer or not. If the informant is arrested for a criminal offense, he or she must be made to understand that working with the police will not provide an escape. Sometimes an informant will tell arresting officers that he or she was committing a crime to maintain cover. Officers who permit this are risking disciplinary action or termination.

The Cooperating Individual Agreement

The cooperating individual (CI) agreement is a necessary ingredient for management of informants and should be taken seriously by all drug-enforcement personnel (Figure 4.2). Basically, it works like a big league contract: no play, no pay! Good-faith efforts don't count in the world of working informants. The only way law enforcement officers can justify to the public giving an arrested person a break is to trade charges against him or her for charges against a larger violator. Therefore, the agreement spells out the expectations of the CI, which include:

- The objectives (people to be investigated, type of drugs to be purchased, etc.)
- The methods to be used (control buys, tape-recorded telephone calls, CI testimony, etc.)
- Other agreements, which release the law enforcement agency from liability in the event the informant is hurt on duty or tries to claim Worker's Compensation or unemployment benefits.

The CI should be told exactly what he or she will receive if the terms of the agreement are fulfilled and a prosecutable case results. Compensation can include a letter to the sentencing judge, reduction of charges, relocation of the CI, etc. Cooperating conditions may include the following:

- The defendant understands that only results will help him or her and not simply good-faith efforts.
- The defendant must be truthful and submit to a polygraph examination or urine analysis upon demand.
- The defendant may be released from his or her obligations at any time. In this case, the government will not be bound to its part of the agreement and there will be no retribution against the CI unless he or she jeopardizes the subsequent investigation.

Informant Payments

From the outset of the relationship it should be determined how the informant will receive compensation, if any, and what is required to receive it. It

CITY POLICE DEPARTMENT
COOPERATING INDIVIDUAL AGREEMENT

I, ______________________________, the undersigned, state that it is my intent to associate myself, of my own free will and without any coercion or duress, with the City Police Department as a cooperating individual.

As a cooperating individual, I understand and agree that I have no police powers under the laws of the State of (______) and have no authority to carry a weapon while performing my activity as a cooperating individual. Further, I understand and agree that my only association with the City of (_________) is as a cooperating individual on a case-by-case or time-to-time basis as an independent contractor, and not as an employee of the police department. Any payment I receive from the City Police Department will not be subject to federal or state income tax withholding or social security. I understand that it is my responsibility to report any income and also that I am not entitled to either workmen's compensation or unemployment insurance payments for anything I do as a cooperating individual.

In consideration for being allowed to associate with the City Police Department as a cooperating individual, and in consideration for any payment I may receive, I agree to be bound by the following terms and conditions and procedures while so associated.

1. I agree that under no circumstances will I purchase or possess any controlled substances or suspected controlled substances without the direction and control of a police officer and then will make a purchase only with monies supplied by him.
2. I agree not to use or sell, dispense, or transfer any controlled substance except that I may use any controlled substance prescribed to be by a licensed physician.
3. I agree to maintain a strict accounting of all funds provided to me by the City Police Department and I understand that misuse of city funds could be grounds for criminal prosecution against me.
4. I agree not to divulge to any person, except the officer with whom I am associated, my status as a cooperating individual for the City Police Department unless required to do so in court, and shall not represent myself to others as an employee or representative of the City Police Department nor use the department or any of its officers as personal references or as credit or employment references.
5. I understand that any violation of the above listed provisions may be grounds for my immediate removal as a cooperating individual and that any violation of law may result in my arrest and prosecution.

I understand that association with the City Police Department as a cooperating individual may involve strenuous physical activity and may become hazardous to my physical well-being and safety. Nevertheless, it is my desire to associate myself with the department, on an independent contractor basis, as a cooperating individual. I am associating myself with the department in this status freely and without any coercion or duress. In consideration of being accepted as a cooperating individual, I release and discharge the City of (_________), the City Police Department and its elected officials, officers, employees, and agents from all claims, demands, actions, judgements, and executions which I may have or acquire and subsequently claim to have against the city for personal injuries and property damage I sustain which arises out of or in connection with my association with the city. I make this release for myself, my heirs, executors, and administrators. Also, I agree not to maintain any action against the City of (_________), the City Police Department, or its elected officials, officers, employees, or agents for personal injuries and property damage I sustain which arise out of or in connection with my association with the City Police Department.

____
Cooperating Individual

____
Date

WITNESSES:

____
Officer

____
Officer

Figure 4.2 A Cooperating Individual Agreement should always be signed by the CI to avoid the problem of informants claiming unemployment or Worker's Compensation benefits.

is better to pay informants on a per diem basis rather than case-by-case to avoid allegations of entrapment later on. Informants also tend to request additional funds for extras such as the telephone bill, car repairs, or groceries in addition to the agreed-upon payments for services rendered. The control officer should discuss these contingencies ahead of time with the informant.

Use of Female Informants

Policy should be established regarding the treatment of female informants by male officers. When male officers are involved, interviews of female informants should be conducted when at least two officers are present. This will minimize any spurious complaints which could possibly be lodged against the officers later. Female informants should be searched by female officers to ensure that they are not armed or are not holding any illegal drugs. A female informant may prove to be as dangerous to the officer as a male informant; their aggressiveness and street smarts should not be underestimated.

Statement of Officer–Informant Relationship

An officer must always remain in control of the officer–informant relationship. For this reason, the officer must be careful not to become too friendly; inadvertently revealing personal information about spouse or children may later reduce the officer's effectiveness or control. Moreover, such information could be revealed during the suspect's trial and be a source of embarrassment for the officer and his or her agency.

Informant Statements

Once an informant has been approved for use, a CI agreement should be signed and kept on file. This agreement states the conditions under which the informant will continue working with the police. There have been cases in which informants have sued law enforcement agencies for Worker's Compensation claims because they considered themselves employees of the city, county, or state. The CI agreement, if properly worded, will eliminate such claims.

After each undercover contact, the informant should provide the officer with a written statement of what occurred, what was said, and what was observed. The informant should sign only the original copy of the statement, which should then be placed in the informant's file; unsigned copies should be placed in the file for later use in court. In the event the informant is compelled to testify, original statements will be used as evidence along with his or her testimony.

Policy on Drug Purchases

Because there are so many different types of drug purchases and the circumstances surrounding them are so variable, a standard policy should be established and understood regarding the informant's role.

Inside Drug Buys

Drug buys are generally safer if conducted on the street or in a suitably wired undercover apartment. If circumstances require that the drug buy take place in the suspect's residence, an officer should be present to corroborate any activity or statements made by criminal suspects. When informants participate in undercover drug transactions, they should always be equipped with concealed transmitters so that officers can monitor and record the conversation for evidence.

Multiple Drug Buys

It is a good practice to make more than one drug purchase from a single suspect. Multiple buys help demonstrate that the dealer was in business and that criminal intent existed for the transaction. This should protect the officer against the suspect's use of the entrapment defense. Multiple buys also help officers identify the dealer's source of supply through repeated contacts.

Controlled Drug Buys (Informant Drug Buys)

Although useful in some circumstances, the controlled buy should be avoided whenever possible. In this type of buy, informants usually make direct contact with the dealer and the informant's testimony is subsequently required. Problems also arise if the informant later decides he or she does not want to testify, and the case is therefore lost (see the section on the controlled drug purchase later in this chapter).

Mutual Agreements and Understandings

All other details of undercover context must be worked out before the informant is placed into service.

The Cover Story

A cover story is crucial to the success of the undercover investigation. An informant may be allowed to suggest a cover story, but the officer should ultimately decide on the details. Both the informant and the undercover officer should be comfortable with the cover story.

Method of Introduction

The manner in which the informant introduces the agent to the suspect should be discussed in detail before the undercover contact. In some cases, the informant might wish to converse with the suspect a few moments before the introduction — sometimes not. In either case, the method should be discussed in advance in order to avoid confusion and misunderstanding.

Negotiating Amounts

It is a good practice for the informant not to be told too far in advance what he or she is supposed to buy or how much. Again, entrapment precipitated by the informant must be avoided at all costs since he or she may be out to "set up" a rival dealer or some other enemy. Which drugs to buy and when to buy them should only be established just prior to the actual transaction. If an earlier meeting is required, officers should record the contact for verification of its legitimacy. Before each drug buy, the informer should be required to phone the suspect (if a phone is available) to reconfirm the drugs to be purchased, the amount, and the quality.

Time of Day

Daylight hours are usually the best time to attempt to purchase drugs. Surveillance officers are better able to notice license tags, addresses, and physical descriptions of associates. In addition, surveillance officers can more easily be hidden in traffic to better cover the informant or undercover officer.

Manipulation of Funds

An informant might advise the officer that a particular drug sells for a specific price, when in reality it sells for less. In this case, the informant is attempting to "skim" the extra money without the officer's knowledge. If this occurs, an ethical (honesty) infraction has occurred and the informant should be declared unreliable and should not be considered for any future use. Moreover, if there is sufficient evidence, the informant should be charged with theft, embezzlement, or any other appropriate criminal charge.

Protection of Informant Identity

Experience has shown that defendants may attempt to injure, intimidate, or even murder people working with the police. Accordingly, the investigator bears an ethical and professional responsibility to safeguard the identity of informants and their families to the best of his or her ability. During initial interviews, investigators should advise potential informants that it is impossible to absolutely guarantee the confidentiality of their identity but that all efforts will be made to do so. The U.S. Supreme Court has ruled that the identity of informants may be kept secret if sources have been explicitly assured of confidentiality by investigating officers or if a reasonably implied assurance of confidentiality has been made. Measures to protect an informant's identity include the following:

1. Direct contact with the informant should be limited to one investigator or the "control" agent (unless the informant is of the opposite sex, in which case, two investigators should be present). Meetings should be brief and held where neither party will be recognized.
2. Telephone conversations between control agents and informants should be kept to a minimum in case someone is listening in on the line.
3. When officers do telephone their informants, they should use a nontraceable telephone since the informant's telephone may have caller ID that others living with them can observe.
4. Meeting places between investigators and informants should be selected by the investigator and should be in a different location each time.
5. Informants should be warned about discussing their association with the police with anyone, including family and friends.

An informant's identity should not be disclosed unless absolutely necessary, and then only to the proper parties. Generally speaking, an informant's identity should not be disclosed if it would create an immediate danger to the informer or cut off a reliable source of information.

The U.S. Supreme Court addressed the issue of protection of the informant's identity in court. In *U.S. Department of Justice v. Landano* (1993), the court required that an informant's identity be revealed through a request made under the federal Freedom of Information Act. In that case, the FBI had not specifically assured the informant of confidentiality, and the court ruled, "The government is not entitled to a presumption that all sources supplying information to the FBI in the course of a criminal investigation are confidential sources."

> It is the right and the duty of every citizen of the United States to communicate all the information he or she has on the commission of an offense against the laws of the United States to officers of government charged with the duty of enforcing the laws. Such information is privileged as a confidential communication which the courts will not compel or permit to be disclosed without the consent of government. Such evidence is excluded, not for the protection of the witness before the policy of law… however, a

> trial court must dispose of the case before it. If what is asked is essential evidence to vindicate the innocence of the accused or lessen the risk of false testimony, or it is essential to the proper disposition of the case, disclosure will be compelled.
>
> *Wilson v. United States*

Generally, there are three possible consequences for an officer's refusal to disclose an informant's identity: the court may uphold the officer's refusal if there is no harm to the defendant, the court may dismiss the charge against the defendant, or the court may find the officer in contempt of court and have him arrested.

The following general guidelines should be observed by all agents to ensure effective management of informants and to ensure officer safety:

- Every attempt should be made to keep track of the informant's independent activities.
- All informant contacts should be made with consideration for optimum officer safety.
- An informant should not be paid until the information has been evaluated.
- All informant information should be verified when possible.
- Prior to any undercover contact, the name of the informant and the location of the contact should be relayed to the police supervisor.
- A receipt for informant payments should be acquired when all payments are made.

Special Informant Problems

Working with informants is an endeavor in human behavior. As such, it is all but impossible to establish a set operational procedure that will apply to all informants, all of the time. Flexibility is the key for the drug investigator. Here are a few of the most common problems that can present themselves throughout the course of a drug investigation.

The Informant with "Cold Feet"

Sometimes an officer will develop an informant, and shortly thereafter the informant will have second thoughts about the arrangement. Often this happens because of fear of retribution from fellow drug dealers. In such cases it is usually best to release the informant (after explaining that the original "deal" is now off). There are three good reasons for officers not to work with informants with cold feet:

1. Frightened informers are seldom productive.
2. Frightened informers may place the undercover agent in dangerous circumstances by acting nervous or by panicking during drug transactions.
3. Informers may be fearful of participation because of the danger involved, and rightfully so. Therefore, they should have the option not to work.

The Informant and the Target's Right to Counsel

There are occasions when the police might wish to use an informer to learn more about a particular prisoner, or after arresting several individuals, place a wire on one of them to learn the defense strategies another might use. It should be remembered that any time the suspect is in custody or has a case pending against him, his right to counsel might become an issue. The rules vary from state to state, but the following points generally should be considered:

1. Generally, once a suspect has asked for an attorney, officers cannot use an informant to try to gain information. The informant would be acting on the part of the police, and thereby would be a "police agent." Once the suspect has been read the *Miranda* warning and has signed a statement of rights and waiver, however, he or she is fair game for a police informant.
2. The above does not apply, however, in the case of an inmate who approaches the informant with information.
3. Once a defendant has been indicted or charged, the right to counsel is "attached." Basically, this means that the police cannot attempt to gain information from him (on the case in which he or she is charged) through an informant. This applies even in a case in which the informant is a codefendant.

These requirements do not necessarily prevent police officers from using an informant to obtain information from the suspect on *other* crimes. If the suspect is planning to murder a witness, the informant has a free hand in attempting to obtain as much information as possible.

Other Problems with Informants

In addition to concerns of entrapment and ethical, moral, and criminal activity on the part of the informant, there are several other areas of concern:

Investigators becoming Too Friendly with Informants

Because investigators and their informers work closely together, it is possible that an officer can become caught up in an informant's personal life and problems. Certainly, the investigator should lend a sympathetic ear when possible, but becoming too close to an informant could jeopardize the investigator's level of control over the person.

Informants of the Opposite Sex

Many investigators have fallen victim to allegations of sexual misconduct with informants of the opposite sex. While some have proven truthful, many have had no basis in fact, but still resulted in disciplinary action against the officer and termination of the investigation. To avoid such allegations, a second officer should always accompany the investigator. The locations of meeting spots with informants should also be considered very carefully, particularly if it is not possible for a second officer to be present.

Crimes Committed by the Informant

During the initial meetings between the investigator and a potential informant, the officer should stress that any criminal activity on the part of the informant will not be tolerated. History has shown that after being arrested for a crime, informants will sometimes mention the name of their control officer at the time of their arrest in hopes of being released or receiving special treatment.

Officers Who "Own" Their Informants

Over the years, some unscrupulous officers have claimed that meetings between themselves and criminals were in fact meetings with informants. Informants should be considered the property of the entire department and should be sufficiently documented. This will avoid any allegations of misconduct on the part of investigators if seen with known criminals.

Legal Concerns: Entrapment

Drug enforcement investigators, by virtue of working in a proactive capacity (investigating crimes *before* they are committed), are faced with some unique legal concerns. As a rule, the issue of entrapment is of the gravest legal concern to investigators and prosecutors alike. At times, information provided by informants is of such value that informants are paid for the information they supply. The investigator should be careful not to pay for information that has not been verified or that is not considered useful in the investigation. Payments should be sufficiently modest to avoid accusations by the defense of entrapment. When this occurs, the defense will maintain that the investigator's payment to the informant was so high that the informant was enticed into "setting up" the suspect solely for the large monetary reward.

Law enforcement organizations have been criticized for going too far in attempting to "fool" suspected criminals. While working undercover or while supervising an informant in that capacity, police officers must be careful that they do not inadvertently coerce someone into committing a criminal act. The defendant may be excused from criminal liability through the use of the entrapment defense if it is demonstrated successfully in court. As summarized by the U.S. Supreme Court in *Sherman v. United States* (1958), *entrapment* is the procurement of a person to commit a crime that he or she did not contemplate or would not have committed, for the sole purpose of prosecuting him or her.

In this case, Sherman was met by a government informant at a doctor's office where they were both being treated for drug addiction. On several subsequent occasions the informant asked Sherman if he knew where some drugs could be obtained. After avoiding the issue on several occasions, Sherman finally offered to supply the drugs. On several occasions thereafter, Sherman furnished the informant with drugs at cost plus expenses. The informant then contacted the FBI and advised of the transactions. Three or more transactions were then arranged, which agents observed. Sherman was subsequently arrested and convicted of the drug offenses. On appeal, the Supreme Court examined the question of whether the actions of the government induced Sherman to commit crimes that he would not otherwise have committed. It was found that entrapment had occurred, and the decision was subsequently overturned. It is not generally considered entrapment if the investigator merely furnishes the opportunity to a person who is already predisposed to commit the crime.

Problems with informants can be seen in cases such as that involving car designer and accused drug smuggler John DeLorean. As an outcome of the criminal trial, the jury was convinced that the government entrapped DeLorean since an FBI informer acting on the government's behalf originally suggested the idea of smuggling cocaine. Consequently, DeLorean was found not guilty.

In a more recent case, the issue of entrapment was addressed in *Jacobson v. United States* (1992). While not a drug case, *Jacobson* addresses the extent to which undercover police should aggressively pursue any target. This relates directly to the use of informants, because informants often operate outside the direct supervision of the police agent and can behave in a manner that can, if left unchecked, legally jeopardize the case. In the Jacobson case, 56-year-old Keith Jacobson was indicted for violating the Child Protection Act. The law made it illegal to knowingly receive through the mail visual depictions of a minor child engaged in sexually explicit conduct. Jacobson claimed that he was entrapped because on numerous occasions agents of the U.S. Postal Service sent him sexually explicit materials through the mail in hopes of getting him to subscribe to one of the publications. Finally, after 26 months of receiving material, Jacobson subscribed to two of the publications. The publications, titled *Bare Boys I* and *Bare Boys II,* contained explicit photos of nude boys in their teens and preteens.

Upon review, the court acknowledged the wrongs of child pornography and upheld the appropriateness of police to employ the use of undercover agents, but the court declared that officers may not originate a criminal design or implant in a person's mind the disposition to commit a criminal act, as happened in this case. The court further held that the government must show that the predisposition to commit the criminal act existed prior to approach by government agents. So in this case, because the defendant had been contacted many times over a two-year period, no such predisposition had been shown.

The Informant in the Courtroom

Investigators should know in advance whether the informant's role in the investigation will necessitate his or her testimony should the case go to trial. The best time to plan for this is while the case is being prepared, and not after the arrest has been made. To reduce the likelihood of testimony being required of the informant the following should be observed:

1. Officers should corroborate as much of the informant's testimony as possible with the use of tape-recordings, surveillance, and other physical evidence.
2. After each contact with the suspect, a statement should be taken from the informant either in longhand or by tape recording for later transcription. Informers, like police officers, must have a means to refresh their memories in the event the case ends up in court. It is usually not satisfactory for the informant to rely on the officer's report, since it could be charged that he is merely memorizing details from the officer's report. In addition, an informant's report will lock him into testimony if he later chooses not to cooperate in the case or to lie on the witness stand.
3. All money paid to the informant should be carefully documented. Defense attorneys may attempt to show that the informant was paid an enormous amount of money to "entrap" the defendant. Adequate records and a proper payment method will invalidate this defense.

The Controlled Drug Purchase

Frequently, undercover officers are unsuccessful in infiltrating trafficking organizations, and must consider other means of penetration. In such cases, police should consider using informants who are already accepted and known by the suspects. It is always better for an informant to introduce an undercover agent to the suspect as a trusted friend than to risk sending the informant alone — there is greater informant control and the case will be strengthened by the officer's firsthand testimony. This, however, is not always possible.

If an informant is the only one who can meet and negotiate a drug transaction with a suspect, the informant's services can be used in two ways: (a) by making undercover purchases for the purpose of later charging the dealer with drug dealing, or (b) by making undercover drug purchases for the purpose of obtaining probable cause for a search warrant of the suspect's residence. Both strategies have distinct advantages and disadvantages. If the drug purchase results in the later arrest of the suspect, the informant will probably have to testify (along with the informant's control officer and any surveillance officers). The defense strategy in this scenario is to attack the credibility of the informant:

1. Is the informant's testimony truthful?
2. Does the informant have a motive that would cause him or her to lie?
3. Does the informant have a history of criminal involvement?
4. Does the informant now or has he or she ever used illegal drugs?
5. Has the informant ever been convicted of a criminal offense involving drugs or honesty?

If the answer is yes to any of these questions, the defense counsel may have an improved basis for defense. Because the defense attorney may cross-examine any prosecution witness, some of the above information may be revealed for the purpose of discrediting and impeaching the testimony of the informant. The defense counsel's ultimate goal is to establish a reasonable doubt in the minds of the jurors, and therefore, seek an acquittal.

If the informant is proven, reliable, and comfortable on the witness stand, he or she might be successfully used for multiple drug buys. If the informant's reliability is untested, a controlled informant purchase for obtaining probable cause will be more appropriate. In either case, however, a strict protocol for handling the informant must be observed. Following this protocol will ensure that the informant's involvement with the suspect was monitored by case officers in order to minimize possible wrongdoing by the informant. Outlined below is a step-by-step process for conducting a controlled drug purchase.

1. Only use informants who have been established as reliable, either in previous drug purchase operations, or by verifying any information they have rendered.

2. Conduct an in-depth interview of the informant. Determine his or her knowledge of various drugs in the community, drug prices, drug packaging, and information on drug dealers. Determine whether the informant is using drugs, and if so, what types.
3. A separate statement should be taken from the informant regarding his or her personal knowledge in dealings with the suspect.
   a. What types of drugs is the suspect dealing?
   b. In what quantities does the suspect deal?
   c. Is the suspect considered dangerous? (If so, why?)
   d. Does the suspect carry a weapon? (If so, what type?)
   e. Who are the suspect's associates?
   f. Does the suspect live alone or with others? (If so, who?)
   g. If employed, where does the suspect work?
   h. What vehicles are involved? (Get descriptions.)
4. Verify the informant's information. A comprehensive utility check should be conducted by the informant's control officer to determine whether other people are living at the residence. A complete criminal history should be acquired on each suspect. This should include teletypes to other jurisdictions for local criminal history inquiries. State driver's license information should also be acquired. Attention must be given to arrests as well as convictions to help profile the suspect.
5. Record the serial numbers of money used for official drug purchases. Serial numbers must be incorporated into the case report and used as evidence in the case. Official funds might later be seized at the suspect's residence as a result of a search warrant. In this event, seized funds are to be used as evidence in the case.
6. Strip search the informant. This must be conducted just prior to the drug buy and should be thorough enough that the officer can later testify that the informant had no illicit drugs concealed on his or her person prior to the meeting with the suspect. If a body cavity search is required, trained medical personnel should be used, not officers. Furthermore, medical personnel (for cavity searches) or officers (for pat-down searches) of the same sex must be used to conduct searches.
7. Equip the informant with a recording device. A concealed transmitter should be placed on the informant to allow surveillance officers to monitor conversations between the informant and the suspect and to record the conversations for evidence. If a transmitter is unavailable, a small tape recorder should be considered. This is a less satisfactory method because officers cannot monitor the conversation, but a recorded tape of the contact will be available as evidence.

8. Search the informant's vehicle. The vehicle used by the informant should be searched by officers for drugs or money. Once the informant and/or the vehicle is searched, neither should be left unattended until after the drug deal is over. This will ensure that both are "clean."
9. Conduct drug buys in populated and open areas where surveillance teams can easily be positioned, and which are familiar to them (such as a shopping center parking lot, a bus station, a city park, etc.). Motel locations should be preselected by officers for accessibility and safety. Do not allow the informant or the suspect to select the location for the drug transaction. If a location is suggested by the suspect, a second or third preselected counter-location should be suggested. Never conduct the deal on the suspect's own "turf."
10. Conduct close surveillance of the informant. The informant must be constantly observed from the time of the strip search to the time he or she meets with the suspect. The informant must be instructed to drive slowly, use proper turn indicators, and go directly to a predetermined location. If the location changes during the deal, the informant should call off the transaction.
11. A set period of time must be given to the informant for the transaction. If the transaction is not completed within the given time, the informant must be advised that the officers will assume the informant is in trouble and storm the location. Officers must carefully log all activities of the informant: times, direction of travel, and any pertinent conversation with the suspect.
12. Informants should be instructed to volunteer as little information as possible. They should instead ask the suspect questions about the transaction (price, quality and purity of drugs, and future drug transactions). If possible, the actual exchange of drugs for money should be observed and photographed by surveillance officers. The informant should be instructed to proceed to a prearranged location after the purchase while officers maintain visual contact. The location should not be the police department in case the informer is followed by the suspects. The drug evidence should be taken from the informant, initialed by both the officer and the informant, and packaged and preserved according to accepted practices of evidence custody.
13. All drug evidence should be promptly transported to the laboratory to protect the chain of custody and for chemical analysis. A second strip search should then be conducted for money and drugs retained by the informant. A statement should be taken from the informant. The statement should include any conversation with the suspect, as well as locations where additional drugs may have been observed.

14. If a search warrant is to be obtained, it should be acquired as soon as possible after the last drug purchase. It will be necessary for the police laboratory to expedite the testing of the drugs. Special arrangements might have to be made. If this is not realistic, the drugs will have to be field tested by officers in order to establish probable cause.
15. Surveillance should be maintained at the location of the intended search in order to identify associates or customers entering or leaving the location. During the search, drugs, paraphernalia, records, weapons, and money should be seized if it can be shown that they pertain to the case. Vehicles should be seized if they were used to facilitate any drug trafficking activity or if they were acquired by illegally obtained drug money.

Summary

The informant is a potentially valuable investigative resource for the drug enforcement officer. The use of informants in drug investigations must be preceded by a thorough understanding of the motivations that underlie their involvement. These motivations may either benefit or hinder investigators in their endeavors.

All investigative personnel must understand procedures for the cultivation and placement of informants. Proper control and management of the informant must be established at the onset of the investigation, and the informant's role should be well defined.

If a task can be accomplished by an undercover officer without the aid of an informant, that should be considered; an uncooperative or unreliable informant may hinder the progress of the case. In many circumstances, however, informants can provide valuable information on people, places, and organizations operating within the drug trade.

Police personnel should take care to use informants in a proper and lawful manner. If they have done so, then the information and evidence obtained through informants can be a significant aid in the successful prosecution of drug traffickers.

Suggested Readings

Lyman, M., *Criminal Investigation: The Art and the Science, 3rd ed.* Prentice Hall, Upper Saddle River, NJ, 2001.

McWilliams, J.C., *The Protectors: Harry Anslinger and the Federal Bureau of Narcotics*, Associated University Press, Canbury, NJ, 1990.

References

1. Police upset by cancellation of *America's Most Wanted, USA Today,* May 16, 1996.
2. Puente, M., A no longer most wanted list, *USA Today,* July 29, p. 3A, 1997.
3. Gray, P., A Heart in Her Hand, *Time,* August 23, p. 43, 1997.
4. DEA, From *Narcotic Investigator's Manual,* 1978, revised 1996.
5. U.S. Department of Justice, Drug Enforcement Administration, *Drug Enforcement Handbook,* U.S. Government Printing Office, Washington, D.C., 1988.

Surveillance Techniques 5

Any investigator will tell you that one way to learn a considerable amount of information about someone is to simply follow them. Doing so can reveal where suspects live, work, hang out, bank, and with whom they associate. Surveillance entails more than just physically following suspects, and is a primary duty of the drug enforcement investigator. Surveillance can be conducted in a number of ways. These include on foot, in a vehicle, or through electronic monitoring or wiretaps.

Police surveillance serves many purposes in ongoing criminal investigations. It is clear, however, that within a covert unit this is an essential function. Specifically defined, surveillance is the surreptitious observation of persons, places, objects, or conveyances for the purpose of determining criminal involvement. The three types of surveillance effectively used by law enforcement agencies are moving, stationary, and electronic.

Surveillance is usually undertaken with certain objectives: to obtain specific details of persons and places suspected of drug trafficking, to verify information, to collect evidence of crimes, to obtain probable cause for search warrants, to apprehend suspects in the commission of crimes, to prevent the commission of crimes, and to locate persons wanted for crimes.

Surveillance is also probably the most time-consuming and tedious task in law enforcement. One key to a successful surveillance operation is reliable intelligence. In addition, the surveillance function can provide invaluable intelligence which might be unobtainable through other sources. Surveillants (officers assigned to make observations) must be creative in their efforts to observe criminal suspects and activity covertly. Ideally, the surveillant's appearance and mannerisms should blend with the surroundings to remain inconspicuous. He or she must also remain alert to details and be resourceful and patient throughout the operation.

To best prepare for surveillance, officers must first study police files for any information pertaining to the case: the suspect's physical description, names, addresses, and physical descriptions of associates, vehicle descriptions, residence and business addresses, and any other known areas the suspect frequents. Appropriate equipment should be made available to each team:

35-mm cameras with telephoto lenses, binoculars, tape recorders for surveillance notes, night viewing devices, and basic items (such as pens, pencils, notepaper for the surveillance log, and change or phone cards for pay phones).

After basic information is gathered, the target area should be reconnoitered to determine the appropriate vehicles and dress. The team should also note surveillance vantage points (where officers can best observe the area), street names, one-way streets, dead-end streets, and traffic conditions in order to avoid problems during the operation.

Surveillance should not be assigned to an officer working alone: two sets of eyes and ears are better than one, and teams better avoid the problem of tedium. A team leader or supervisor should also be present during the surveillance to add cohesiveness and direction to the operation. If the surveillance becomes mobile, a system of communication must be established to reduce confusion and avoid excessive radio traffic. As surveillances are often lengthy, relief officers are necessary. The supervisor must establish procedures to guarantee that each new shift is apprised of any advancements or changes in the case. The briefing should include identification of new suspects, vehicles, residences, and locations. Depending on the case, different methods will be employed to best document the actions of criminal suspects.

Moving Surveillance

Mobile surveillance is usually much more difficult to manage than stationary. Mobile surveillance can be accomplished by foot, vehicle, or a combination of both. The likelihood of officers being noticed by suspects is greater in mobile surveillance, and backup officers must be available to continue the surveillance without raising the suspicions of the suspects. We will now consider the various methods of surveillance.

One-Man Foot Surveillance

One-man foot surveillance may occasionally be necessary, but it is not generally considered the best method. There is personal risk to the officer, and a single officer has more chance of being detected than multiple officers. When conducting a one-man foot surveillance, the officer should keep the suspect in view at all times, which means that the surveillant must constantly remain close to the suspect. Pedestrian traffic can afford a certain amount of cover; if the officer is observing the suspect from across the street, he or she must generally stay even with the suspect to avoid losing him or her when entering buildings or turning down streets.

A suspect who notices a surveillance officer can generally lose him or her without much effort. Officers who sense that the suspect is becoming suspicious should pull off and reestablish surveillance later so as not to "burn" the investigation. The surveillant must also be aware of any countersurveillance employed by the suspect. This is becoming more common, and it poses not only a threat to the investigation but, more importantly, to the officer's safety. At times an officer may think he or she has been spotted and overreact in an effort to appear "normal." Overreactions, however, may actually draw attention to the surveillance officer.

The ABC Method

The ABC method uses three officers, and it is considered the best technique for foot surveillance. Officers will find their jobs much easier and safer with two support officers. A greater variation exists when three officers participate in a surveillance. In this case, one officer can have the point (lead) for a period of time and then periodically trade off with the other officers to avoid detection.

Ideally, the point officer "A" maintains visual contact with the suspect while a second officer "B" maintains visual contact with "A." The third officer "C" will usually walk across the street and watch for countersurveillance. Occasionally, one officer may be positioned in front of the suspect for variation and if pedestrian traffic is too heavy, all three officers may be positioned on the same side of the street.

Generally, when the suspect is observed approaching an intersection, "C" (who should be across the street) should lead the suspect and reach the intersection first. By pausing at the corner or crossing the street, "C" continues visual contact with the other officers and through hand signals informs them of the suspect's actions. If the suspect stops, then "A" should cross the intersection before proceeding in the same direction as the suspect. If the suspect remains stopped, then both "A" and "B" may be forced to continue on ahead of the suspect, relying on "C" to maintain visual contact. Officer "C" will then have to signal when the suspect moves on. Any time the suspect turns a corner, the officers have a chance to rotate positions.

The "Leap-Frog" Method

The leap-frog method uses two surveillance officers. It is not considered as successful as the ABC method because of the time involved, but it can be of some value in locating a suspect's hiding place. In leap-frog, one officer follows the suspect while the other officer moves well ahead, usually on the opposite sidewalk. When the suspect passes, the lead officer moves in behind. The leap-frog method works well inside large stores. When used on the street, it might be easier to facilitate if the suspect takes the same route every day. If, however, the suspect follows a different route daily and officers are not very alert, the suspect will most likely get away.

Generally, if the suspect is believed to be aware of the surveillants, the surveillance should be called off and resumed later. If continued surveillance is deemed necessary, the surveillants should watch for the possible following countersurveillance traps that could be set by the suspect:

1. A suspect can view reflections in a store-front window as in a rearview mirror.
2. A suspect may enter a restaurant, observe who enters behind him or her, and then leave abruptly midway through a meal.
3. A suspect may drop a worthless piece of paper to see if a suspected officer picks it up.
4. A suspect may drive the wrong way down a one-way street or make an illegal U-turn to see if anyone follows.
5. A suspect may drive down an alleyway to see if anyone follows. This could also be a set up for hijacking.
6. A suspect may approach the officer directly and accuse him or her of following or being an officer.

When foot surveillance officers need to communicate with eash other, small radios may be used. If these are too obvious (or too expensive for the department), a system of hand signals should be used. These signals must be clearly understood prior to the surveillance operation to eliminate confusion. Taking off (or putting on) a hat, tying a shoe, turning up one's collar, placing a newspaper under an arm, or throwing away a newspaper are all examples of clear signals.

Combined Vehicle–Foot Surveillance

If only one car is available, surveillance may be conducted by using both foot and vehicular surveillance. In such cases, it is a good idea to place two officers in the car and place it behind and to the right of that of the suspect. The distance behind the suspect's vehicle will vary depending on the amount of traffic in the area. In moderately heavy traffic, it is wise to allow one to two vehicles between the surveillance vehicle and the suspect's car. This creates cover for the officers' vehicle, allowing them to see the suspect without being seen themselves. In rural areas, the suspect must be given a considerable lead so as not to attract attention to the officers' vehicle. This should not pose a problem on the highway, but on section line roads or small town streets, the risk of detection is much greater.

In nighttime surveillance, the officer's vehicle should not have any distinguishing lights (i.e., bright lights or running lights that can be easily recognized). The same is true for burned-out headlights or parking lights, which might be remembered by the suspect after he or she has seen them more than once.

Multiple Vehicle Surveillance

When the two-car method is used, both cars are normally positioned behind the suspect's vehicle. A variation of this method, which works fairly well, is for one car to follow the suspect on a parallel street while the others stay behind the suspect. The parallel vehicle's job is to arrive at intersections just prior to the suspect so the suspect's direction of travel can be noted and conveyed to the others by radio.

Three cars give the surveillance officers still more flexibility by being able to change positions. When three vehicles are available, the "leap-frog" method is sometimes used: surveillance vehicles are located along a known route. After the suspect's car passes a surveillant's car, the surveillant then proceeds to pass the suspect at high speed, enabling the surveillant to take up a position beyond the other official vehicles. This allows the officer to keep track of a suspect without actually following him or her. This system does not work when the suspect takes a route unknown to the officers.

In Figure 5.1 we see that the "set" is in the corner of 81st St. and Amsterdam Avenue. This location can be very effectively covered from the roof observation point. The officers at this location can advise other units of any pertinent information. (Never assign only one man to a rooftop surveillance. Always assign at least two; one to make observations and one to watch the other's back.)

The units are situated where visual observation of the establishment (the bar) can be conducted, and at the same time the officers can ready themselves for moving surveillance should it become necessary. If it does become necessary, each vehicle is in position to cover (tail) any direction in which the suspect travels, while the other three units arrange themselves so they can aid the point vehicle in perimeter and parallel observation of the suspect. However, if there is no movement of the suspect by automobile, the mobile units remain stationary and allow the observation units to report back any observations.

The observation truck unit (unit #3) should have been parked at least one hour prior to the time of the transaction in order not to arouse suspicion. From the truck, surveillants can watch not only the "set" but can attempt to observe the location of the "stash," as well. This unit will be the first to arrive on the scene and the last to leave, remaining about an hour after the transaction to observe possible additional suspects and to take photographs of the transaction and the suspects.

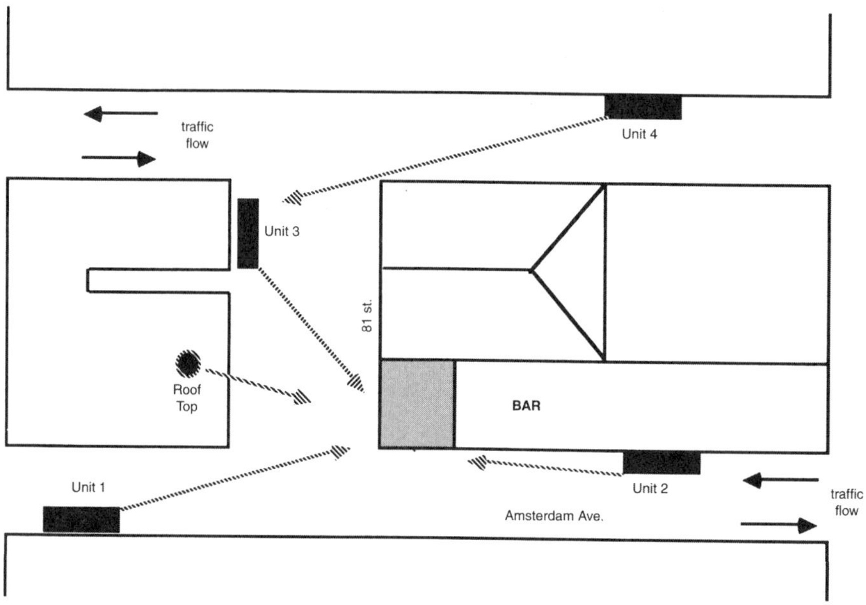

Figure 5.1 The tactical plan and surveillance setup.

Stationary Surveillance

Stationary (fixed) surveillance is used when the suspect is expected to come and go from a particular location. This method (a stake-out) is considerably easier; many of the factors contributing to confusion and lack of safety in a moving surveillance are minimized. Sometimes stationary surveillance can be conducted from a specially outfitted house or apartment. This is also called a "base," and it should be located to afford maximum observation of the target location's entrances and exits.

It is more common, however, for stationary surveillance to be conducted from a vehicle; in some cases, the vehicle may be an undercover vehicle or a special "decoy" vehicle (possibly disguised as a telephone or utility truck). In stationary surveillance conducted from a vehicle, certain factors should be considered:

1. The type of vehicle used must fit in with the area.
2. When conducting surveillance in a residential neighborhood, the vehicle's license tags should be local rather than out-of-state in order to avoid looking suspicious.
3. Policy should be established for explaining the surveillants' presence in the neighborhood in case the police or curious neighbors question them.

4. In cold weather, an idling vehicle will emit exhaust fumes, which can easily be seen by neighbors. Moreover, exhaust fumes may make the surveillants drowsy and inattentive.
5. If more than one vehicle is used, one should have the point while others are nearby for relief or for use in case the surveillance becomes mobile.
6. To safeguard against suspects monitoring police radio frequencies, surveillants should use a radio "scrambler," a device that garbles radio traffic and is affixed to each officer's radio.

Although vans have traditionally been used in surveillance, suspects are now alert to such parked vans, thus requiring drug enforcement personnel to consider other types of vehicles. One possible alternative is a "drone." Basically, a drone is an unmanned, nondescript type of vehicle (such as an older Ford Taurus or Toyota Camry) that contains surveillance equipment. Most of the monitoring equipment is placed in the truck, and a pin-hole camera lens is mounted in the headrest and focused on the target. Because the vehicle is an older car and because no equipment is visible, the drone can sit unobtrusively while surveillance equipment is left running. To help safeguard equipment stored in the trunk, a motion-sensor auto alarm may be installed to prevent tampering.

Another application for vehicles of this type is to remove the rear seat and darken the glass of the vehicle. As the vehicle appears unoccupied, surveillance officers can occupy the vehicle for short periods to observe suspects or locations. Occasionally, surveillance vehicles may be used in conjunction with the base for optimum coverage.

Whether conducted from a base or a vehicle, officers engaged in stationary surveillance must maintain a chronological log of all activity associated with the location: descriptions and times of individuals and vehicles coming and going, and any items brought to or taken from the location. The log may allow officers to trace evidence of other crimes such as illicit laboratory activity or fencing of stolen property. As previously mentioned, all of the basic equipment — cameras, binoculars, tripod, video camera, paper, and pencils — should be on hand.

Electronic Surveillance

Electronic surveillance is the documentation of persons, vehicles, or locations by electronic means; electronic devices are frequently used in conjunction with foot or vehicle surveillance. In order to secure a conviction in a drug case, most prosecutors now require not only the testimony of officers and police chemists, but also supportive evidence such as photographs of the defendant, a recorded tape of the defendant's voice, or a videotape showing the defendant's criminal involvement. Many devices are available, and their quality and expense will vary from manufacturer to manufacturer. Basically, electronic surveillance devices fall into two categories: audio and visual.

Audio Surveillance

The ability to record the suspect's voice before, during, and after a criminal transaction is an asset to any case. Even during the initial negotiations — long before any transactions have taken place — recorded conversations can provide valuable evidence of a suspect's "criminal intent."

Typically, undercover operatives wear concealed transmitters, or so-called body-mikes, when personal contacts are made. Officers should always test the unit before it is used because a body transmitter may occasionally transmit over cable channels inside a suspect's residence. Body transmitters are also usually expensive; a small tape recorder may serve as a substitute.

Another way to record conversations with a suspect is to have an undercover agent or informant phone the suspect and record the call with "induction coil pickup." An induction coil pickup is relatively inexpensive and is readily available at most electronic stores. It is also easy to use: simply attach the pickup to a telephone receiver and insert the plug into a standard tape recorder microphone jack. This procedure is not considered an illegal wiretap because one party of the conversation (the undercover officer) has given permission for the recording.

Another method of recording criminal conversations is the use of the "spike-mike." When a suspect is located in a particular location (e.g., an apartment or motel room), the spike-mike can be placed against an adjacent wall and conversations can be monitored (Figures 5.2, 5.3). Here, however, the suspect's constitutional rights must be protected. If no agency personnel is participating in the conversation, use of a spike-mike must first be authorized by the local prosecuting attorney.

The Legality of Audio Recording

In order to monitor and/or record a private conversation between two suspects lawfully (third-party interception), officers must first obtain a court order. The U.S. Supreme Court has held that people have a "reasonable expectation of privacy" when conversing under certain circumstances. Such circumstances include a meeting between two suspects at a private room or when conducting a private telephone conversation (when no party line is involved).

Bumper Beepers

For a moving surveillance, a vehicle-tracking device (or so-called bumper beeper) might be considered. A bumper beeper is an electronic transmitting

Figure 5.2 A radio frequency (RF) surveillance setup where an adjacent motel room is "wired," permitting agents to monitor conversations between the undercover agent and the suspects.

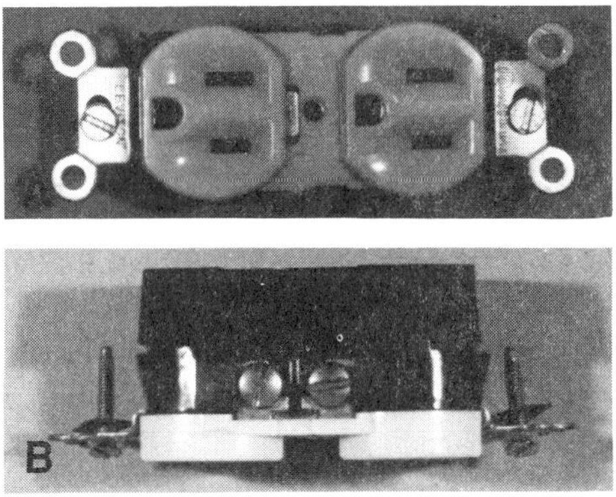

Figure 5.3 (A) A seemingly innocent looking wall outlet is (B) actually a well concealed microphone for recording conversations in a room.

device, usually attached to the underside of the suspect's vehicle, which emits a signal that is picked up by special receiver. The receiver indicates which direction the suspect is traveling by emitting a series of "beeps"; the beeps are rapid when the suspect is close, and spaced out when the suspect is further away. A bumper beeper makes it easier to maintain a "loose tail" on a suspect. A bumper beeper, however, can be installed on a vehicle only pursuant to a court order.

Bumper beepers can be somewhat problematic. Ideally, they are connected to the car's battery (12 volt), but the hookup could be discovered by the suspect. Failing this, one can rely on the beeper's internal 9-volt batteries. However, these are only good for short periods of time, thus making it necessary to retrieve the unit periodically and replace the batteries. Finally, the suspect may discover the beeper, thus jeopardizing the investigation and losing the unit (usually incurring a financial loss, and perhaps embarrassing the department).

Wiretaps

The wiretap is the most commonly discussed form of electronic surveillance. The wiretap is a sensitive technical method of electronic surveillance. Although it may be legally authorized under federal law (and most state laws), a few states still have legislation that forbids wiretapping or eavesdropping.

Even in states where a wiretap may be legally used, it still must be the last resort in the investigation process: officers must show that all other avenues of investigation have been tried and have failed, or they must show that those not tried are too dangerous to attempt. Furthermore, all details of the previous investigation attempts (and the reasons why other techniques should not be tried) must be specifically documented in the application (affidavit) for the court order authorizing the wiretap. Moreover, the courts have ruled that to conduct electronic eavesdropping lawfully, officers must do everything reasonably possible to respect the suspect's right to privacy. This means that should a wiretap be authorized, officers can only listen to criminal conversations and therefore must "minimize" intrusions into conversations not relating to criminal conduct.

In addition to being legally complicated, wiretap investigations are also expensive and time-consuming. In addition to carefully planning a wiretap investigation, it should be remembered that a wiretap merely facilitates a conspiracy investigation. It is a means of documenting an agreement between two suspects to commit a particular criminal act. Because an overt act is necessary to prove a conspiracy, surveillance officers must be on 24-hour standby to properly observe and document the subsequent overt act. This represents a considerable commitment of time and manpower; many departments often cannot justify its use.

If a wiretap is employed, however, it can prove to be a good investigative tool. It permits law enforcement officers to record criminal conversations, and the recordings provide excellent evidence for the prosecution of conspirators.

Recording Telephone Conversations

If an undercover officer is a party to a conversation, he or she is not violating the suspect's reasonable expectation of privacy; therefore the recording of the conversation is lawful. This enables officers and informants to record (and thus document) valuable and incriminating conversations in the course of drug investigations.

Another area of misunderstanding involves recording suspect phone calls by officers in an undercover apartment. Caution should be observed because even though the officers may be renting both the apartment and telephone, a suspect still has a reasonable expectation of privacy when using the telephone outside the presence of informants or undercover officers.

Use of Concealed Transmitters (Body Mikes)

Drug enforcement agents frequently conceal transmitters when meeting suspects to allow support officers to monitor and record conversations. Monitoring is desirable for two reasons: (a) to determine if the undercover officer is in any danger during the transaction, and (b) to record the conversation for later use as evidence for the prosecution of the suspect. Concealed microphones are also commonly used in suspects' residences or in other locations where criminal conversations are anticipated.

As with recording telephone calls, the circumstances surrounding the appropriate use of a concealed transmitter must always be considered by investigators. There are times when recordings may be made lawfully and times when they are unlawful.

If officers wish to listen to a suspect's conversation and there is no police agent (either an officer or informer) in the room with the suspect, a court order is required. Any time a police agent is not part of the conversation, it is considered eavesdropping. Eavesdropping is a violation of the suspect's civil rights and an intrusion of his or her reasonable expectation of privacy (*Katz v. United States, 1967).*

If a police agent is present, officers may lawfully monitor the conversation. The suspect's reasonable expectation of privacy is not violated provided the police agent is participating in the conversation or is present while the conversation is taking place; therefore, a court order is not required. If, however, the police agent leaves the room where the suspect is located, surveillants may not continue to monitor the suspect's conversations in the officer's absence. This reverts back to the rules governing third-party intercepts (specifically the rule of minimizing), and, absent a court order, it is unlawful.

The exclusionary rule requires that any evidence obtained against a suspect be accomplished according to the requirements of the Fourth Amendment. Electronic surveillance, under certain circumstances, is considered a form of search. Any third-party interception (such as a wiretap or concealed microphone) must be based on probable cause and authorized by a magistrate.

Finally, if an informant is used to contact a suspect, the case officer should obtain written authorization to record the conversation between the informant and the suspect. This protects the officer in the event the informant later claims that no such permission was given.

Passive Monitoring

Passive monitoring (that is, without electronic equipment) of suspect conversations is permitted under certain circumstances. The same considerations with regard to the suspect's reasonable expectation of privacy, however, still pertain.

An example of permissible passive monitoring would be when two suspects are discussing a drug deal while standing at a pool table in a public tavern. If an undercover agent was legally present in the tavern (posing as a customer) and close enough to overhear the conversation, the suspect's reasonable expectation of privacy would not have been violated. Any conversation overheard regarding criminal activity could then be used against the suspect in court.

Video and Photo Surveillance

Whenever possible, visual surveillance equipment should be used to corroborate audiotape recordings or testimony of prosecution witnesses. The most typical (and underrated) means of visual recording is the camera. Whether it is a 35-mm or even a small 110 camera, it can provide a reproduction of all or parts of the crime for prosecution. If budgets are not too restricted, a 35-mm camera with a full array of attachments (such as infrared filters, telephoto and fiber optic lenses) will give officers clear and detailed photographs. Many cameras are equipped with a device that automatically dates each print at the time it was taken.

The use of video cameras is also generally accepted in sophisticated criminal surveillance operations. Generally, videotaped evidence provides a more comprehensive reproduction of a crime than a still photograph (even though still photographs often afford greater detail and clarity). Unit managers, especially, should be aware that video technology is constantly changing, and they should try to stay current with what is available. The newer smaller cameras, for example, are more easily concealed and may be worth the additional expenditure.

Because many covert operations involve nighttime maneuvers, methods should be developed to use cameras and video equipment at night. The starlight scope, for example, will illuminate an otherwise almost totally dark area, and may be used with or without a camera (Figure 5.4). The starlight scope produces a greenish, somewhat grainy image, but it permits acceptable-quality photos of nighttime meetings between suspects and police agents

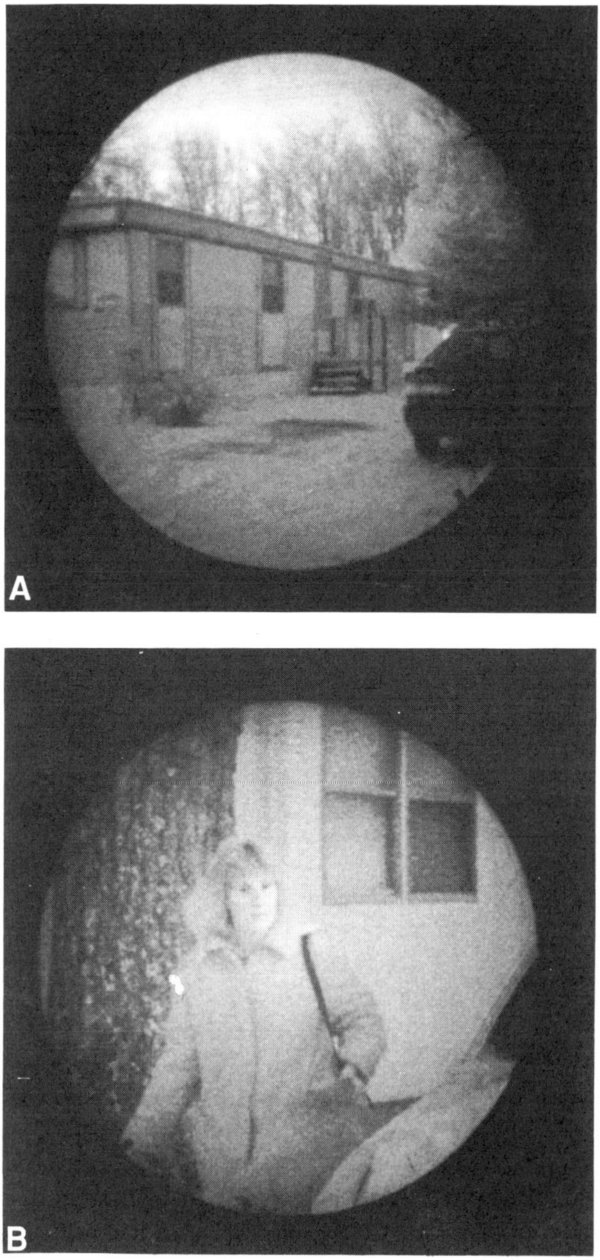

Figure 5.4 At first glance, these photos (A & B) would appear to be of poor quality, but considering that the picture was taken in total darkness with the use of a starlight scope, they are useable and identifiable surveillance photos.

Figure 5.5 A starlight scope enables investigators to see objects at night with a passive light source, such as moon or stars.

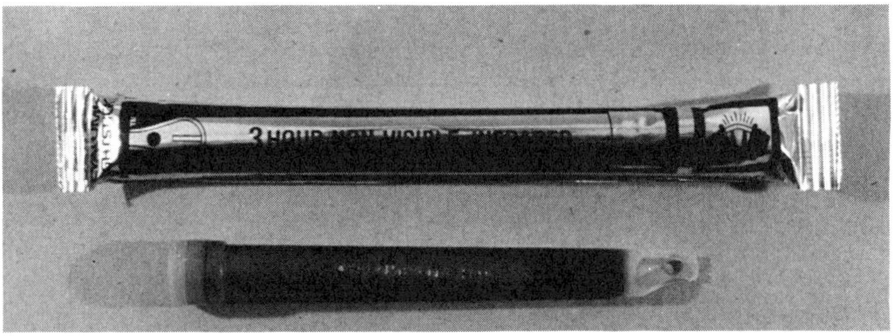

Figure 5.6 Infrared Cyalume lightsticks emit an invisible light source that will adequately illuminate subjects when used with a camera equipped with an infrared lens.

(Figure 5.5). In the case of total darkness, the starlight scope will, however, require some light source to provide an image. The source cannot be too great, such as a nearby streetlight, but a mild source of light (starlight, mild moonlight) will create sufficient illumination to an otherwise dark area, permitting suspect identification, the reading of automobile license tags, and tracking of undercover agents.

Another solution to the problem of nighttime surveillance is the use of a 35-mm camera with an infrared lens. An infrared lens allows excellent quality photos under minimal lighting conditions. One source, which provides more than sufficient lighting, is a Cyalume® infrared lightstick (Figure 5.6). The Cyalume lightstick is an inexpensive light source that, when broken in half, emits ample light for infrared photography while the light source itself remains literally invisible to the naked eye. Suspects will be unable to detect anything unusual unless they, too, are using infrared equipment for countersurveillance.

Infrared lightsticks have other benefits. An infrared lightstick can be placed in an undercover agent's jacket pocket, thus allowing surveillants using infrared equipment to more easily distinguish the agent from suspects during the nighttime contact. In office buildings, when it is not feasible to turn on the indoor office lights, lightsticks placed in a ceiling vent will emit enough light for infrared photography or visual surveillance. Even in a room that appears totally dark to the naked eye, infrared lighting will illuminate the room so that a positive identification of suspects is possible through an infrared camera system.

Undercover Apartments

A highly recommended surveillance tactic is the use of a specially equipped undercover apartment as a meeting place between undercover officers and suspects. The apartment should be selected for its strategic location and for ease in incorporating surveillance equipment. Ideally, the undercover apartment should be a two-bedroom dwelling in which a bedroom and the living room share a common wall; such a layout enables support officers to more closely monitor meetings between undercover officers and suspects. When locating an appropriate apartment, however, a background check of all neighbors should be performed to ensure that known felons are not living nearby.

In the undercover apartment there should be a specific item — such as a sofa or chair — in the main surveillance room upon which video cameras, microphones, and special lighting will be targeted. This is where the undercover officer tries to have the suspect sit so that the suspect's image and words can be clearly recorded. The officer should be trained to be able to lead the conversation to what the officer wants to discuss.

The undercover officer must have the ability to read the suspect's body language in order to detect nervousness. The undercover officer must also feel comfortable in front of the camera. It is important that he or she does not talk too much, act nervous, or otherwise fail to think clearly during the undercover contact. To prepare officers for the videotaped encounter, it might be advisable *not* to tape the first transaction in an investigation. When subsequent transactions are made, the officer should be more comfortable with both the camera and the suspect. If the subsequent videotaped drug buy goes smoothly, the officer may choose not to file charges on the unrecorded initial purchase.

The proper placement of low-light video cameras is crucial to the proper documentation of meetings between undercover officers and suspected drug violators. The cameras may be placed in almost any location within the room

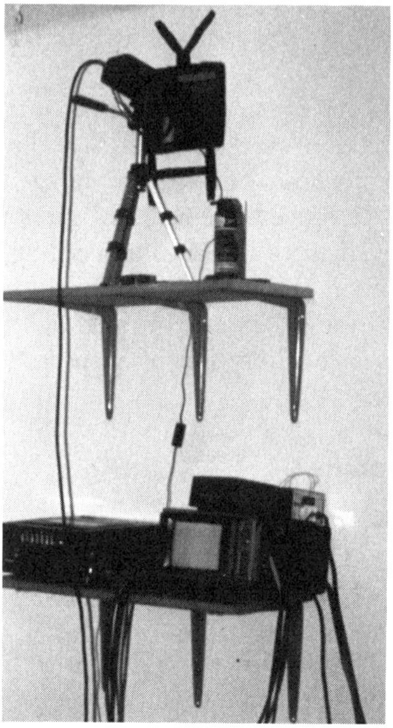

Figure 5.7 A video camera located behind a wall and focused through a heating vent in an undercover apartment.

where both the officer and suspect can be filmed, but to avoid detection, they should never be placed at the suspect's eye level. People have a tendency to look around at eye level more often than they do above or below it. Good locations for camera placement include ventilation vents, stereo speakers, flowerpots, and behind posters and pictures (Figure 5.7).

Two-way mirrors, although still used, are no longer recommended. Their use is somewhat dated, and suspects may expect that cameras are concealed behind them. If mirrors are used, however, a black cloth should be positioned behind the mirror so that surveillance cameras cannot be detected. In addition, if concealed cameras are employed, steps must be taken both to shield the cameras from view and to position the cameras so that light reflections from the lenses do not give away their hiding places.

When placing a video camera in an undercover apartment, officers must take care to position it where images can clearly be recorded. Preferably, a 17-mm to 25-mm wide-angle lens should be used, as the field of view will most likely take in the entire room. When placing the camera, a rule of thumb is to manipulate the suspect to an area of the room where the image of his head appears on the video monitor just slightly larger than a thumb when placed on the monitor screen over the image. If a clear image is unobtainable

Figure 5.8 A video editing system, which is necessary for making tape duplications and photos from video tapes.

on the videotape (Figure 5.8), subsequent identification of the suspect may be difficult in court proceedings, thereby jeopardizing the case.

Other technical modifications can be made to not only conceal surveillance cameras but also to more easily cloak the surveillance process. Such modifications include installation of silent plastic gears in camera autowinders, appropriate interior lighting in undercover apartments, and the placement of specially designed concealed power microphones, which can clearly transmit voices within a particular room.

Surveillance of Undercover Personnel

When surveillance of undercover personnel is anticipated, surveillants must consider several important factors. First, it should be understood that once the undercover officer assumes his or her role in a contact, the officer's ability to control the overall safety of the meeting is diminished. Even if the undercover officer is the case agent, he or she will not be able to observe the "big picture." Basically, this means that the undercover officer cannot observe countersurveillance by suspects or new and unforeseen circumstances. These are the provinces of the support officers conducting the surveillance.

Second, it should be remembered that the surveillance officer has several basic functions while assisting the undercover officer. All of these functions are important and should be remembered at all times. These include the following:

- To protect the undercover officer by monitoring his contacts with suspects
- To locate any possible countersurveillance suspects in the area
- To accurately log any activity associated with the undercover contact; for example, people coming and going, vehicle descriptions, etc.

Observation of an undercover officer may pose other surveillance problems:

- Neon signs and large buildings tend to reduce the transmitting range of the body transmitter (RF transmitter).
- Officers conducting surveillance in parking lots where transactions are scheduled may be observed by employees of businesses in the area. The local police may be called in this circumstance because of the employees' belief that the officers are would-be burglars or armed robbers.

Summary

The effective use of covert surveillance in drug investigations cannot be overemphasized. It is through this process that much is learned about the activities of suspect traffickers. Employment of surveillance agents to monitor contacts with traffickers is necessary in drug enforcement, since this protects the undercover officers and successfully documents actions, conversations, and other evidence that will later benefit the prosecution of the case.

Techniques for a proper surveillance include vehicle, foot, and electronic methods; all are designed to permit the officer to observe without being observed. Investigative personnel must be cognizant of the suspect's right to privacy and the need to gain the proper authority to observe the suspect in various circumstances.

In addition to the techniques of observation in surveillance, it is often necessary for the officer to be trained in the use of sophisticated electronic devices, which enhance the officer's ability to conduct his surveillance duties. The use of these devices will enhance images of suspects so that identification can be made in court proceedings. Such devices will also increase the degree of safety afforded to the undercover officer during his contacts with suspects.

Suggested Readings

Lyman, M. and Potter, G., *Criminal Investigation,* 2nd ed., Prentice Hall, Upper Saddle River, NJ, 1999.

Levine, M., *Deep Cover,* Delacorte Press, New York, 1990.

Search and Seizure 6

One of the most important tools possessed by the drug enforcement investigator is his or her authority to search and seize evidence. It is this function that drives all investigations and that is aimed at the arrest of persons responsible for drug trafficking, manufacturing, distribution, etc. in our communities. But search and seizure is a complex undertaking if done correctly. Think about it; the investigator must know what to look for. That is, he or she much be able to recognize packaging, containers, and other materials related to drug dealing. That in itself is no easy task. Next, the investigator must be aware of criminal and constitutional law, as well as standard operating procedures which relate to this effort. Doing so ensures that all of his or her efforts will hold up under legal scrutiny. Next, the investigator must be on guard against hazards while searching: explosives, contaminated blood, sharp objects, corrosive solvents, etc. Failure to be aware of hazards could result in severe health complications for an investigator immediately or down the road. Having a general understanding of these concerns is the focus of this chapter.

The body of constitutional law addressing searches and seizures by police is immense and includes thousands of case decisions from courts in virtually all levels of government. Of paramount importance in criminal investigations is the officer's ability to be aware of and work within constitutional (and departmental) guidelines. Issues such as what to search, when to search, and how to conduct a search play vital roles in determining what is fair in the eyes of the U.S. Supreme Court. In this chapter, we examine some of the more crucial principles of searches and seizures, and how officers must conduct themselves to present a legally sound criminal case.

Due Process and the Constitution

In addition to affording protection by ensuring separation of powers within the government, the U.S. Constitution also oversees operations of the criminal justice system. This is done by granting individual freedoms in what is called the Bill of Rights, which was added to the Constitution in 1791. Initially, the Bill of Rights applied only to the manner in which the federal government operated in the justice system. However, in 1868 the Fourteenth Amendment was passed and extended due process to each of the states as well. Under this amendment, citizens are basically guaranteed three classes of rights:

1. Privileges and immunities of citizens of the United States
2. Due process of law
3. Equal protection under the law

For more than 30 years, the U.S. Supreme Court's interpretation of the Constitution has served as the basis for the establishment of legal rights of the accused. The fundamental principles that govern criminal investigations are required by the Bill of Rights. Therefore, we consider here the implications of the Fourth, Fifth, and Sixth Amendments, which limit and control the manner in which government officials operate in our justice system.

1. **The Fourth Amendment:** Two clauses of this amendment are most significant in the realm of criminal investigation.
   - Unreasonable Searches and Seizures Clause: "The right of the people to be secure in their persons, houses, papers, and effects, against unreasonable searches and seizures, shall not be violated."
   - Warrants Clause: "No warrants shall issue, but upon probable cause, supported by oath or affirmation, and particularly describing the place to be searched and the persons or things to be seized."
2. **The Fifth Amendment:** The principal component of this amendment is the self-incrimination clause.
   - Privilege against Self-Incrimination Clause: "No person…shall be compelled in any criminal case to be a witness against himself."
3. **The Sixth Amendment:** This amendment guarantees people the right to confront their accusers and to have legal representation.
   - Right of Confrontation Clause: "In all criminal prosecutions, the accused shall enjoy the right…to be confronted with the witness against him."
   - Right to Counsel Clause: "…to have the assistance of counsel for his defense."

The Fourth, Fifth, and Sixth Amendments limit and control the manner in which government officials operate in the justice system.

Legal Guidelines for Searches

Investigators must remember that they not only must have legal grounds to begin a search, but that while conducting the search, they must not contaminate any evidence. Doing so will result in the dismissal of such evidence in the courtroom. Additionally, searches must first be justified under law. Officers do not always follow the rules, as the case histories discussed in this chapter show.

The Probable Cause Requirement

For the last three decades, courts have scrutinized virtually every phase of the Fourth Amendment. The probable cause requirement is one of the most important components to the Fourth Amendment because it lies at the heart of the police officer's authority to search, seize, and make arrests. Simply put, *probable cause* is the minimum amount of information necessary to warrant a reasonable person to believe that a crime has been or is being committed by a person who is about to be arrested. Officers generally establish probable cause through their own observations. For example:

- Did the suspect attempt to run away when approached by the officer?
- Did the suspect admit to any part of the alleged crime?
- Did the suspect behave furtively as if he or she were trying to hide something?

It is unlikely that a single fact or circumstance will establish probable cause, but several such facts put together might. Probable cause is the minimum amount of information necessary to cause a reasonable person to believe that a crime has been or is being committed by a person who is about to be arrested.

It is also common for probable cause to be established through hearsay information provided by third-party sources, typically informants. Here, officers must be careful that the information is reliable, verifiable, and is not based on rumor or suspicion, as such information is not sufficient to establish probable cause.

The Exclusionary Rule

The *exclusionary rule* relates primarily to cases involving issues of search and seizure, arrests, interrogations, and stop-and-frisk violations. In addition, it pertains to any evidence obtained illegally. The exclusionary rule states that courts will exclude any evidence that was illegally obtained even though it may be relevant and material.

The exclusionary rule originated with the 1914 case of *Weeks v. United States* but was geared to apply to federal, not state governments. Although the Weeks case was virtually ignored by the courts, the subsequent Mapp decision (*Mapp v. Ohio,* 1961) expanded the scope of the exclusionary rule by applying it to both federal and state courts. In 1957, Cleveland police officers went to the residence of Dolree Mapp while acting on information that a fugitive was in hiding there. Mapp refused to admit officers to the residence without a search warrant. The officers then left and maintained surveillance on the residence. Three hours later more officers arrived and forced their way into the Mapp residence. By this time, Mapp's attorney had arrived, but the officers ignored him. Mapp then demanded to see a search warrant, at which time one of the officers held up a piece of paper, claiming it to be a search warrant. Mapp grabbed the piece of paper and stashed it in her blouse. A struggle ensued and officers retrieved the paper and arrested Mapp for being "belligerent." The officers then searched the entire home. Although they never located the fugitive they were looking for, they ran across some obscene material for which Mapp was subsequently arrested and convicted. The U.S. Supreme Court overturned the conviction, stating that the methods used by officers to obtain the evidence were a violation of her constitutional rights.

The question in the Mapp case was whether the illegally seized evidence was in violation of the Fourth Amendment's search and seizure provisions, which would render it inadmissible in the state trial, which found Ms. Mapp guilty. Although the state supreme court in Ohio upheld the conviction, the U.S. Supreme Court overturned it. In addition to imposing federal constitutional standards on state law enforcement personnel, the court pointed out that there is a relationship between the Fourth and Fifth Amendments which makes up the legal basis for the exclusionary rule.

Since the early days of the exclusionary rule, other decisions have highlighted the fact that the Fourth Amendment protects people, not places. Stated differently, while the old saying "a man's home is his castle" has a great deal of validity within the context of constitutional law, people have a reasonable expectation to privacy in "homes" of many descriptions: apartments, duplexes, motel rooms, even cardboard boxes or otherwise makeshift dwellings of the homeless. Indeed, all of these places are protected under the Fourth Amendment. For example, in *Minnesota v. Olson* (1990), the U.S. Supreme Court extended the protection against warrantless searches to overnight guests residing in someone else's home. The deciding factor in one's capacity to claim the protection of the Fourth Amendment depends on whether the person who makes that claim has a legitimate expectation of privacy in the place searched.

The "Fruit of the Poisoned Tree" Doctrine

With its ruling in *Silverthorne Lumber Co. v. United States* (1918), the court built further on the rules of evidence. The Silverthorne case articulated a new, far-reaching principle of *due process* which has become known as the fruit of the poisoned tree doctrine. Complicated police cases may be jeopardized if criminal lawyers are able to show that the prosecution's case was based originally on a search or seizure that violated due process. In such cases, it is likely that all evidence will be declared "tainted" and thrown out of court. Prior to the Warren Court era, however, most U.S. Supreme Court decisions were regarded as applicable only to federal law enforcement agencies.

Search Incident to Lawful Arrest

We will now consider a search immediately following an arrest. *Chimel v. California* (1969) dealt with areas searched without a warrant that were not in plain view. The case also addressed arrest activities by police. Ted Chimel was approached in his home by police officers who possessed a valid arrest warrant for him. The officers then advised Chimel that they wanted to "look around" and proceeded to search the premises without Chimel's permission. After a one-hour search, some coins were located and seized as evidence in a crime. Although initially convicted, Chimel later appealed the case, which was reversed by the U.S. Supreme Court because the coins were not found lawfully. Although the coins were found "incident to a lawful arrest," the evidence was excluded because it was not in plain view and the officers did not have a warrant to search Chimel's residence, only an arrest warrant. The Chimel decision established that a search made incidental to a lawful arrest must be confined to the area around the suspect's immediate control.

The point in the Chimel case is that the officers who searched Chimel's house went far beyond any area where he might have either hidden a weapon or been able to destroy any evidence. Therefore, there was no constitutional basis for an extended search of the house. The Chimel case is important as it relates to criminal investigation because it changed the policy with regard to the *scope of the search* as it relates to an officer's authority to search incident to an arrest. Prior to *Chimel*, officers had more leeway to search the area around an arrested suspect. Since *Chimel*, however, officers can search only the arrested person and the immediate physical surroundings under the defendant's control (e.g., within arm's-length of the defendant). To search further, officers must obtain a search warrant. Searches of the immediate area are for weapons or to safeguard against the destruction of evidence.

In 1990, the U.S. Supreme Court further defined the circumstances under which officers may conduct a limited search in the home of an arrested person. In *Maryland v. Buie* (1990) the court held that a protective sweep during an arrest in a home is allowed if justified. Of course this case authorized only a "protective" warrantless sweep for additional suspects who might be located in the residence.

In 1989, the U.S. Supreme Court clarified the basis upon which law enforcement, lacking probable cause to believe that a crime has occurred, may stop and detain a person for investigative purposes. In *United States v. Sokolow* (1989), the court ruled that the legitimacy of such detainment must be evaluated according to a "totality of the circumstances" criterion in which the defendant's entire behavior is taken collectively to provide the basis for a legitimate stop. In this case the defendant, Sokolow, appeared suspicious to police because, while traveling from Honolulu under an alias, he paid $2100 in $20 bills (taken from a larger sum of money) for a round-trip airline ticket to Miami, where he spent a considerably short period of time. Sokolow was noticeably nervous and had checked no luggage. A warrantless airport investigation by DEA agents revealed more than 1000 grams of cocaine on the defendant. Upon appeal, the court ruled that while no single activity was proof of illegal activity, taken together they created circumstances under which suspicion of illegal activity was justified.

Exceptions to the Exclusionary Rule

Since the Mapp and Chimel cases, the Supreme Court has developed several exceptions to the exclusionary rule. These play a considerable role in shaping the manner in which police officers are allowed to behave before, during, and after a search and seizure of evidence.

The Good Faith Exception

Since the Weeks and Silverthorne cases, the U.S. Supreme Court has been criticized for "chipping away" at the exclusionary rule. One such case emerged in the summer of 1984. The laws dealing with search and seizure changed dramatically in *United States v. Leon* (1984), when the first good-faith exception to the exclusionary rule was decided. During the course of a drug trafficking investigation by the Burbank, California Police Department, officers secured a search warrant for the residence of Alberto Leon. The warrant was reviewed by three prosecutors prior to its being issued by a state court judge. The subsequent search netted large quantities of drugs, and Leon was arrested and charged with drug trafficking. The defense challenged the validity of the warrant based on the unreliability of the informant and moved to suppress the evidence. The district court and the U.S. Court of Appeals both held that the affidavit was insufficient, but the U.S. Supreme Court supported the prosecution, holding that the exclusionary rule was designed only as a deterrent for the abuse of police authority. The court specified that evidence might be excluded (1) if police officers were dishonest in preparing the affidavit, and (2) if the warrant was deficient on its face (e.g., a wrong or missing description of the place to be searched) such that no officer could reasonably serve it, or (3) if the magistrate was found not to be neutral.

The practical effect of *Leon* is that any evidence seized through a search warrant is immune from suppression even if the judge signing the warrant was wrong and there was not probable cause to believe that contraband or other evidence would be discovered under the warrant. The Leon case allows the use of evidence obtained by officers acting in reasonable reliance on a search warrant issued by a neutral magistrate but that is ultimately found invalid.

Another case decided by the U.S. Supreme Court the same year was *Massachusetts v. Sheppard* (1984), which reinforced the concept of good faith. In the Sheppard case, officers served a search warrant that failed to describe accurately the property to be seized. Although they were aware of the error, they were assured by the magistrate that the warrant was valid. After conviction of the defendant, the Massachusetts Supreme Court reversed the conviction of the trial court, but upon review, the U.S. Supreme Court supported the good faith exception and allowed the original conviction to stand.

The scope of the exclusionary rule was diminished further in another case, *Illinois v. Rodriguez* (1990). In the Rodriguez case, Gail Fischer, who was badly beaten, complained that she had been assaulted in a Chicago apartment. She led police to the apartment, which she claimed she was sharing with the defendant, and produced a key and opened the door. The defendant, Edward Rodriguez, was found inside asleep on a bed with cocaine and drug paraphernalia spread around him. Rodriguez was arrested and charged with assault and possession of drug paraphernalia and cocaine.

After his conviction, Rodriguez demonstrated that Fischer had not lived with him for at least one month and argued that she no longer had legal control over the apartment, so the defense claimed that Fischer had no authority to give police warrantless access to the apartment. The Supreme Court disagreed, stating that there was no Fourth Amendment violation because the police "reasonably believed" at the time of their entry that Fisher had authority for consent.

The Inevitable Discovery Doctrine

The inevitable discovery exception to the exclusionary rule was developed in the 1984 *Nix v. Williams* case. This exception states that evidence that has been seized illegally or evidence stemming from illegally seized evidence (e.g., fruit of the poisoned tree) (*Wong Sun v. United States,* 1963) is admissible if the police can prove that they would have inevitably discovered it anyway by lawful means. On Christmas Eve a 10-year-old girl disappeared from the YMCA in Des Moines, Iowa. Shortly thereafter, Williams was seen leaving the YMCA carrying a large bundle wrapped in a blanket. A young boy who had helped Williams carry the bundle reported that he saw skinny white legs in it.

The next day Williams' car was located near Davenport, some 160 miles away. The police assumed that the girl's body would be located somewhere between the YMCA and Williams' car and began conducting a massive search. In the meantime, Williams was located and arrested in the town where the car was located. Williams' lawyer was told that Williams would be transported back to Des Moines without being interrogated. During the trip back, however, the officer had a conversation with Williams in which he suggested that it would be nice if the girl could be located before a predicted snowstorm, and have a Christian burial. As Williams and the officer neared the town where the body was hidden, Williams directed the officer to the body, a location about two miles from one of the search teams.

At the trial, the motion to suppress the evidence was denied and Williams was convicted of first-degree murder. On appeal, the U.S. District Court declared that the evidence was wrongfully admitted at Williams' trial. At his second trial, the prosecution did not offer Williams' statements into evidence and did not attempt to show that Williams led officers to the body. The court held that if Williams had not led police to the body, it would have been found by searchers anyway. Williams was convicted of murder a second time.

So, because the *Miranda* warnings were not read to the defendant before he confessed, evidence that was seized was excluded at the first trial. However, because the evidence would have been discovered anyway as a result of the police search, the court admitted the evidence.

The Computer Errors Exception

In the 1995 *Arizona v. Evans* case, the court created a computer errors exception to the exclusionary rule. The exception held that a traffic stop which led to the seizure of marijuana was legal even though officers conducted the stop based on an arrest warrant stored improperly in their computer. The case was initiated in 1991 when Issac Evans was stopped in Phoenix, Arizona, for driving the wrong way on a one-way street in front of a police station. A routine computer check revealed an outstanding warrant for Evans, who was taken into custody. Police then found marijuana in the Evans car, and he was later convicted on drug charges. After the arrest, however, police learned that the arrest warrant reported to them by their computer had actually been quashed a few weeks earlier but had not been removed from the computer. The court upheld Evans' conviction by reasoning that officers should not be held responsible for a clerical error made by a court worker and concluded that the arresting officers were acting in good faith based on the information available to them at the time of the arrest.

Searches with a Warrant

The *search warrant* is one of the most valuable tools in criminal investigation. It authorizes the search of homes, businesses, and vehicles of suspects; it typically results in the arrest of multiple suspects, and expedites investigation and subsequent case closure.

Advantages of Searching with a Search Warrant

Among the many tools afforded the criminal investigator, the search warrant has proved to be of substantial worth. It represents an authorization by the court for officers to enter a designated location or structure and search for specific items. It can be useful to a criminal investigator in many situations. The search warrant can be used to:

- Recover stolen property
- Seize drugs or other contraband
- Seize any other type of property used in the commission of a crime

The search warrant must contain specifics about the location to be searched, the objects being sought, the probable cause that indicates that there is property to seize, and a signature of the judge authorizing the search. Evidence obtained through the use of a search warrant may also be more readily accepted by courts than if seized without a warrant or incident to arrest. In addition, the officer is protected from civil liability when a warrant is obtained. A search warrant also benefits the prosecutor by shifting the legal burden to the defendant. Instead of the prosecutor having to justify a presumably unreasonable search, it becomes the burden of the defendant to show that the evidence was seized illegally. This factor alone has encouraged officers to obtain search warrants when possible.

Structuring the Warrant

A search warrant cannot be issued unless it meets with constitutional guidelines. In addition, for the warrant to be legal, it must meet specific legal requirements. The legal requirements for a search warrant are:

- It must be authorized by the proper official.
- It must be issued only for specifically authorized objects.
- It must be issued on probable cause.

The search warrant *affidavit* presents facts that the officer believes constitute probable cause to justify the issuance of a warrant. Authorization of the warrant is through the judicial branch of government. If a magistrate agrees that probable cause exists, he or she signs the affidavit and issues the warrant.

The warrant must contain the following information:

- Reasons to request the search
- Name of the officer requesting the warrant
- Items to be seized

- Specific place to be searched
- Signature of the issuing judge

Once issued, a warrant should be executed promptly. During the course of a search, other items of contraband should not be sought unless they are specified in the search warrant. The seizure of items other than those listed in the warrant is not considered "within the scope of the search" and will probably be excluded from the trial as evidence obtained illegally. The search warrant process consists basically of three stages: the affidavit, the search warrant, and the search warrant return.

The Affidavit

The search warrant affidavit (Figure 6.1) must be prepared before obtaining a search warrant. The affidavit tells the judge three things.

1. What is being searched for?
   - Contraband
   - Instrumentation of crime
   - Weapons
   - Fruits of crime
2. Where is the search to occur?
   - Residence
   - Business
   - Vehicle
3. Why is the search to be conducted?
   - Probable cause adequately outlined
   - Facts establishing probable cause

The Search Warrant

Basically, the search warrant (Figure 6.2) sets forth the same facts as outlined in the affidavit. The affiant (the officer) prior to signing the affidavit, must be first sworn in by the judge. The judge must then sign and date all pages of the affidavit and warrant.

The Search Warrant Return

The *search warrant return* (Figure 6.3) is an itemized inventory of all property and material seized by officers at the location of the search. A copy is left with the defendant, and the return itself is returned to the issuing judge. In most cases the officer who executes the warrant is the one to return it, and this must be accomplished within 24 hours after the search.

IN THE DISTRICT COURT OF THE FIFTH JUDICIAL DISTRICT IN AND FOR:
BOONE COUNTY, MISSOURI

Before ________________ Judge, District Court of
Boone County, Missouri

State of Missouri }
Boone County

Affidavit of Search Warrant

On this _____ day of ______, 20___, ___Agent Brian Johnson___being first sworn, upon oath deposes and says:

That a certain Residence within said County and State, located and described as follows, to wit:

2304 N. W. 38th Place, Columbia, Missouri located in Boone County being a single-family wood frame dwelling facing South, and under the control of Samuel Thomas Lawrence, and wife Dorothy. The garage area of the house is to the West end of the South side. The house is on the North side of the street with tan colored brick along the lower third of the front, while being fenced in, with a chain link fence, around the back yard area.

The same being the residence of Samuel Thomas and Dorothy Lawrence whose more full, true and correct name is unknown to the affiant, there is located certain property particularly described as follows, to-wit:

Controlled substance to include marijuana, Schedule I, LSD, Schedule I, Cocaine, Schedule II, and one (1), one hundred dollar bill ($100.00) UPS. currency bearing serial number JO3744496B, and any other records or documents showing illicit business dealings in controlled drugs.

which said property is subject to search and seizure as set out by the laws of Missouri for the following grounds, to-wit:

Violation of the state criminal code controlled substances section RsMo 195.233.

and that the probable cause of the affiant believing such facts as follows, to-wit:

1) Your affiant is a sworn police officer with the City Police Department, who has been a full time narcotics investigator for three years and seven months. 2) On April 30, 2002, at approximately 1630 hours, Officer Johnson purchased one (1) kilo of marijuana for $1500 from Dorothy Lawrence which was contained in a black trunk located in the hallway of the residence. 3) On April 30, 2002, at approx. 1945 hours Officer Johnson purchased 100 units of LSD for 4300 from Samuel Lawrence which he acquired from the freezer area of the kitchen. 4) On April 30, 2002, Samuel Lawrence also displayed approx. one (1) ounce of white powder claiming it to be cocaine which was also kept in the refrigerator area of the kitchen.

____
Affiant

Subscribed and sworn below me this ____ day of ____, 20___

____
Judge, District Court of
Boone County, Missouri

Figure 6.1 Sample Affidavit of Search Warrant — to be prepared before obtaining a search warrant.

IN THE DISTRICT COURT OF THE FIFTH JUDICIAL DISTRICT IN AND FOR:
BOONE COUNTY, MISSOURI

BEFORE _______________ JUDGE, DISTRICT COURT OF
BOONE COUNTY, MISSOURI

State of Missouri} ss.
Boone County

SEARCH WARRANT

In the name of the State of Missouri, to any sheriff, constable, marshal, policeman, or peace officer in the County of Boone, State of Missouri.

Proof by affidavit having been this day made before me, by *Agent Brian Johnson* that there is probable cause for believing that in the herein described *residence* is located the following property particularly described as follows to-wit:

Controlled substances to include marijuana, Schedule I, LSD, Schedule I, and Cocaine, Schedule II, and one fifty dollar bill U.S. currency bearing serial number: J3744496B

And that the herein described *residence* should be searched by reason of the following grounds to-wit:

Possession of the above described controlled dangerous substances and currency is evidence of violation of the state criminal code controlled substance section RsMo 195.233.

YOU ARE THEREFORE COMMANDED at any time of day or night to make immediate search of the *residence* of *2304 N.W. 38th Place, Columbia, Missouri* whose more full, true and correct name is unknown, located and described as follows, to-wit:

A single-family wood frame dwelling facing south, and under the control of Samuel Thomas Lawrence, and wife Dorothy. The garage area of the house is to the West end of the South side. The house is on the North side of the street with tan colored brick along the lower third front, while being fenced in, with a chain link fence, around the back yard area.

For the said property above described, and, if you find the same or any part thereof to bring it forthwith before me at my office in Columbia, Boone County, Missouri.

Dated this *1st* day of *May 2002.*

____
Judge, District Court of
Boone County, Missouri

Figure 6.2 Sample Search Warrant — sets forth the same facts outlined in the affidavit.

The search warrant return should include the following information:

- The name of the officer serving the warrant
- The date the warrant was served
- An itemized list of all property seized
- The name of the owner of the place searched

SEARCH WARRANT RETURN

Received this writ _____ day of ______, 20____.

Executed the same on the _____, 20___ by going to the within designated place where I found and seized the following property, to-wit:

____

____

____

____

____

and brought the same before the within named court.

____
Sheriff – Peace Officer
Marshal – Policeman

Executed the same day on the ______ day of _____, 20___ by searching the within designated place, where I could find none of the above described property.

____
Sheriff – Peace Officer
Marshall – Policeman

OFFICERS FEES

Executing writ ________________________________ $ ______________

Mileage ____________________________________ Miles $ ____________

Total: $ ________

____
Sheriff – Peace Officer
Marshall – Policeman

Figure 6.3 Sample Search Warrant Return form — an inventory of all property and material seized by officers at the location of the search.

- The signature of the officer who served the warrant (this is usually signed in the presence of the judge)
- The signature of the issuing judge and the date of the return

Execution of the Warrant

Once issued, the search warrant is basically an order by the court to execute it. The officer has no choice but to do so. If the warrant is valid on its face, has been authorized by the proper official, and is executed correctly, the officer is protected from both civil liability and criminal prosecution. Certain procedures should be adhered to carefully when executing the search warrant. Search warrant execution guidelines include:

- The search warrant may authorize a specific officer (the affiant) to execute it. Typically, however, a class of officers will be authorized to execute the warrant, so that anyone within that class may do so.
- Time limitations must be adhered to. Although the word reasonable has not been defined by the courts, execution of the warrant must be within what a rational person would consider reasonable. To deal with this issue, many states have outlined a specific period in which the warrant must be issued. Periods may range from 48 to 96 hours. If the warrant cannot be executed within the designated period, it is invalid.
- Only necessary force can be used in executing the search warrant. The U.S. Code requires that officers announce their purpose and authority, and if refused admittance, break both outer and inner doors to gain entry. Denial need not be specific, or even be inferred, such as the occupants refusing to answer the door.
- Some states may authorize a "no-knock warrant." If such a warrant is obtained, specific information must be contained in the affidavit justifying why the no-knock warrant is necessary.

Warrantless Searches

Officers must remember that the rules that apply to searches differ from those applying to arrests. An arrest and a search are two completely separate and distinct law enforcement procedures. For example, depending on certain statutory restraints, an officer might be empowered to make an arrest without an arrest warrant, provided that probable cause exists. In addition, arrests are permissible even though there may be time for the officer to go get a warrant.

For searches the rules are different. The Fourth Amendment says that all searches must be preceded by the officer obtaining a search warrant. Regardless of how much probable cause the officer may have, if he or she searches without a search warrant, there is a legal presumption that the search is unconstitutional. Several exceptions have been developed in which a warrantless search is authorized under law:

- Consent searches
- Searches under exigent circumstances
- Searches incident to lawful arrest
- Stop-and-frisk searches
- Plain-view searches
- Moving-automobile searches
- Open-field searches

Search by Consent

Police can search without a warrant when a suspect gives them permission to do so. Searches in this instance must, of course, be subsequent to an initial detention that was lawful. As a case in point, *Florida v. Royer* (1983) held that evidence obtained as a result of a *consent search* (Figure 6.4) when the detention was made without probable cause is a violation of the defendant's Fourth Amendment rights and will be excluded.

The consent search can be especially useful in cases in which officers have no legal basis for obtaining a search warrant. It is important to remember, however, that a consent search must be authorized voluntarily, with no coercion from officers. This was affirmed in *Bumper v. North Carolina* (1968), in a decision in which the U.S. Supreme Court held that a search is not justified on the basis of consent when consent was given only after the officer conducting the search asserted possession of a warrant. Although it is legal for officers to search on the word of the suspect, it is a better idea to have the person sign a consent-to-search waiver authorizing the search in writing. For the consent to be valid, officers must first establish that the person giving consent has legal authority to do so. So, just because a suspect is present in a particular residence, he or she may not have legal authority to grant a search. Dominion and control can be verified through the seizing of utility bills, for example, that bear the name of the suspect and the associated address.

One interesting aspect of a consent search is that the suspect does not have to be given the *Miranda* warning or be told that he or she has the right to withhold consent for the search to be valid (*Schneckloth v. Bustamonte,* 1973). In the event that the suspect changes his or her mind about the search, officers must cease searching or obtain a search warrant to continue.

Another problem with consent searches is that the person giving permission to search can limit the scope of the search. Permission to search can be withdrawn at any time, and any area or container within the search area can

CITY POLICE DEPARTMENT
CONSENT TO SEARCH

DATE ____________

LOCATION ____

I, ______________________________, having been informed of my constitutional right not to have a search made of the premises hereinafter described without a search warrant and of my right to refuse to consent to such a search, hereby authorize ____, officers of the City Police Department, to conduct a complete search of my:

Premises ___

Curtilage ___

Vehicles ___

These officers are authorized by me to take from my premises any letters, papers, materials, or other property which they may desire, after receipting me for same. I further state that I am the proper person to give the consent and authorization referred to herein.

This written permission is being given by me to the above named officer(s) voluntarily and without threats or promises of any kind.

____
Signature

WITNESSES:

____

____

____

Figure 6.4 Sample Consent to Search form.

be specifically exempted. What if an area or container that might reasonably hold the object of the search isn't specifically exempted? In the case of *Florida v. Enio Jimeno* (1991) the court held that a person's general consent to search the interior of a car includes, unless otherwise specified, all containers in the car that might reasonably hold the object of the search. In this case a Dade County police officer began following a car after overhearing the driver, Enio Jimeno, make arrangements on a pay phone for a drug transaction. When

Jimeno failed to come to a complete stop before turning right at a streetlight, the officer pulled him over. The officer advised Jimeno that he was going to receive a traffic citation for failure to stop at the red light. Next, since he had reason to believe that Jimeno was involved with a drug transaction, the officer asked for permission to search the automobile. Jimeno agreed, claiming that he had nothing to hide. As a result of the search, the officer found one kilo of cocaine in a brown paper bag located on the passenger side of the floorboard. Jimeno was arrested and charged.

The issue here is that since Jimeno had not given specific permission to search the bag, the Florida courts ordered the cocaine suppressed as evidence. The courts claimed that although the officer was proper in asking for permission to search the vehicle, permission was not extended to the bag under the floorboard or any other containers in the car. The U.S. Supreme Court didn't agree. In his delivery of the majority opinion, Chief Justice William Rehnquist stated:

> The scope of a search is generally defined by its expressed object. [The officer] had informed Jimeno that he...would be looking for narcotics in the area. We think that it was...reasonable for the police to conclude that the general consent to search [the] car included consent to search containers within that car which might bear drugs.

Rehnquist further explained that a different degree of privacy should attach to a paper bag than to a locked suitcase and that it is probably unreasonable for an officer to think that a person who gives consent for a search of his vehicle has also given consent to pry open a locked bag inside the car, but it probably isn't unreasonable for the officer to open a paper bag under the same circumstances. Rehnquist went on to say that

> a suspect may of course delimit as he chooses the scope of the search to which he consents ...but if his consent would reasonably be understood to extend to a particular container, the Fourth Amendment provides no grounds for requiring a more explicit authorization.

In a related case, *Florida v. Bostick* (1991), the U.S. Supreme Court permitted warrantless sweeps of inner city buses. In *Bostick* the court ruled that law enforcement officers who approach a seated bus passenger and request consent to search the passenger's luggage do not necessarily seize the passenger under the Fourth Amendment. The test applied in such situations is whether a reasonable passenger would feel free to decline the request or otherwise terminate the encounter. In the Bostick case the defendant was traveling from Miami, Florida to Atlanta, Georgia. When the bus stopped in

Fort Lauderdale, two police officers involved in drug interdiction efforts boarded the bus, and lacking reasonable suspicion, approached the defendant. After asking to inspect his ticket and identification, they then requested and were given consent to search the defendant's luggage for drugs. Cocaine was found as a result of the search.

The Florida Supreme Court ruled that the cocaine had been seized in violation of the Fourth Amendment. In doing so, the court noted that the defendant had been illegally seized without reasonable suspicion and that an impermissible seizure necessarily results any time that police board a bus, approach passengers without reasonable suspicion, and request consent to search luggage. The U.S. Supreme Court reversed the Florida court's decision and held that this type of drug interdiction effort may be permissible as long as officers do not convey the message that compliance with their request is required. The court noted that previous cases have permitted the police, without reasonable suspicion, to approach individuals in airports for the purpose of asking questions, verifying identification, and requesting consent to search luggage.

Emergency Searches

In the case of an emergency or *exigent circumstances*, a search may also be conducted without a warrant provided that probable cause exists. This exception is generally applied when one of three circumstances exists: there is (1) a danger to life, (2) a threat of the suspect escaping, or (3) a threat of the removal or destruction of evidence (e.g., flushing it down the toilet). Any one of these circumstances may create an exception to the Fourth Amendment's warrant requirement. It is incumbent upon investigating officers to demonstrate that a dire situation existed which justified their actions. Failure to do so will result in the evidence seized being deemed illegal.

The need for emergency searches was first recognized by the U.S. Supreme Court in *Ker v. California* (1963) and *Cupp v. Murphy* (1973) when they decided that police may enter a dwelling unannounced in cases in which a delay in the search would result in the destruction of evidence. In a related decision, the court held that it was lawful for police to enter a residence without a warrant if they were in pursuit of a fleeing robber (*Warden v. Hayden*, 1967). In another case, *Mincey v. Arizona* (1978), the Supreme Court held that the "Fourth Amendment does not require police officers to delay in the course of an investigation if doing so would gravely endanger their lives or the lives of others." Finally, in the 1995 case of *Wilson v. Arkansas*, the Supreme Court ruled that police officers generally must knock and announce their identity before entering a dwelling or other premises with a search warrant. However, in certain emergencies, officers armed with a search warrant need not knock or identify themselves.

Searches Incident to Arrest

As we learned earlier, the Chimel decision authorized a search of an arrested suspect and the immediate area around him or her. This is justified by an officer's right to search a suspect for weapons before being transported to jail. The area around the suspect is searched because it is considered lunging distance, where a suspect could conceivably acquire a weapon. When the suspect is arrested in a vehicle, the immediate area is defined as the entire passenger compartment of the vehicle, including closed but not locked containers (*New York v. Belton,* 1981). In circumstances in which a thorough search is desired pursuant to an arrest, a search warrant should be obtained.

Stop-and-Frisk Searches

Although searches without warrants are often challenged in court, officers must frequently act without them. Indeed, the public expects officers to act when a crime is suspected to be occurring. This responsibility extends to stopping and questioning suspects on the street who are suspected of involvement in a crime. Two circumstances can be identified in which officers are required to stop and possibly search people:

1. To investigate suspicious circumstances
2. To make identification of a subject

The first circumstance is illustrated in the landmark *Terry v. Ohio* (1968) decision. In this case a plainclothes policeman with over 35 years of experience observed two men standing on a street corner. The men were acting suspiciously, walking up and down while peering into a store window, seemingly "casing" the store. A third man soon joined them, spoke briefly, and quickly left the immediate area. The officer, after observing the two men join the third man a couple of blocks away, approached them, identified himself, and asked for identification. After receiving a mumbled response, the officer patted down the outer clothing of the three men. Weapons were found on Terry and one other man. They were charged and convicted of carrying concealed weapons.

The issue under *Terry* is whether it is lawful under the Fourth Amendment for an officer to *stop and frisk* a suspect. The court found that the practice of stop and frisk is valid. However, in a 1993 case, the Supreme Court reaffirmed that a frisk that goes beyond *Terry* is invalid (*Minnesota v. Dickerson*).

Plain-View Searches

Police officers have the opportunity to begin investigations or confiscate evidence without a warrant, based on what they find in plain view and open to public inspection. This has become known as the *plain-view doctrine,* a doctrine first stated in the Supreme Court ruling in *Harris v. United States* (1968). A police officer found evidence of a robbery while inventorying an impounded vehicle. The court ruled that "objects falling in the plain view of an officer who has a right to be in the position to have that view are subject to seizure and may be used as evidence." This doctrine has been widely used by investigators in such cases as crimes in progress, accidents, and fires. An officer might enter an apartment, for example, while responding to a domestic disturbance, and find drugs on a living room table. He or she would be within his or her rights to seize the drugs as evidence even though there was no search warrant.

The criteria for a valid plain-view search were identified in *Coolidge v. New Hampshire* (1971). In that decision the court identified three criteria that must be present:

1. The officer must be present lawfully at the location to be searched.
2. The item seized must have been found inadvertently.
3. The item is contraband or would be useful as evidence of a crime.

Prior to 1990, the courts required that all items found in plain view be found inadvertently, but in *Horton v. California* (1990), the court ruled that "inadvertent discovery" of evidence is no longer a necessary element of the plain-view doctrine. Other cases supporting the plain-view doctrine include the 1958 *United States v. Henry* decision, in which the court ruled that if an officer discovers evidence of another crime "unexpectedly," that evidence is seizeable. In 1978, coinciding cases *Michigan v. Tyler* and *Mincey v. Arizona* concluded that while officers are present on a person's premises carrying out legitimate emergency responsibilities, any evidence in plain view is seizeable. In another case, the court held that the officer needn't know that the evidence is contraband, only that it is associated with a crime (*Texas v. Brown,* 1983). In this case the officer's personal knowledge that heroin was transported in balloons was sufficient to seize a balloon without knowing exactly what it contained.

The plain-view doctrine, has, however, been restricted by more recent court decisions such as the case of *United States v. Irizarry* (1982), where the court held that officers cannot move objects to gain a better view of evidence otherwise hidden from view. This was affirmed in *Arizona v. Hicks* (1987), which stated that evidence seized must be in plain view without the need for officers to move or dislodge it.

In *Hicks,* officers responded to a shooting in a second-floor apartment where a bullet had been fired through the floor, injuring a man in the apartment below. The premises of James Hicks were in considerable disarray when investigating officers entered. As the officers looked for the person who fired the weapon, they discovered a number of guns and a stocking mask that might have been used in some local robberies. The items were seized. In one corner, officers noticed two expensive stereo sets. One of the officers approached the equipment, suspecting that it might be stolen, and read a few of the serial numbers from where it sat, but in order to read the remaining serial numbers, the equipment was moved away from the wall. After calling in the serial number, the officer learned that the equipment had, in fact, been stolen. Hicks was then arrested and later convicted of armed robbery, because of the seized property. On appeal the U.S. Supreme Court decided that the search of Hicks' apartment became illegal when the officer moved the stereo set away from the wall to record the serial numbers. The court found that Hicks had a reasonable expectation of privacy, which means that the officers, although invited into the apartment, should have acted more like guests than inquisitors.

Automobile Searches

The precedent established for warrantless searches of automobiles is the automobile exception, or Carroll Doctrine (*Carroll v. United States,* 1925). This decision established that the right to search a vehicle does not depend on the right to arrest the driver but on the premise that the contents of the vehicle contain evidence of a crime.

In this case, George Carroll, a bootlegger, was convicted for transporting intoxicating liquor in a vehicle, a violation of the National Prohibition Act. At the trial, Carroll's attorneys contended that the liquor need not be admitted into evidence because the search and seizure of the vehicle were unlawful and violated the Fourth Amendment. Because of the mobility of the automobile, the warrantless search under *Carroll* is justified. Following the Carroll decision, there existed some uncertainty about the moving vehicle doctrine. Much of this doubt was laid to rest in 1970, however, when the U.S. Supreme Court reaffirmed the right of officers to search a vehicle that is moving or about to be moved out of their jurisdiction, provided that probable cause exists that the vehicle contains items that officers are entitled to seize.

Since the ruling of the Carroll doctrine, related cases have raised the question of whether officers searching under *Carroll* also have the right to search closed containers in a car. In a 1981 decision, the U.S. Supreme Court held that warrantless seizures of evidence in the passenger compartments of a car, after a lawful arrest, are valid (*New York v. Belton,* 1981). Before this decision, there was some confusion about the authority of police to search within the vehicle but outside the driver's "wingspan." The court authorized a search of the entire passenger compartment of the vehicle, including the back seat. It also authorized the opening of containers in the vehicle that might contain the object sought. The following year the court held that after a lawful arrest, police may open the trunk of a car and containers found therein without a warrant, even in the absence of exigent circumstances (*United States v. Ross,* 1982). This case further defined the scope of police search-and-seizure authority in vehicle searches. The Ross case therefore has expanded the scope of warrantless searches only to what is "reasonable." It should be noted, however, that police may not open large containers taken from the car, such as footlockers, without a warrant, provided that there is time to obtain one.

In a high-profile case, *California v. Acevedo* (1991), much of the confusion about vehicle searches was eliminated. Federal agents in Hawaii intercepted a package of marijuana being sent via Federal Express to Santa Ana, California. At that time officers staked out the Santa Ana Federal Express office. The man who claimed the package was then followed to his apartment, where he went inside and came back out a few minutes later with an empty carton, which he pitched into a dumpster. At that time, one officer left the area to obtain a search warrant while the other officers maintained surveillance on the residence.

Before the officer returned with the warrant, Acevedo drove up and entered the apartment. In about 10 minutes he exited the apartment with an object in a paper bag which was about the same size as a brick of marijuana. Acevedo placed the bag in his vehicle trunk and began to drive away. In an effort to stop Acevedo before he would be lost to chase, the officers pulled him over and searched his trunk. The bag was discovered and was found to contain marijuana. Although the trial court found Acevedo guilty, on appeal the California Court of Appeals ruled that the officer's probable cause was attached to the bag and not the vehicle: therefore, they should have obtained a warrant pursuant to the Chadwick rule. The U.S. Supreme Court didn't agree. Its response included a statement by Justice Harry A. Blackmun, who wrote:

> The [Chadwick] rule not only has failed to protect privacy but it has also confused courts and police officers and impeded effective law enforcement.... We conclude that it is better to adopt one clear-cut rule to govern automobile searches and eliminate the warrant requirement for closed containers. We therefore interpret *Carroll* as providing one rule to govern all automobile searches — the police may search an automobile and containers within it where they have probable cause to believe contraband or evidence is contained.

Stated simply, the Acevedo case holds that if an officer has probable cause to believe that a container in an automobile holds contraband, the officer may open the container and seize the evidence, provided that the evidence is in fact contraband.

The law on vehicle searches has changed dramatically over the past 15 years, enabling police officers more latitude in their search and seizure authority. For example, in *Pennsylvania v. Labron* (1993), the Supreme Court ruled that there is no need for a search warrant in vehicle searches if the vehicle is readily mobile, even if there is time to obtain a warrant. In a related case, the court held that police officers with probable cause to search a car may inspect passengers' belongings found in the car that are capable of concealing the object of the search (*Wyoming v. Houghton,* 1999).[1]

Vehicle Inventory Search

In 1970 the U.S. Supreme Court reaffirmed the right of officers to search a vehicle that is moving or is about to be moved, provided that there is probable cause to believe that the vehicle contains items that are legally seizeable. In *Chambers v. Maroney* (1970), the court referred to the earlier case of *Carroll v. United States* and determined that a search warrant is unnecessary provided probable cause exists that contraband is contained in the vehicle, that the vehicle is movable, and that a search warrant is not readily obtainable. This doctrine applies even if the vehicle has been driven to the police station by a police officer and there was time to secure a search warrant.

In the Chambers case, officers received a report that a service station had been robbed. After receiving a description of the station wagon the robbers were driving and a partial description of the suspects, officers stopped a vehicle matching the description and arrested the occupants. After the suspects were arrested, the officers took the vehicle to headquarters to be searched. Although a search warrant could have been obtained, one was not. During the search, officers located two .38 caliber handguns concealed under the dashboard, some small change, and credit cards belonging to a service station attendant who had been robbed previously.

At the trial, the court rejected the search incident to lawful arrest because the search was made at the police station some time after the arrest. On appeal, however, the U.S. Supreme Court stated that there were alternative grounds for the search. When a vehicle is seized, its contents are routinely inventoried to prevent subsequent claims by the defendant that items were taken. The search and the inventory are, however, two separate processes under law but can be conducted simultaneously, as was the case in *Chambers*. Evidence located as a result of the inventory search is admissible in court. It has been recommended, however, that in the case of an automobile that is rendered immobile or one that has been transported to the police station, a search warrant should be obtained as a precautionary matter.

Open-Field Searches

In *Oliver v. United States* (1984), the U.S. Supreme Court reaffirmed its position that open fields are not protected by the Fourth Amendment. This differs from constitutional protection over buildings, houses, and the area surrounding them, known as curtilage. A yard is considered curtilage; thus both the house and yard are protected and cannot be searched without a warrant or one of the exceptions mentioned. Open fields and pastures outside the curtilage are not protected by the Constitution; thus searches made by the government of those areas are not considered "unreasonable."

In the Oliver case, police officers, acting on reports that marijuana was growing on Oliver's farm, proceeded to investigate, but without a warrant or probable cause. They drove past a locked gate with a sign that read "No Trespassing." However, a path was also observed leading around the side of the property. After following the path around the gate, officers found a field of marijuana located over a mile from the house. Oliver was subsequently charged and convicted of manufacturing a controlled substance.

This case is significant because the court essentially stated that a person's "reasonable expectation of privacy" under the Fourth Amendment does not apply when the property involved is an open field.

Defining Curtilage

In a 1987 decision, *United Sates v. Dunn*, the Supreme Court ruled that the warrantless search of a barn that is not part of the curtilage is valid. Out of this decision came four factors that laid out whether an area is considered a part of the curtilage:

1. The proximity of the area to the home
2. Whether the area is within an enclosure surrounding the home
3. The nature and uses of the area
4. The steps taken to conceal the area from public view

The Dunn decision, while still subject to imprecise application, is helpful because it narrows the definition of what buildings should be considered curtilage of the main residence.

Beginning the Search

Once an investigator has documented a crime scene, the actual search must begin. Evidence discovered at the crime scene will generally serve four objectives: (1) to determine the facts of the crime, (2) to identify the lawbreaker, (3) to aid in his or her arrest, and (4) to aid in the criminal prosecution of the perpetrator.

History has shown that there are many different ways to search a crime scene for evidence, and methods for crime scene searching vary according to the types of crime scenes and evidence at hand. Varieties of crime scene evidence include firearm evidence, trace materials, tool-mark evidence, body fluids, fire and explosion evidence, outdoor crime scene evidence, evidence from vehicle searches, and evidence from interior and victim searches.

The search of the crime scene consists of several distinct phases:

- Surveying the crime scene
- Documenting the crime scene through sketches and photographs
- Recording all physical evidence
- Searching for fingerprints

Search Patterns

Regardless of the method used, the search of the scene should be conducted in a systematic way. The most common search patterns include the spiral search method, grid method, strip or line-search method, and quadrant or zone-search method. Some methods of searching are best suited for outdoor scenes, whereas others are more applicable to indoor crime scenes. Other scenes present unique problems and are discussed next. Whichever method is adopted, the rule to remember is that the search must be thorough.

Indoor Crime Scene Searches

It is generally recommended that at least two officers search an indoor crime scene. This may best be accomplished by dividing the room in half and having each investigator search half (the quadrant or zone search method). At the conclusion of the search, the investigators switch halves. In this fashion, each half of the room is searched twice.

Outdoor Crime Scene Searches

In most cases the outdoor crime scene covers a broader area than one that is indoor, so more investigators will be required. Accordingly, with the increased size of the scene, a more systematic searching method must be employed. One way is to rope off the scene into a grid. Each square, averaging about 6 square feet, represents a specific search area that is a manageable size for each investigator (the grid search method).

Nighttime Crime Scene Searches

If possible, investigators should wait until daylight to search a crime scene. Obviously, circumstances can require investigators to proceed with the search at night. These may include inclement weather or other emergency circumstances. In the event that such a search is to be conducted, lighting generators should be employed to provide sufficient illumination for the search.

Vehicle Searches

The search of a vehicle requires the same degree of attention as indoor and outdoor searches. Obviously, the nature of the crime will dictate the area of the vehicle to be searched. For example, a drug smuggling or murder case will require closer examination of the interior of the vehicle, whereas a hit-and-run investigation will necessitate examination of the exterior of the vehicle. Like an interior search, a vehicle should also be searched for fingerprints. This should be done after other trace evidence has been sought.

Strip Search

A strip search must be conducted in a private and controlled environment. This technique requires the suspect to undress completely, and all clothing is searched. In some cases the suspect's body cavities may need to be searched. Officers are allowed to search the ears, mouth, and nose visually, but they must exercise caution, as only authorized medical personnel may search the vaginal and rectal areas. It is also recommended that investigators communicate with the prosecutor before conducting a strip search of any suspect to safeguard against possible procedural errors.

Searching the Scene

Evidence of crimes is dynamic. That is, it is unique, often fragile, and may constantly be undergoing change. Experience tells us that there is usually only one chance to search a crime scene properly, so for this reason it is a good idea to survey the scene carefully before embarking on the search process. As a first step, the investigator should consider all information provided to him or her by officers who arrived earlier on the scene. Such information includes the officers' perceptions of what occurred and the nature of the evidence. Next, investigators should rationalize the importance of the evidence items that seem to play the greatest role in the alleged crime. The principal concern at this point is to observe and document the scene rather than take action.

Of specific importance in the observation phase is the relative distance of any object to the victim. The distance between an object and a victim may play a greater role in the evidence collection phase than the item itself. For example, if the crime scene consists of a dead person who has apparently been shot, and a 9-mm handgun, the locations of spent shell casings could indicate the angle of the weapon or the position of the victim at the time it was discharged. Such a determination could point to either suicide or homicide, and may subsequently alter the character of the investigation. As indicated, while observations are being carried out, notes should be taken to organize the sequence of events. Witness statements should be taken as well, regarding the victim(s) or related information. Additionally, videotapes and photographs should be made during this phase to document the scene adequately for future reference. Both of these considerations are discussed in greater detail later in the book.

Collecting Evidence

There is a tendency on the part of many investigators to rush the evidence collection process and focus attention on the obvious. Understandably, the task of observing firsthand the scene of another's misfortune is a difficult one for many, and one might appreciate the desire for expeditiousness on the part of the investigator. It is a fact, however, that much critical evidence, often seemingly unimportant, can be located in and around the scene of almost every crime. As discussed in the earlier section on crime scene searches, investigators must choose which method of searching is best suited for the crime in question. Regardless of which method is used, evidence must be collected in a comprehensive, nondestructive manner, within a reasonable period, and with a minimum of unnecessary movement about the scene. Although every criminal case is unique and should be evaluated on an individual basis, experience has shown that the following general recommendations are beneficial in organizing the search and preventing errors.[2]

General Rules of Crime Scene Searching

> If there is an indication that evidence is deteriorating significantly with time or by the elements, these have first priority. Crime scene investigators should always wear protective clothing to protect evidence from contamination and to safeguard themselves as well.
>
> All of the major items are examined, photographed, recorded, and collected, as appropriate, taking them in the order that is most logical, considering the requirement to conserve movement. Making casts and lifting latent prints from objects to be moved from the scene are done as necessary. Items should not be moved until they have been examined for trace evidence. Fingerprints should be taken, or at least developed and covered with tape, before the object is moved. When an (obviously) deceased person is involved, the evidence items lying between the point of entry to the scene and point of exit from the scene and the body are processed; then the detailed search of the deceased is conducted. After that search, the body should be removed and the processing of obvious evidence continued as noted earlier.

After processing the more obvious evidence, the search for and collection of additional trace material is begun. Trace evidence should be searched for and collected before dusting for fingerprints. After the trace materials have been collected, other latent prints are lifted. When sweeping or vacuuming, surface areas should be segmented, the sweepings from each area packaged separately, and the location of their point of recovery noted. Normally, elimination fingerprints and physical evidence standards are collected after the preceding actions have been completed.

Gathering and Preserving Evidence

Once the initial crime scene search has been completed, and following the sketching and photographing of the scene, evidence should be collected. The manner in which evidence is collected must be consistent with each law enforcement agency's policies and procedures, and should be in keeping with accepted rules of evidence. The evidence collected first is usually that which is most fragile. Therefore, fingerprints should be lifted as a priority. Next, other fragile evidence, such as blood and other trace evidence, should be collected. It is important for officers to search the crime scene a second time after the evidence has been collected. This should uncover any evidence accidentally overlooked. When possible, one investigator should serve as the evidence collector. This designation ensures that all evidence gets recorded and processed at the scene in a uniform manner. It also ensures that evidence will be moved only when the collector decides that it can be moved.

When the case goes to court, both the investigator who discovered the evidence and the collector will usually be required to testify. The greatest advantage to using this system is that all evidence is collected in a uniform manner, and one officer is responsible for packaging and marking the evidence and filling out necessary paperwork. This reduces the need to tie up additional officers at the office for such a task.

The Chain of Custody

Evidence that has been collected must be safeguarded until the case goes to court. During the trial, if it is determined that labels are missing, evidence is not properly initialed, or evidence is otherwise missing or altered, the evidence may be considered inadmissible and the case might be thrown out. The total accounting of evidence is known as the *chain of custody*. This is made up of all persons (usually law enforcement personnel) who have taken custody of the evidence since its collection and who are therefore responsible for its protection and storage. The chain of custody is established by adhering to certain guidelines:

- The number of persons handling evidence from the time that it is safely stored should be limited. If the evidence leaves the possession of an officer, he or she should record in the notes to whom the evidence was given, the date and time, and the reason it was turned over.
- Anyone who handles evidence should affix his or her name and badge number to the package containing evidence.
- A signed receipt should be obtained from the person accepting the evidence. In turn, the investigator should sign a receipt or log when the item is returned.
- When a piece of evidence is turned in, the investigator should check his or her identification mark on it to ensure that it is the same item.
- After an item is returned to the investigator, he or she should determine if the item is in the same condition as when it was discovered. Any change in the physical appearance of the evidence should be called to the attention of the court.

Evidence can be stored in vehicle trunks, strongboxes, property rooms, locked file cabinets, evidence lockers, or vaults. The only stipulation is that it be marked properly and protected from tampering or destruction. Most evidence is turned over to an evidence custodian, who is usually an employee of the crime lab. This person will sign off on an evidence form as the recipient of the evidence. The seizing officer can then indicate in his or her investigative report the person to whom the evidence was given.

Marking the Evidence

Another important rule to remember during the evidence collection process is that all evidence must be marked immediately upon its seizure to enable proper identification later. It is common for the officer who seizes evidence to identify it at the trial. Such testimony ensures the integrity of the chain of custody. Proper marking of each piece of evidence also ensures organization of all items of evidence for restructuring the events of the crime and the questioning of witnesses. Generally, it does not matter how the officer marks evidence as long as both the initials of the seizing officer and the date of the seizure are clearly indicated on the seized item and on any container used to enclose the object, such as an envelope or cardboard box.

In many cases, the officer's department will require additional information. Such information includes the assigned case number, the type of crime, the victim's name, and the defendant's name, address, and date of birth. After physical evidence has been marked, sealed, counted, weighed (if necessary), and placed within a sealed container, a label is affixed containing identifying information. The following details should be included on the evidence label:

- Case number
- Exhibit number (when numerous items are seized)
- Date and time of seizure
- Name and description of articles
- Location at time of discovery
- Signature or initials of officer making the discovery
- Name or initials of others witnessing the discovery

Special Cases in Evidence Handling

Just as evidence can be damaged or destroyed in the mishandling of a crime scene, improperly collected and managed evidence can also sabotage an otherwise successful investigation. Improperly handled evidence, if contaminated, may either result in investigators reaching inaccurate conclusions or wasting time trying to correct the problem. The question commonly arises as to whether an object is or is not evidence. The decision is based on the officer's ability to consider the facts and circumstances at the crime scene, as well as his or her good judgment, common sense, and past experience. When any doubt exists, the object should be collected and processed as evidence. The object can be reevaluated later. We shall now examine some of the ways that certain types of critical evidence should be dealt with on the crime scene.

Infected Evidence

Among the many dangers encountered by law enforcement officers in the performance of their duties is the threat of street violence and even death. The rising specter of acquired immunodeficiency syndrome (AIDS) has created a new health concern for criminal investigators charged with collection and preservation of crime scene evidence. Problems in collection of suspected infected evidence arise out of the fact that unlike many health care professionals, crime scene investigators are operating in an uncontrolled environment and often under extremely adverse conditions. Even the use of protection devices such as gloves and masks may not provide the investigator with adequate protection from communicable diseases such as AIDS, tuberculosis, and hepatitis B. This is partly due to the fact that such protective measures often fail to protect against cutting or puncturing, which can be a means of transmitting disease and infection through blood and other bodily fluids. Implements such as weapons, drug paraphernalia, razor blades, and hypodermic needles, which can be secreted in pockets, drawers, and in automobiles, all pose threats to crime scene technicians.

An unfortunate side effect of the AIDS epidemic is that it is likely that officers who lack adequate protective equipment, are uneasy about the prospect of contracting certain diseases, or lack training on how best to deal with such problems, might tend to limit their searches, intentionally or inadvertently, for fear of contracting an infecting organism. This could result in the attitude "it's just not worth it," which could have many negative side effects for the overall investigative process, including inadequately seized evidence, resulting in a poorly investigated case which would, in turn, result in weak prosecution of the defendant. The National Institute of Justice has offered a list of recommendations on how best to deal with the problem of infected evidence.[3]

Recommendations for Dealing with Infected Evidence

- Human Bites. Viral transmission through saliva is unlikely; however, if bitten, after milking the wound, rinse well and seek medical attention.
- Spitting/Urine/Feces. Viral transmission through saliva is unlikely. In urine, the virus is isolated in very low concentrations, and not at all in feces. No AIDS cases have been associated with urine or feces.
- Cuts/Puncture Wounds. When searching areas hidden from view, use extreme caution to avoid sharp objects. Cases involving needle-sticks are very low.
- CPR/First Aid. A minimal risk is associated with CPR but it is a good idea to employ the use of masks/airways and gloves when in contact with bleeding wounds.
- Body Removal. As with all crime scenes, when in contact with a dead body, always wear protective gloves.
- Casual Contact. No AIDS cases or infections have been associated with casual contact.
- Any Contact with Body Fluids or Blood. Wear protective gloves if contact with blood or body fluids is likely. If contact is made, wash the area thoroughly with soap and water. Clean up spills with one part water and nine parts household bleach.
- Contact with Dried Blood. No cases of infection have been traced to exposure to dried blood. The drying process itself seems to deactivate any viruses in blood. However, it is still a good idea to wear protective clothing such as gloves.

Firearms

Extreme care should be taken when handling firearms because of the types of trace evidence typically found on such evidence. The guidelines are as follows:

- The firearm should be carefully handled by the grip or the sides of the trigger guard.
- Never stick anything, such as a pencil, into the barrel of a firearm; this could destroy valuable trace evidence.
- There should be no attempt to fire the gun, dismantle it, or to interfere with the mechanism in any way.

If the weapon is a revolver, mark empty cases or live cartridges and the rear edge of the cylinder with a code to show the chambers in which each empty case or live cartridge rested at the time of its removal.

Bullets, Cartridges, and Empty Cases

Bullets, cartridges, and empty cases should be handled with particular attention to the portions used in identification. Such evidence can be beneficial in determining the type of weapon used by a criminal. A laboratory analysis may also determine the exact caliber of weapon. Investigations have revealed instances in which criminals have purposely used one gun for the commission of a crime and a second gun to fire rounds into walls or the floor to confuse investigators. Certain areas of cartridges are typically used for identification: (1) the base, and (2) the rim or cannelure (just above the base of the case).

The exact location of spent cases should be noted. Bullets must be removed carefully from their point of impact and the location where they were found must be recorded accurately. In many cases, it is not advisable for a crime scene investigator to attempt to remove spent bullets. If possible, the investigator should try to remove the material encasing a spent bullet (part of a door, wall, etc.) and transport it to the laboratory to be examined there. A spent bullet can be ruined by attempting to dig it out of an enclosure with a pocketknife. Care must be taken so that the drill, saw, or other cutting instrument does not damage the bullet. Bullets should be handled as little as possible and packaged to prevent movement and to protect the side portions used in ballistic comparison and identification. Rather than attempting to mark a bullet directly, it should be packaged individually and the container marked appropriately.

Stains

Many types of crimes result in some type of characteristic stain being left at the crime scene. Typically, blood is the stain found most commonly. Blood can provide an investigator with much valuable evidence. Investigators should remember that not all bloodstains found at a crime scene belong to the victim. Indeed, a bloodstain may belong to the perpetrator, who might have been injured while committing the crime. In any case, it is usually a good idea to adhere to the following guidelines when considering the collection of blood:

- Good photos and videos should be taken of bloodstains.
- Samples should be taken from all locations where blood is found.
- Blood samples may easily rot, so they should be swabbed and air-dried prior to storage.

Glass

Glass fragments can result from many circumstances. For example, a bullet can shatter glass by passing through it, or glass purposely broken will leave behind fragments at the crime scene and on the perpetrator. When collected, glass could be used to:

- Show the direction of travel of a projectile
- Show the sequence of impact of a projectile
- Match other broken glass

Impressions

Many crimes result in the formation of impression marks. Such crimes include burglary and rape, but almost any crime could produce such evidence. In all cases, impression evidence should be regarded as valuable and must be protected. Examples of impression evidence include:

- Tool marks: usually found on metal doors or window frames and on locked metal desks, cabinets, and safes
- Tire impressions
- Foot impressions
- Teeth impressions: sometimes located on partly eaten food at crime scenes

Investigators should locate the object that made the impression so that a comparison can be made in court.

Drugs

Studies have revealed that drug abuse is the greatest contributor to the commission of crime. Many illicit drugs exist and may appear quite different from one another in form. Therefore, great care must be practiced by evidence collectors (1) to preserve such substances for court, (2) to transport the substances, and (3) to protect themselves from the possible harmful effects of certain drugs. Most illicit drugs come in one of several forms: plant, powder, liquid, and tablet or capsule. Each requires specific attention from the evidence officer to avoid danger. For example, some drugs, such as liquid PCP and liquid LSD, may be absorbed accidentally through the skin. Others, such as marijuana, are more benign in nature and don't pose such a notable physical threat to handle. However, certain general considerations apply in any collection process.

Plant Material. Because plant material is organic, it will decompose in time. To preserve plant evidence best, it should be placed in a porous container such as a paper bag. For large amounts of plant material, such as evidence collected at a marijuana-growing site, samples of the material should be collected and the remainder destroyed after weighing in metric units. This is only done, of course, after authorization of such action is obtained from the prosecutor expected to handle the case.

Powdered Material. Powdered material such as heroin, cocaine, and methamphetamine can generally be packaged in plastic envelopes that are sealed to prevent loss of powder. Officers should also compute the net weight of the powder seized. This is done by weighing the entire exhibit to obtain a gross weight. The actual weight of the container should then be determined and subtracted from the weight of the exhibit.

Liquid Material. Depending on its composition, liquid material may be stored successfully in a glass bottle. Caution should be shown here, however, as many liquids are explosive, corrosive, or dangerous because of their composition. Here a chemist is needed for advice. Liquid evidence should also be weighed for content in metric units.

Tablets or Capsules. This type of evidence is typically packaged in a clear plastic envelope that has been sealed and marked properly. Investigators must also remember to weigh this evidence as well as count each dosage unit. The resulting weight should then be reported in the police report as an "approximate" weight.

Precautionary Rules for Collecting Drug Substances. If an illicit laboratory is encountered and a chemist from the crime laboratory is not present, do not attempt to shut down the operation. Ventilate the area, call for assistance, and wait outside. If an illicit laboratory operation is anticipated, include a chemist from the crime lab as a member of the raid team. Never taste or smell any material suspected of being a controlled substance. Do not handle controlled drugs more than is absolutely necessary. After drugs have been handled, wash hands thoroughly as soon as possible.

All chemical materials must be handled with care. They may be highly flammable, corrosive, or susceptible to explosion. Care should be practiced when searching a drug suspect, an automobile containing drugs, or any area believed to contain drugs. Investigators might encounter hypodermic needles, which could be contaminated with drugs or even with the acquired immunodeficiency syndrome (AIDS) virus.

Summary

For generations, search and seizure has been one of the greatest legal powers of the criminal investigator. It enables the investigator to obtain evidence to be used in a court of law against drug defendants. Typically, evidence searched for and seized by drug investigators other than the drugs themselves are paraphernalia, weapons, drug-manufacturing equipment, and papers and effects that might help the investigator prove ownership or residence of the defendant.

This chapter began with a review of search and seizure as it relates to the Constitution and the doctrine of due process. It went on to explain the probable cause requirement for law enforcement officers to search and seize, followed by a brief explanation of the exclusionary rule which protects defendants from illegal search and seizure on the part of the government. Of importance to the criminal investigator is the fact that there are exceptions to the exclusionary rule as well as exceptions to the search warrant requirement under law.

The chapter explains the process of searching with and without a search warrant. It is vital to the drug investigator to know what he or she can and cannot legally do in each circumstance. Specifics are offered as to structuring of the affidavit, the warrant, and the search warrant return.

Search by consent (which is another form of searching without a search warrant) was then discussed. Emergency searches, searches incident to arrest, stop-and-frisk searches, and plain-view searches are also discussed. Next, automobile searches were covered, since this is a common practice for today's drug investigator.

The chapter concludes with a section on conducting the search. This differs from the drug raid (discussed in Chapter 10) which is a method by which a residence or location is secured for a search. In this section, search methods are examined. Last, some basic rules for evidence collection are discussed and should be well noted; the drug investigator who has deficiencies in this area may very well find a criminal case being lost in court.

The actions taken by the crime scene investigators often have a vital effect on subsequent investigation and prosecution of the case. Indeed, the success or failure of any criminal investigation could hinge on the competency of the crime scene investigator and on his or her treatment of the crime scene.

Suggested Readings

Lyman, M. and Potter, G., *Drugs in Society: Causes, Concepts and Control, 3rd ed.*, Anderson Publishing, Cincinnati, 1998.

References

1. Del Carmen, R.V. and Walker, J.T., *Briefs of Leading Cases*, Anderson Publishing, Cincinnati, 2000.
2. Fox, R.H. and Cunningham, C.L., Crime Scene Search and Physical Evidence Handbook, U.S. Department of Justice, Washington, D.C., 1985.
3. National Institute of Justice, *Investigators Who Perform Well*, U.S. Department of Justice, Washington, D.C., September, 1987.

Making an Arrest

7

The arrest is the culmination of the drug investigator's efforts and is one of the most dangerous tasks of any law enforcement officer. As with all other aspects of police work, no police officer can have too much training on how to arrest a suspect. The arrest must be done with tactical precision while observing legal constraints of the Constitution, criminal law, and agency standard operating procedure.

The Fourth Amendment reads:

> The right of the people to be secure in their persons, houses, papers, and effects, against unreasonable searches and seizures, shall not be violated, and no warrants shall issue, but upon probable cause, supported by Oath or affirmation, and particularly describing the place to be searched, and the persons or things to be seized.

It has been said that an estimated 80% of a criminal investigator's duties are uneventful, routine, and unglamorous. However, the successful completion of an investigation will end in the arrest of a suspect, who will then be prosecuted. This process is far from routine. The arrest is one of the most critical aspects of an investigator's responsibilities. Arrests are always dangerous and may result in an injury to, or even the death of, the arresting officer. Therefore, there are certain considerations that the professional investigator must keep in mind before exercising this important police function.

Defining Arrest

One of the fundamental charges of criminal investigation is to identify a suspect in a crime and take him or her into custody. Indeed, when a suspect has been arrested pursuant to the filing of criminal charges, or when an officer invokes the criminal process pursuant to the filing of charges, the officer must be familiar with certain critical legal guidelines.

What Is an Arrest?

The term arrest has many different interpretations. It is the official interaction between a peace officer and a suspected lawbreaker when the suspect is captured and delivered before the court. It may also be the simple restriction of one's freedom by an agent of the government. There may not be the announcement "You're under arrest" by the arresting officer, nor may *Miranda* warnings be given. In some cases the suspect may not even consider himself or herself to be under arrest. When a person is arrested, he or she forfeits many constitutional rights. Consequently, because of the severe legal implications, the arresting officer must ensure fair and lawful treatment of the arrestee and the legal process of criminal apprehension.

The Legal Arrest

Laws of arrest will vary from one jurisdiction to another, but peace officers are generally authorized to make an arrest on the authority of an arrest warrant for either a misdemeanor or a felony offense. In many cases, the only restriction placed on the officer in these circumstances is the time of day that the arrest is authorized. As a general rule, misdemeanor arrest warrants are authorized for service only during the daytime hours, whereas felony warrants are typically authorized for daytime or nighttime service. Under the strictest interpretation of the U.S. Constitution, warrants should be required for all arrests. However, the courts have loosely interpreted this requirement in allowing officers to arrest without a warrant if they personally observe any violation of the law.

Realistically speaking, an arrest results after a situation between the officer and suspect develops, and the officer requests information from the suspect. Only when the suspect attempts to leave and tests the limits of the officer's response may the suspect realize that he or she is really under arrest. The "free to leave" test was created in 1980 in *Stansbury v. California* in an effort to create a criteria to determine the point at which an arrest had been made. The Stansbury case involved the interrogation of a suspected child molester and murderer, and the court attempted to clarify the issue of arrest. It held that "when determining when a person is in custody, the court must examine all of the circumstances surrounding the interrogation, but the ultimate inquiry is simply whether there [was] a formal arrest or restraint on freedom of movement of the degree associated with a formal arrest."

The most common type of arrest is that which follows the questioning of a suspect. Once a decision to arrest is reached, the officer must come to the conclusion that a crime has been committed and that the suspect is probably the one who committed it. The presence of these elements constitutes the probable cause needed for a legal arrest. Under any circumstance, probable cause is the minimum requirement for arrest, and where a suspect is caught in the process of committing a crime, the officer has the immediate probable cause required for arrest. Most jurisdictions permit a felony arrest without a warrant when a crime is not in progress, provided that probable cause has been established. In *Payton v. New York* (1980), the U.S. Supreme Court ruled that unless the suspect gives permission or an emergency exists, an arrest warrant is necessary if the arrest requires entry into a suspect's private residence.

In a related Supreme Court ruling, *County of Riverside v. McLaughlin* (1991), a person arrested without a warrant must generally be provided with a judicial determination of probable cause within 48 hours of arrest. Arrests are authorized under the following conditions:

- When the officer has probable cause to believe that the person to be arrested has committed a violation of the law "in his or her presence"
- When the officer has probable cause to believe that the person to be arrested has committed a felony but "not in his or her presence"
- When the officer has probable cause to believe that the person to be arrested has committed a felony, whether or not a crime has been committed

The in-presence requirement generally refers to the context of sight, but court rulings have supported prudent use of all five senses to support probable cause for a warrantless arrest. Other cases also have addressed the significance of the probable cause requirement. For example, *Draper v. United States* (1959) found that specific information as to the location of a suspect, when provided by a reliable informant, can also constitute probable cause for an arrest. In *Brinegar v. United States* (1949), the courts underscored the importance of the probable cause requirement as it relates to arrests by stating that a relaxation of the requirement would leave law-abiding citizens at the mercy of the personal whims of police officers.

Detention vs. Arrest

What constitutes an arrest? How does an arrest differ from an investigative detention? In many situations it might appear that an officer has arrested someone, but he has not. Adams states that police intervention may be classified as a contact, a consensual encounter, a detention, or an arrest.[1]

- *Contact*: In this situation, the subject is free to walk away if he or she so desires. It is the sole decision of the subject whether or not to cooperate with an officer.

- *Consensual encounter*: In this situation, the officer may not exert any authority over the subject. Officers can continue to seek the subject's cooperation, but cannot demand it.
- *Investigative detention*: This is defined as something less than an arrest but more than a consensual encounter. Generally, this is when a person thinks that he or she cannot just walk away (*Terry v. Ohio*).

Probable Cause

- An officer has probable cause to make an arrest whenever the totality of facts and circumstances known to the officer create a fair probability that a particular person is guilty of a crime.
- Probable cause is analogous to reasonable suspicion in all ways but one: probable cause requires evidence that establishes a higher probability of guilt.
- The Fourth Amendment requires probable cause for four different purposes: (1) a warrantless arrest, (2) issuance of an arrest warrant, (3) issuance of a search warrant, and (4) warrantless search and seizure.

Investigatory Stops

Terry v. *Ohio* (1968) is the seminal case that recognized investigative stops (the investigative detention) as a separate category of seizures allowed on a lower degree of suspicion. Three constitutional requirements exist for a *Terry Stop* to be lawful:

1. The officer must be able to point to objective facts and circumstances that would warrant a reasonable police officer in linking the detainee's conduct with possible criminal activity.
2. The officer must proceed with the investigation as expeditiously as possible to avoid unnecessarily prolonging the period of involuntary detention.
3. The officer must stay within the narrow investigative boundaries of reasonable suspicion allowed for *Terry Stops*.

In order to satisfy the reasonable suspicion standard, the officer must possess objective grounds for suspecting that the person detained has committed, is committing, or is about to commit a crime. To satisfy this standard, the officer must be able to point to specific facts that, taken together with inferences that arise from them, provide a rational basis for suspecting the detainee of criminal activity.

Whether the facts known to the officer provide objective basis for reasonable suspicion is determined from the vantage point of a trained police officer. Courts consider "rational inferences that arise from the facts" as well as the facts themselves, in deciding whether the officer's information was sufficient to satisfy the reasonable suspicion standard. In drug enforcement, information surfaces in numerous ways. Examples of how reasonable suspicion may impact criminal investigators follows.

- *Criminal profiles*: Criminal profiles are groupings of behavioral characteristics commonly seen in a particular class of offenders. While police are allowed to consider criminal profiles in evaluating the evidentiary significance of things they observe, the fact that a suspect exhibits characteristics included in the criminal profile is no guarantee that a court will find that the officer possessed sufficient reasonable suspicion.
- *Tips from the public*: Police officers may not act on information received from members of the public without independent corroboration, unless they have a rational basis for believing this information to be reliable.
- *Officer-to-officer information*: An officer who makes an investigatory stop (or an arrest) at the direction of another police department or officer need not be informed of the evidence that supports the action. However, if the officer making the stop lacks grounds to support the action, the stop will be constitutional only if the department or officer requesting the action had grounds to support it.

Investigatory stops are allowed on a lower degree of suspicion than arrests because they are designed to be less intrusive than arrests. When police officers sever lawful boundaries of an investigatory stop, the stop automatically escalates into an arrest, resulting in a violation of the detainee's Fourth Amendment rights unless probable cause for an arrest has already been established.

Some investigatory techniques are too intrusive for a *Terry Stop* to be validated by reasonable suspicion alone. The police should never do the following unless they already have probable cause for an arrest:

- Take a suspect against his or her will to the police station (*Hayes v. Florida*)
- Search the suspect for nondangerous contraband without his or her consent

Police should also avoid doing the following during a *Terry Stop*:

- Give *Miranda* warnings before police have developed grounds for an arrest, unless highly intrusive safety measures become necessary during the stop

- Perform a weapons frisk without a reasonable suspicion that the detainees may be armed or dangerous
- Transport the detainees to a second location, unless this action is necessary for the officer's safety or to further the investigation
- Display weapons, use handcuffs, place the detainees in a patrol car, or perform other acts traditionally associated with an arrest, unless these precautions appear reasonably necessary for the officer's safety or to further the investigation

A Terry Stop Must Be the Following:

1. Brief (90 minutes maximum)
2. Conducted efficiently to avoid unnecessarily prolonging the period of involuntary detention
3. Confined to investigating the suspicion that prompted the stop unless articulable grounds for reasonable suspicion of unrelated criminal activity developed during the stop

When Is a Person under Arrest?

In most cases, the answer is easy: a suspect is taken into custody based on a warrant or probable cause, handcuffs are applied, and the suspect is read his or her *Miranda* warning and transported to jail. The question has arisen, however, whether a person is under arrest when the officer simply displays his or her "authority" to arrest (e.g., turning on the red lights on the police car, ordering a person to stop). Such actions may not constitute a legal arrest.

The courts have held that a suspect is seized within the meaning of the Fourth Amendment when he or she is restrained of his or her liberty and brought under the officer's control, either through submission to a show of legal authority or physical restraint.

1. **Seizure by Submission to a Show of Legal Authority:**
   The test for whether there has been a show of authority is objective — whether a reasonable person in the suspect's situation would feel that he or she was not free to ignore the officer's request and walk away.
2. **Seizure by Physical Restraint:**
   If the suspect does not submit to the officer's show of legal authority, no seizure occurs until the suspect is actually brought under the officer's control.

This issue was considered in *California v. Hodari* (1991), where the court ruled that a Fourth Amendment seizure does not occur when law enforcement officers are chasing a fleeing suspect unless the officers apply physical force or the suspect submits to the officers' show of authority. A juvenile named Hodari was standing with three other youths on a street corner in downtown Oakland, California. When an unmarked police car was observed approaching, the youths ran in different directions. An officer exited the police car, pursued Hodari, and finally caught up with him. Just before being tackled, Hodari tossed away a bag containing crack cocaine that was later used as evidence to convict Hodari of possession of cocaine.

On appeal, the California Court of Appeals held that Hodari had been constructively seized as soon as the chase began; therefore, an arrest had taken place. The officer's display of authority was sufficient to place him under arrest. However, since there was no probable cause for the arrest before the cocaine was discovered, it was inadmissible as evidence. The conviction was overturned.

Upon review by the U.S. Supreme Court, the justices considered the issue of whether or not an arrest had been made. There was no doubt that the officer had displayed his authority, that he had wanted Hodari to stop, and that the suspect had recognized all of this. However, even though the suspect had not submitted to arrest, was an arrest made? In a majority decision, Justice Antonin Scalia said: "An arrest requires either physical force … or, where that is absent, submission to the assertion of authority." He later added: "Neither usage nor common-law tradition makes an attempted seizure a seizure." The conviction was reaffirmed.

When there is no physical contact between an officer and a suspect, the totality of the circumstances must be considered when deciding if an arrest has been made. It must be shown that the officer's words or actions would have led a reasonable person to believe that he or she was not free to leave before attempting seizure of the person. Also, the person must somehow show his submission to the officer's authority before the seizure actually occurs. Other factors affecting the legality of an arrest include the following:

1. The officer must have the appropriate legal authority to do so (e.g., jurisdiction).
2. Arresting officers must be sure that people arrested fall under the authority of the law (e.g., being physically placed into custody by the officer or submitting to the assertion of authority).

Other related U.S. Supreme Court decisions include the following:

1. *County of Riverside v. McLaughlin* (1991): Detention of a suspect for 48 hours is presumptively reasonable. If the time to hearing is longer, the burden of proof shifts to the police to prove reasonableness. If the time to hearing is shorter, the burden of proof of unreasonable delay shifts to the suspect.

2. *Florida v. Bostick* (1991). The test to determine whether a police/citizen encounter on a bus is a seizure is whether, taking into account all of the circumstances, a reasonable passenger would feel free to decline the officer's requests or otherwise terminate the encounter.

Fourth Amendment Requirements for a Constitutional Arrest

There are two kinds of arrests: (1) formal (i.e., intentional) arrests, and (2) detentions that last too long or are too invasive to constitute a *Terry Stop.*

- The Fourth Amendment requires probable cause for an arrest.
- An arrest warrant is mandatory under the Fourth Amendment only when the police make a nonconsensual entry into a private residence to arrest someone inside. (*Payton v. New York.*)

An arrest warrant has two advantages over an arrest without a warrant. It ensures that evidence seized during the arrest will be admissible, and it immunizes the officer from civil suit. However, both of the advantages above will be lost if the officer deliberately or recklessly includes false information in his or her affidavit, or fails to include enough factual information to enable the magistrate to make an independent determination of whether probable cause exists for the arrest.

A defendant who is arrested without a warrant and not released on bail is entitled to a judicial determination of probable cause without undue delay after the arrest. Absent extraordinary circumstances, this determination must take place within 48 hours after a warrantless arrest.

Use of Force

Police are granted specific legal authority to use force under certain conditions, but the authority of officers to use force is limited. Penalties for abuse of authority can be severe, so police officers must be clear on what they can and cannot do. The management of force by police officers is a constant challenge facing law enforcement managers. Balancing issues of a violent society with the safety concerns of police personnel creates many obstacles and concerns in developing departmental policies and procedures. The prevailing police perspective is based on a serious concern for the welfare of officers who must cope with the constant threat of a violent society. In contrast, citizens are fearful that police officers may exceed their legal bounds and use force as a means of punishment rather than control.

Public awareness of police brutality was sparked by an unfortunate incident in Brooklyn, New York, during the summer of 1997. On Saturday,

August 9, a fight between two women broke out in a bar and the police were called. Haitian immigrant Abner Louima, a thirty-year-old bank security guard, was taken into custody in connection with the incident. As Louima was being driven to the station house he was beaten, and upon arrival he was stripped, searched, and sodomized with a wooden stick attached to a toilet plunger. Louima suffered a ruptured bladder, a punctured lower intestine, and several broken front teeth.

Police officers deal every day with people who are violent, under the influence of drugs or alcohol, mentally deranged, or who are just desperate to avoid arrest. To cope, officers are granted specific legal authority to use force under constitutional law and the laws of most states. However, the authority of officers to use force is limited. Those limitations may be enforced through criminal prosecution, civil lawsuits, and disciplinary actions. Our society recognizes three legitimate and responsive forms of force:[2]

1. The right of self-defense, including the valid taking of another person's life to protect oneself
2. The power to control those for whom some responsibility for care and custody is granted an authority figure, such as a prison guard.
3. The institution of a police group that has relatively unrestricted authority to use force as required

Police officers are taught that the penalties for abusing their authority to use force can be severe. To avoid harsh penalties, police officers must be aware of the rules that govern the use of force. Such rules are included in state law, federal law, and department policy. The federal standard for police use of force was established by the U.S. Supreme Court in *Graham v. Connor* (1989). In that case, the court recognized that the police officer's duty to make arrests and to conduct searches and investigatory stops carries with it the authority to use force reasonably or threaten the use of force. The Graham decision allows officers to use force for two reasons only: defense and control, but not punishment. One must remember that the Fourth Amendment protects the "right of the people to be secure in their persons…against unreasonable searches and seizures and shall not be violated…." Because a police officer's use of force constitutes a seizure, using excessive force is a violation of a citizen's rights under the Fourth Amendment.

Based on the totality of the circumstances, three key factors can be used to evaluate the extent of an officer's use of force:

1. The severity of the crime committed
2. Whether the suspect poses an immediate threat to the safety of the officer or others
3. Whether the suspect actively resisted or attempted to evade arrest

When police are compelled to use force, a court will use the following standards to determine whether such force was reasonable. First, the officer's conduct will be compared to that of a "reasonable officer" confronted by similar circumstances. Second, when the judge and jury evaluate the officer's actions, they must do so from the "standing in your shoes" standard. This means that they can only make use of what information the officer had at the time he or she exerted force. So 20/20 hindsight cannot be considered in this analysis.

Use of Force in Making an Arrest or Other Seizure

Use of excessive force is regulated by three provisions of the Constitution — the Fourth, Eighth, and Fourteenth Amendments. The Fourth Amendment standard used to evaluate whether unconstitutional force has been used in making a seizure is whether a reasonable police officer on the scene would have considered this amount of force necessary. This is called the objective reasonableness standard. Physical force may be used for the following three purposes only:

1. To protect the officer or others from danger
2. To overcome resistance
3. To prevent escape

One of the confusing aspects about the use of force is that there are no clear-cut answers regarding how it is applied. Police officers who take the wrong course of action on the street face severe penalties. We know that numerous dangerous situations confront police officers every day. From time to time, officers are required to use force — it's inevitable. After a police officer makes the decision to use force, his or her department and the courts will take considerable time scrutinizing the situation to determine whether such actions were appropriate.

Remember, today's police officer must not only know how to use force techniques, such as the swinging of a baton, but when to apply those techniques. The use of force by police officers stems from the premise that in a modern democratic society, citizens are discouraged by law from employing force to solve personal disputes. Instead, they are expected to rely on the justice system to arbitrate and resolve conflicts. With few exceptions, such as cases involving self defense, this restriction applies to most situations.

Defining Use of Force

The authority to use force carries with it awesome responsibilities. The fear of criticism can cause officers to second-guess themselves and hesitate, which could be dangerous. People have different ideas about what constitutes force and police brutality. Police officers, in particular, have specific ideas of what justifies the use of force. Generally speaking, force is defined through the concepts of assault and battery.

Battery

Battery is generally defined as an intentional, nonconsensual bodily contact that a reasonable person would consider harmful. Certainly, hitting someone with fists or a baton or shooting someone would be considered offensive, harmful, and forceful by a reasonable person. However, battery also includes any intentional, nonconsensual contact associated with the body. The terms battery and assault are usually used together. However, under most criminal statutes, there is a significant difference between them.

Assault

Assault means to intentionally put someone in fear of immediate battery or to threaten someone while having the apparent ability to carry out that threat. Although battery requires actual contact, the legal concept of assault doesn't necessarily include actual bodily contact. It's wrong to think that an officer uses force only when striking someone. An officer who displays his or her weapon while shouting, "Stop or I'll shoot!" fits within the definition of assault. So even though the officer doesn't fire in that situation, force has been used. Acting in any manner that implies a threat, such as raising fists, mace, weapons, or batons, constitutes the use of force.

Understanding Reasonableness

Under the Graham decision, the court identified three key factors based on the totality of the circumstances to use in evaluating the reasonableness of an officer's use of force:

1. The severity of the crime committed
2. Whether the suspect posed an immediate threat to the safety of the officer or others
3. Whether the suspect actively resisted arrest or attempted to evade arrest by flight

According to the Graham decision, active resistance to arrest includes any physical actions by the suspect that make the arrest physically difficult to accomplish. Active resistance to arrest includes pushes and shoves as well as more obscure actions, such as holding on to the steering wheel while being removed from a car. An interesting finding of the Graham decision was an explanation of the standards under which an officer's conduct should be judged by a jury and trial judge. First, the actions of the officer will be compared to actions of a "reasonable officer" involved in a similar situation. Second, the court said that when the judge and jury evaluate the officer from within the point of view of the officer under review, they must make their decision based on the information the officer had at the time that he or she took action. So hindsight cannot be used to consider the behavior of an officer in question.

Levels of Force

In 1991, the Christopher Commission, which investigated the behavior of the Los Angeles Police Department in the Rodney King beating incident, found that a significant number of officers regularly used force against the public and often ignored departmental guidelines for the use of force. Under departmental guidelines, officers were required to exercise the minimum amount of force necessary to control a suspect. While these guidelines mainly apply to uniform police officers, plainclothes officers will be faced with an array of circumstances during the course of an arrest. The commission set forth guidelines that identify five levels of force and the permissible use of force techniques within each level:

1. Verbalization
2. Firm grip
3. Compliance holds
4. Intermediate force: baton, kicks, swarm, chemical gas, saps, taser
5. Deadly force: upper body, control holds (e.g., carotid), firearms

Although it is important to consider this continuum in determining the various levels of force, it is also important to consider operational basics that apply to all police officers regarding the use of force. For example, experience tells us that while modern aerosol sprays can cause considerable discomfort, they seldom (if ever) result in bodily injury. In comparison, use of a baton can result in serious tissue damage, depending on the area targeted by the officer. So since aerosol spray has a lower propensity for causing pain or injury, it has a low level of force.

Another example is the use of impact weapons, such as a baton or a flashlight. The flashlight has a greater propensity to create damage than the baton, and although the flashlight is commonly used as an impact weapon, it is not designed for this use. In comparing the two, it is easy to see that a flashlight would be on a higher level of force than a baton. Officers should constantly consider their options when approaching what they perceive to be a dangerous situation. In doing so, if the need to use force becomes a reality, proper application of force will be available quickly.

Deadly Force

In 1967, the President's Commission on Law Enforcement and the Administration of Justice noted that most police departments had no policy to guide them on the use of deadly force. At the time, most state laws were extremely broad in defining the circumstances under which officers could employ deadly force. In its most commonly used parlance, the term deadly force refers to actions of police officers that result in the killing of a person. As a rule, such actions result from situations where individuals are fleeing the police, assaulting someone, or attempting to use lethal force against another person (including a police officer). If deadly force is used improperly or illegally, the officers responsible may be criminally liable, and both the officers and the police department may be sued in a civil action. Most rules regarding the use of deadly force come from federal statutes and case law, and as a rule, are concerned with police use of deadly force to arrest fleeing felons engaged in nonviolent felonies. These cases are different from those pertaining to suspects committing violent felonies, such as murder, assault, rape, robbery, or other types of behavior that represent a substantial risk of bodily harm or death.

The Fleeing Felon Rule

Until the mid-1980s, the shooting of a suspect by police was tolerated by many police agencies. Although this is currently not the case, it was prevalent in the early development of policing when most felonies were punishable by death and there was an assumption that all felons would avoid arrest at any cost. Therefore, the fleeing felon rule was developed during a time when apprehension of felons was considered more dangerous than it is today. Police officers in those early days often worked alone and lacked sophisticated communications technology with which to track suspects who were wanted by police.

The concern was that felons would escape arrest and retreat to another community where they could begin a new life of crime. As time went by and more efficient means were developed for apprehension, arrests became easier for law enforcement officials. For a period of time, police still relied on the ability to use deadly force, even though some felons were not considered dangerous and posed no particular threat to the officer or the community. Prior to 1985, police officers were legally authorized by most states to employ the use of deadly force in apprehending fleeing felons.

Over the years, many states modified the fleeing felon rule, but some still allowed rather broad discretion about when to use deadly force. In a watershed decision by the U.S. Supreme Court in March 1985, it was determined that Tennessee's fleeing-felon law was unconstitutional. *Tennessee v. Garner* (1985) involved the police shooting and subsequent killing of an unarmed boy as the youth fled from an unoccupied house. In this case, the officer could see that the suspect was a youth and that he was unarmed. The officer argued, however, that if the youngster was able to leap a fence, he would be able to escape. The state statute in Tennessee at the time permitted officers to shoot fleeing felons to prevent escape. Pursuant to *Garner*, the court ruled that for the employment of deadly force by police to be lawful, it must be "reasonable." Reasonable deadly force is authorized under three circumstances:

1. To prevent an escape when the suspect has threatened an officer with a weapon
2. When there is a threat of death or serious physical injury to the officer or others
3. If there is probable cause to believe that the suspect has committed a crime involving the infliction or threatened infliction of serious physical injury and, when practical, some warning has been given by the officer

In some instances, the Tennessee statute allowing an officer to shoot a fleeing felon may be constitutional, but the special circumstances in the Garner case, in which the suspect was an unarmed juvenile involved in a nonviolent crime, made the shooting both unreasonable and unlawful. The use of force by police is necessary and appropriate, but only when used properly. Otherwise, it violates the rights of others and can result in serious injury or death, as well as a loss of confidence in the police department.

The Deadly Force Triangle

One way to help officers decide when to use deadly force is the deadly force triangle (Figure 7.1). This is a time-tested model that enhances an officer's ability to respond to a deadly force encounter, while at the same time keeps him or her within the limits of the law and departmental policy. The three sides of an equilateral triangle represent three factors: ability, opportunity, and jeopardy. All three factors must be present to justify deadly force.[3]

Ability. According to this model, ability means the suspect's physical capacity to harm an officer or another innocent person. This is widely interpreted as a suspect's being armed with a weapon, such as a firearm, knife, or club, capable of inflicting death or serious physical injury. Ability also includes personal physical capabilities, such as those possessed by martial arts practitioners, agitated suspects under the influence of drugs, or a powerfully built person.

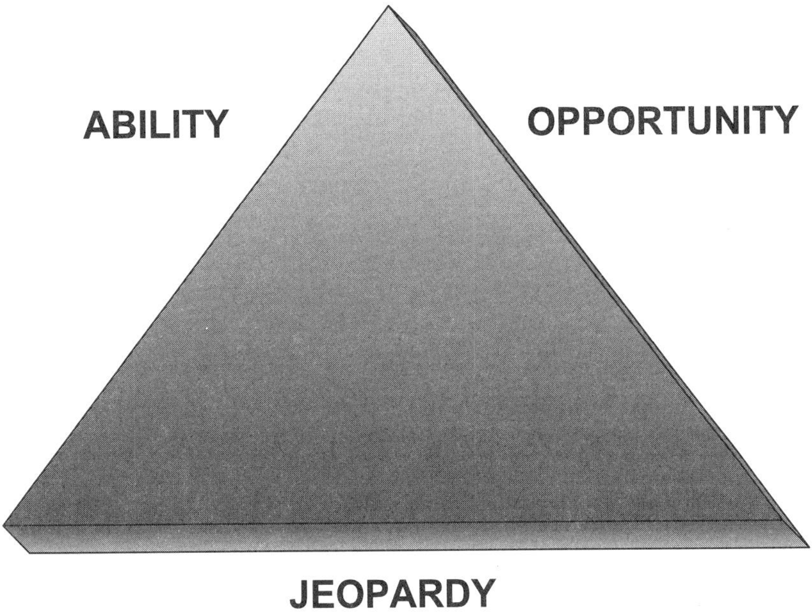

Figure 7.1 Decision model: deadly force triangle — all three factors must be present to justify deadly force. (Source: FBI, 1998.)

Opportunity. Opportunity is described as the suspect's potential to use his or her ability to kill or seriously injure. An unarmed but large and powerfully built suspect might have the ability to kill or injure a smaller individual who is not in comparable physical shape. However, as a rule opportunity does not exist if the suspect is more than 50 yards away. Accordingly, a suspect armed with a knife has the ability to kill or seriously injure but might lack opportunity if he or she is too far away to make use of their weapon.

Jeopardy. Jeopardy exists when suspects take advantage of their ability and opportunity to place an officer or another person in imminent physical danger. For example, an armed robbery suspect's refusal to drop a weapon when ordered to after a foot pursuit would constitute jeopardy.

Off-Duty Arrests

A simple fact of policing is that police officers are off duty more than they are on; accordingly, many departments require off-duty officers to carry firearms. Although the likelihood of an armed encounter is unlikely for the off-duty officer, volatile situations do present themselves at times. Any encounter with which an off-duty officer may be confronted will be much different from one that occurs while the officer is on duty. For example, an on-duty officer is typically in uniform, has access to handguns as well as a shotgun, has access to radio communication, and has backup nearby. In addition, the on-duty officer can generally plan the encounter so that he or she has a tactical advantage. Conversely, the off-duty encounter usually occurs when the officer is alone or accompanied by friends or family. No radio is available to call for help, shotguns are not available, and spare ammunition is probably scarce. Another problem for an off-duty encounter is the likelihood of potential harm from responding officers because of mistaken identity.

If an officer observes a crime while off duty, an assessment of the situation should be made before taking action. If the crime appears to be one in which no one is in immediate jeopardy, the officer is best advised simply to assume the role of a good witness — a role for which officers are well trained. After the suspects have exited the area, the off-duty officer should then contact "911" and provide the dispatcher with a detailed description of the suspects and the vehicle they are driving. In the event it is determined that intervention is needed, officers should remember that criminals often work in teams. Therefore, officers might risk being the target of gunfire from the suspect's accomplices. If accompanied by friends or family, officers should move far enough away to minimize the risk of innocent people getting hurt. When intervening, officers must identify themselves as quickly as possible so that the innocent people in the area are aware of the identities of both the suspects and the police.

Summary

The arrest is the culmination of the drug investigator's efforts. The arrest occurs after the investigator has collected a sufficient amount of evidence to prove in a court of law that the defendant was criminally involved in some aspect of drug trafficking. This chapter began with a brief discussion of the definition of arrest and what makes a legal arrest. A subtle distinction is also identified between an arrest and a detention, since detentions are common among drug trafficking crime scenes.

Law enforcement officers may not effect an arrest until such time as they have probable cause to believe that the individual in question has committed a violation of the law. In recent years, the U.S. Supreme Court has dealt with the issue of "What constitutes a legal arrest?" This topic is also discussed in this chapter.

Criminal defendants will often offer considerable resistance to arrest. In this case, law enforcement officers are legally authorized to make use of an increasing level of force to accomplish the arrest. The various levels of force to be used are discussed. Finally, the use of deadly force is discussed in detail and the investigator is reminded that this action can only be pursued under very specific legal circumstances.

Suggested Readings

Lyman, M. *Criminal Investigation: The Art and the Science, 3rd ed.*, Prentice Hall, Upper Saddle River, NJ, 2001.

References

1. Adams, T., *Police Field Operations, 2nd ed.*, Prentice Hall, Upper Saddle River, NJ, 1990.
2. Peak, K. J., *Policing America: Methods, Issues and Challenges,* Prentice Hall, Upper Saddle River, NJ, 1993.
3. Olson, D. T., Improving deadly force decision making, *FBI Law Enf. Bul.*, February. pp. 1–8, 1998.

Interview and Interrogation 8

Once the suspect in a crime has been arrested, the drug investigator's job is not finished. The matters of proof and prosecution remain. It is the duty of each investigator to attempt to secure a confession from suspects they have arrested. If successful, the legally obtained confession is one of the most powerful pieces of evidence in a case. However, legal considerations are the key and must always be observed to ensure that any statement made by the defendant is admissible in court. Interviews and interrogations are a fascinating aspect of drug enforcement. It is the phase of the investigation where the investigator wears a different hat, so to speak. Putting the officer's psychological talents to work may come into play to enhance the chances of a suspect admitting his or her role in a crime.

Interview vs. Interrogation

To be a good interviewer or interrogator, the investigator must apply certain physical and psychological techniques to the person being interviewed to persuade him or her to divulge information. In the case of the interview, it's the drug investigator's job to create an atmosphere in which the subject can be relaxed enough to recall and explain details of a suspected crime. When a criminal suspect is interrogated, the investigator must gently and skillfully break down the subject's defenses to gain an admission or confession, and do so while staying within the constraints of constitutional law. In some countries, physical and mental stress is used to coerce information from both witnesses and suspects. It is generally accepted that a person will confess to anything if enough pressure or intimidation is applied. But is a "confession" really a truthful statement under these circumstances? Certainly not!

During the course of an investigation, an investigator will probably conduct many interviews and several interrogations. The distinction between an interview and an interrogation is often blurred, but it can be expressed in terms of the purpose of the contact. An *interview* is a relatively formal conversation conducted for the purpose of obtaining information. Notes are taken and major points are reviewed. Interviews, however, may involve virtually anyone, including informants, witnesses, victims, cooperating citizens, and even the suspect. In brief, the interview process occurs either before the case focuses on a particular person or in a place where the suspect can clearly terminate the interview at any time. By comparison, an *interrogation* is the systematic questioning of a person suspected of involvement in a crime, for the purpose of obtaining a confession. Legal guidelines affecting the two activities differ considerably as the probability increases that the person being questioned may incriminate himself or herself.

The Interview Process

The interview is a form of communication used extensively by law enforcement. Interviewing is used to screen job applicants, to extract information from witnesses or victims of a crime, or to obtain a confession from a criminal suspect. Interviews of cooperating citizens and witnesses are often conducted outside the office. More often than not, however, the investigator will have a more productive interview if it can be conducted at a location where the subject is mentally relaxed, such as his or her own home or place of business. In any case, because of legal and technical considerations, investigators should try to follow certain guidelines when conducting an interview.

Investigators should take time to prepare properly for the interview. Sometimes this preparation must be done quickly and may consist of no more than a mental review of details of the case. In any event, some kind of preparation should precede the actual contact with the interview subject. The most common interviews that investigators deal with involve witnesses, cooperating citizens, victims, informants, and suspects.

Interviewing Witnesses, Citizens, and Victims

Investigators must remember that although the interview process is geared toward those believed simply to have information about a crime, witnesses often turn out to be suspects. Sources for interviews include the victim, witnesses, and the complainant. These subjects should be separated before questioning begins. The following considerations should be observed during the interview process.

Develop a Plan of Action

The investigator should be familiar with pertinent data about the incident in question before initiating the interview. He or she should take care to develop questions designed to elicit the particular task at hand. For example, questions directed to a witness should be tailored to obtain specific facts for the police report. Questions that are prepared in advance will tend to add to the flow of conversation and give direction to the interview.

Conduct the Interview in Private

It is sometimes easier to fulfill this requirement than other times, depending on the circumstances. In any case, it is important to provide interviewee the greatest amount of privacy possible both to encourage clarity of thought and to protect the confidentiality of the interview.

Place the Interviewee at Ease

Most interviews involve a great amount of stress and emotional distress for the interviewee. This is usually created by a sense of uncertainty about the expectations of the investigator and the uniqueness of the situation. If a degree of fear develops in the person being interviewed, he or she may withhold information. The investigator's personality will be tested rigorously during the preliminary phase of the interview. The investigator should therefore take great care to make the person being interviewed as comfortable as possible and to build rapport. In addition, he or she should attempt to uncover any reasons for an interviewee's reluctance to cooperate. It is also important to put the person being interviewed at ease, as comments made by a calm person are easier to evaluate than those made by someone who is nervous. This can be accomplished by beginning the interview casually with friendly conversation. A strained or awkward initial contact with the subject might convey the message that the investigator doesn't like something about the interviewee. A friendly approach will help defuse any negative feelings in the subject and reinforce positive ones.

Be a Good Listener

Once the communication barrier is lifted, the investigator must let the interviewee speak freely. Indeed, this is a great shortcoming for many investigators, as many feel the need to interrupt or share their personal opinions with interview subjects. It is the job of the interviewer to listen closely and evaluate not just *what* is being said, but *how* it is being said. In short, it is the responsibility of the investigator to control the interview, but not to dominate it.

Ask the Right Questions

Not only is it important to know what questions to ask the subject, but how those questions should be asked. During the conversation, the investigator's emotions should be in check at all times, while attempting to make the questions easy to comprehend. The phrasing of questions is critical to the success of the interview. For example, *closed-ended questions* requiring a simple yes or no response should be used sparingly. This type of question doesn't elicit personal information from the subject, because it simply permits the person to confirm or deny information being offered. A preferable technique is to ask *open-ended questions* that force the interviewee to relate in his or her own words what was observed. *Hypothetical questions* should also be avoided, as they tend to make the interviewee guess at a certain response or tell the interviewer what he or she wants to hear. Finally, the interviewer should avoid asking *loaded* or *leading questions* that contain the answer and require the person being interviewed to choose between the lesser of two evils.

Don't Dispute the Subject's Answers

The emotional reactions of the investigator must be kept under control at all times. Once the subject gives his or her interpretation of what happened, the investigator can later go back and document any discrepancies.

Maintain Control of the Interview

Frequently during an interview, the subject might try to steer the conversation away from the subject at hand. Again, proper preparation is the key to having a good plan and to staying on track.

Take Brief Notes

Once the interviewee begins to talk freely, the investigator should avoid interruptions. An attempt to take complete notes while a citizen is narrating a story will probably disrupt the flow of information. This generally occurs because the witness sees the investigator writing profusely and will slow down just to accommodate him or her. In doing so, the witness may become distracted and forget important details. Furthermore, some people are just naturally nervous speaking in the presence of someone recording everything they say. Brief notes are therefore the prescribed method of recording the conversation. These generally consist of names, addresses, and certain phrases that will outline the narrative for review. Most important, however, the investigator should listen carefully and not lose eye contact with the witness.

Adjourn the Interview Properly

Just as the interview process begins with a proper introduction, it should also end appropriately. Generally, a concluding remark is sufficient, such as: "OK, you may leave — thank you for your time." It might also be advisable to summarize the interview briefly with the witness before dismissal. Such expressions of courtesy during and after the interview create a favorable atmosphere and encourage further cooperation.

Interviewing Confidential Informants

Certain considerations govern the interview procedure when dealing with informants. As with the interview of the citizen, the investigator must learn to control the interview of the criminal informant. Although the general rules of interviewing apply (as discussed previously), the investigator must keep personal safety considerations in mind and safeguard any information given. The location of the interview should be selected by the investigator but should be away from the investigator's office and the informant's residence or place of business. Instead, a neutral site, such as a motel room, is selected. Once the informant becomes active, the investigator can briefly gain some information over the phone. Factors governing the interview of a new informant should include the following:

1. Safety of the investigator
2. Privacy, so that the interview cannot be observed by others
3. Time, so that the interview is not interrupted
4. Sufficient space to take notes and perform other administrative activities

The interview should follow the process already outlined, with the inclusion of several other considerations.

1. Sympathize with the informant about any personal problems that he or she may be experiencing, especially if they may affect the informant's performance.
2. Learn whatever motivations the person may have for becoming an informant.
3. Ask information that is already known to check the informant's reliability.
4. If certain information is known to be worthless, do not reveal this to the informant. The investigator should protect his or her secrets during the interview and not unwittingly become the person being interviewed.

The investigator must be careful not to reveal his or her own knowledge through the phrasing of the questions. For example, an inquiry about a specific person reveals that police already know about that person. Investigators must learn to move from very general, purposely vague questions to specific ones that have particular value. Accordingly, the investigator might act passively about important disclosures to protect the fact that such information is of interest to the police.

The Interrogation Process

During any case it is important for information to be obtained by means of a direct interview with a suspect. It is not uncommon during the progress of a case for a person who was interviewed as a witness or victim to become a primary suspect at a later date. In that event, as the case progresses, the investigator can use information learned in the earlier interview.

Goals of the Interrogation

The interrogation is designed to match new information with a particular suspect, to secure a confession. The goals of the interrogation process are as follows:[1]

- To learn the truth of the crime and how it happened
- To obtain an admission of guilt from the suspect
- To obtain all facts to determine the method of operation and the circumstances of the crime
- To gather information that enables investigators to arrive at logical conclusions
- To provide information for use by prosecutors in possible court action

Legal Requirements of the Interrogation

According to early English common law, the confession of a suspect was by far the most important type of evidence against an accused person. In many cases, failure to produce such evidence was the equivalent to not having any evidence at all. Therefore, investigators vigorously pursued confessions at all costs, with little regard for the rights of those accused or the fairness of their methods. Techniques for obtaining a confession included submersion in water, stretching, branding, and other types of physical and psychological torture. Today, such tactics have been replaced with legal guarantees of fairness, such as the Bill of Rights, the Constitution, and statutes prohibiting the use of coercion or duress in the interrogation process. Still, the confession reigns as one of the most influential types of evidence in a court proceeding.

Preparation for the Interrogation

In preparation for the interrogation, the investigator should review all important details of the case and be prepared to seek answers to basic questions such as what, when, why, where, and how? In addition, the investigator should give some thought as to what information would be of the most value to the investigation. A series of questions can be drawn up and referred to unobtrusively during the interrogation.

The Interrogation Setting

In addition to the manner in which the interrogator treats the suspect, it is also important to consider the physical surroundings where the questioning occurs. Because of pressure from peers and family members who might be present at the scene, it is important to remove the suspect from familiar surroundings and take him or her to a location with a more sterile and less threatening atmosphere. A key psychological factor contributing to successful interrogations is privacy. This encourages the suspect to feel comfortable in unloading the burden of guilt. The structure of the interrogation setting should also be conducive to obtaining confessions. Its surroundings should reduce fear and therefore encourage the suspect to discuss his or her role in the crime. Consequently, the interrogation room should reflect a more businesslike atmosphere than a police-like environment.

The interrogation should be conducted in a room specifically designed for that purpose. It should be isolated from the bustling activity of the rest of the office, the sound of police radios, overhead intercoms, and other interruptions. Ideally, a soundproofed room best serves this purpose. The interrogation room should be well lit but not to the extent that its lights are glaring. In addition, it should be protected from interruptions and equipped with some means of communicating with the outside, such as a buzzer or office intercom. Furnishings should be minimal, consisting of chairs, preferably without a desk, and containing pencil and paper but otherwise nondescript, with no distracting decorations.

The Interrogation Procedure

As a rule, two investigators handle the interrogation: one conducts the questioning, and the second acts as a witness to statements made by the suspect. The two investigators should meet before the interrogation to discuss their "roles." Frequently, one investigator will assume one approach to the suspect and the other assumes a different and sometimes contrasting style. The suspect may be more receptive to one approach than the other.

Interrogation Styles

Investigators have developed a variety of interrogation styles and techniques over the years. The choice of style can depend on many factors, including the personality of the suspect, the personality of the interrogator, and the nature of the case. Some of the most common styles of interrogation are described below.

Logical

In a case in which the evidence seems to be overwhelming, such as a drug trafficking case involving a drug purchase from an undercover agent, the investigator may try to appeal to the suspect's sense of logic. In doing so, it is hoped the investigator will persuade the suspect that cooperation is the only way in which the charges against him or her can be lessened. It is important to note here that promises of leniency should not be made without direct authorization from the prosecuting attorney. The only promise that should be made is that his or her cooperation will be brought to the attention of the prosecutor for consideration of some kind of leniency.

Sympathetic

If the investigator thinks that the suspect is easily affected by an emotional appeal, the sympathetic approach might be a good technique. The interrogation is conducted by speaking in low tones and includes expressions of concern and understanding for the suspect, his or her spouse, children, business, and so on. The investigator stimulates feelings of self-pity in the suspect when he or she blames others for his or her plight. Ideally, further relief of guilt is achieved by the suspect agreeing to cooperate with the investigator.

Indifferent

In this technique, the investigator acts as though he or she does not really care if the suspect cooperates or not, but thinks that he or she must go through the motions of making the opportunity available to the suspect. The investigator's manner suggests that the investigator would rather see the suspect punished severely by the court rather than give him or her the opportunity to gain leniency through cooperation.

Face Saving

In this approach, the investigator will attempt to give the suspect a "way out" that will justify his or her participation in the crime. By systematically rationalizing the suspect's actions up to the point of the violation, describing them as natural consequences of some other problem, the investigator tries to get the suspect to start talking about his or her actions. Periodically, the investigator interjects comments that tend to diminish the importance of the suspect's own involvement in the crime.

Egotistical

In this case the investigator plays on the suspect's sense of pride and precision in the commission of the crime. It is pointed out how daring and difficult the crime was to implement and that it took a great degree of planning and intelligence to pull it off. This approach encourages the suspect to brag about his or her involvement in the crime and to provide additional details to impress the investigator.

Lying and Deception

Because of certain psychological and cultural differences, a perceptive investigator can sometimes readily identify the manner in which people lie. The trained listener will observe a pattern of evasiveness in the suspect, and after a period will be able to identify lies or efforts to deceive.

Verbal Signs of Deception

Research has shown that vocal changes occur 95% of the time when a person lies. A liar's speech rate and voice pitch will also increase 95% of the time.[2] In addition, liars will usually stall before giving an answer, to give them time to decide if they should lie or tell the truth, or to decide just how big a lie to tell. Liars will always attempt to con the investigator. They may choose to tell a big lie, a misleading statement, or the complete truth. In most cases, they will attempt to dodge the truth. For example, they may restate the question or ask to have it repeated. They might say that they can't remember or that they don't understand the question. If the subject stammers, stutters, or has a mental block before answering the question, most of the time he or she is lying.[2]

Physical Characteristics of Lying[3]

Head position

- Tilted: cooperative, interested, probably truthful
- Jutting forward, no tilt, jaw up: angry, aggressive, stubborn
- Chin on chest, no tilt: depressed, bored, probably lying

Eyebrows

- Both raised with mouth partly open: surprised, truthful
- One raised: confused, skeptical, probably truthful
- Squeezed together and lowered: angry, worried, confused

Eyes

- Breaks eye contact (1 to 2 seconds is common): suddenly tensed, probably lying; may not resume eye contact until new subject is discussed
- Looks at ceiling and blinks: just decided to confess
- Pupils fully dilated: high degree of emotional arousal, probably lying
- Closes eyes: trying to mentally escape, probably lying
- Narrowed eyes: looking for trouble, anticipating the worst
- Rapid blinking: nervous, probably lying

Hands

- Covers both eyes: probably lying
- Hands over mouth: probably lying
- Hand on chin: probably truthful
- Touches or rubs nose while talking; probably lying
- Hands clasped together, holding back of head; probably truthful

Legs

- Men with crossed legs: probably lying

Feet

- Moves feet beneath chair: probably lying
- One foot tucked beneath the other: probably truthful.

Lying Techniques

People often lie by using *specifics*. For example, the suspect may say, "I don't even own a gun!" Although this could be a true statement at face value, he or she might have borrowed a gun to commit the crime but is relying on the fact that the statement is a true one, and the investigator will, it is hoped, infer that the suspect didn't commit the crime. Liars tend to admit only to what the investigator can prove and deny what can't be proved. In addition, they will sometimes make an issue out of trivial things. For example, if a suspect complains about the manner in which the government has treated him in the past, he is probably attempting to swerve away from the real issue. Other commonly used lying techniques include the following:

- The suspect tries to confuse the interviewer by arguing about trivial points rather than addressing the real issues.
- A debating tactic is used in which the suspect tries to discount the investigator's argument in advance. For example, if the investigator makes a statement regarding a piece of evidence, the suspect replies, "You don't really expect anyone to believe that, do you?" The big lie or repeated assertion is based on the assumption that if you say something over and over, people will start to believe it. Repeated denial of the violation only reinforces the suspect's ability to lie.
- The "You don't understand" tactic is used by experienced liars to block an in-depth interrogation. This is attempted by saying, "You wouldn't understand," "You don't know how these things work," or "How would someone like you be expected to know?"
- The "loophole" liar is a dodger who is unsure just how much the investigator knows about the crime. Loophole liars typically respond by saying, "I can't remember," or "to the best of my recollection." This technique gives them a way out in case they are later confronted with contradictory evidence.

Safeguarding against Police Misconduct

Several types of behavior have been identified as improper (even illegal) for police investigators and will result in any confession obtained from the suspect being deemed inadmissible by the courts. These behaviors include coercion or duress, physical constraint, unreasonable delay in arraignment, and refusing legal counsel during interrogation.

Coercion and Duress

Coercion and duress are similar in that they both create an environment of intimidation during the interrogation process. *Coercion* is defined as the use or threat of the use of illegal physical methods to induce a suspect to make an admission or confession. *Duress* is the imposition of restrictions on physical behavior, such as prolonged interrogation or deprivation of water, food, or sleep. In *Brown v. Mississippi* (1936), the court ruled that physical coercion used to obtain a confession was a violation of the Fourteenth Amendment. Following this ruling, the Supreme Court focused its attention on cases in which "psychological" rather than physical coercion was used to prompt a confession.

In a related case, *Ashcraft v. Tennessee* (1944), a prolonged interrogation resulted in a confession that was overturned because the police used duress, intimidation, and other psychological pressures to evoke a confession. One such measure was not allowing the suspect to phone his wife until after he confessed. Although no physical force was used against the suspect in this case, psychological intimidation was ever present and was consequently considered illegal.

Unreasonable Delay in Arraignment

Confessions obtained without coercion or duress may still be deemed unconstitutional and inadmissible if the suspect confessed before being allowed to see a magistrate within a reasonable period after arrest. The case of *McNabb v. United States* (1943) first illustrated this vital principle. In this case, McNabb was involved in bootlegging, along with several members of his family. After the murder of several federal officers in Tennessee, McNabb was arrested for the crime. After his arrest, he was held in custody and was not taken before a magistrate for a considerable period of time. Subsequently, he confessed and was convicted. The court held that the government's failure to take McNabb before a committing officer was a violation of his constitutional rights; therefore, the confession was inadmissible. What made this case particularly significant is that, for the first time, a confession obtained voluntarily and freely was still considered illegal because officers failed to comply with other constitutional procedures.

A subsequent ruling in *Mallory v. United States* (1957) reaffirmed that an officer making an arrest must take the accused without unnecessary delay before the nearest available magistrate and that an official complaint must be filed without delay. These decisions are based on the due process clause of the Fourteenth Amendment of the U.S. Constitution. The Supreme Court has taken into consideration whether or not a case in its entirety represents a good picture of the civilized standards expected in this country.

The Suspect's Right to Legal Counsel

The legal guidelines to protect the rights of the accused were defined further by the Supreme Court in such cases as *Escobedo v. Illinois* (1964) and *Miranda v. Arizona* (1966). Surprisingly, before 1964 there were no legal rules requiring the presence of an attorney during the interrogation of a criminal suspect. In a ruling in May 1964, the Supreme Court reversed the conviction of a lower court because prosecutors had used incriminating statements made by the defendant to a friend that were overheard by a federal agent. The remarks were made after the defendant was indicted and while he was out on bail. The court held that the statement was made by the defendant without the advice of his attorney, who he had already retained. So, according to the court, the defendant was deprived of his Sixth Amendment right to an attorney.

In *Escobedo v. Illinois* (1964), Escobedo was arrested without a warrant and interrogated in connection with a murder. On the way to the police station, officers told Escobedo that he had been implicated as the murderer and that he should admit to the crime. He then requested to speak to an attorney. After arriving at the police station, his retained lawyer arrived and asked to speak with his client. His request was denied on several occasions. In addition, Escobedo requested to speak with his attorney on several occasions and was told that his attorney did not want to speak to him. Subsequently, the defendant made an admission to the crime and was later found guilty.

The legal question here is: does a suspect have a right to an attorney if he or she requests one during a police station interrogation? The answer is yes. Following this decision, states were directed to require police to advise every person arrested for a felony that they have a constitutional right to counsel and silence. Despite this, the guidelines for police in interrogation settings were still unclear.

The *Miranda* Warning

Two years following the Escobedo decision, the U.S. Supreme Court reversed an Arizona court's conviction in a kidnapping and rape case that further defined the Escobedo decision and the rights of the accused. In *Miranda v. Arizona*, a 23-year-old man, *Miranda*, was arrested and transported from his home to the police station for questioning in connection with a kidnapping and rape. He was poor and uneducated. After two hours of questioning, officers obtained a written confession that was used against him in court. He was found guilty of the kidnapping and rape.

The legal question in this case is: do the police have a responsibility to inform a subject of an interrogation of his or her constitutional rights involving self-incrimination and a right to counsel before questioning? Again, the answer is yes.

> A person being interrogated has the right to remain silent; any statement may be used in a court of law. The person also has the right to have an attorney present during questioning. If the suspect can not afford one, one will be appointed for him or her before questioning.
>
> *Miranda* Warning

In addition to being informed of these rights, the suspect must also agree, freely and voluntarily, to waive them before police can begin questioning (Figure 8.1). Accordingly, the suspect may invoke his or her right to stop answering questions any time during the interrogation. Several court cases have arisen over the years that relate to *Miranda* and custodial interrogations. For example, *Rhode Island v. Innis* (1980) interpreted the meaning of interrogation by stating that, in addition to direct questioning, interrogation also refers to any actions or remarks made by police that are designed to elicit an incriminating response.

In another case, *California v. Prysock* (1981), the court found that *Miranda* warnings do not have to be given in any specific order or with precise wording. Further, in *Edwards v. Arizona* (1981), the court established a "bright line" rule for investigators. The court found that all police questioning must be discontinued once a suspect who is in custody has requested an attorney, even if the *Miranda* warning was given a second time. However, in yet another related decision, *Oregon v. Bradshaw* (1983), the court found that the Edwards decision doesn't apply if the suspect simply inquires "What is going to happen to me now?" In this case, police were allowed to continue questioning the suspect. However, in *Minnick v. Mississippi* (1990), the court ruled that once a custodial suspect requests counsel in response to *Miranda* warnings, law enforcement officers may not attempt to reinterrogate the suspect unless the suspect's counsel is present or the suspect initiates the contact with officers.

In related cases it has been determined that probation officers need not read the *Miranda* warning to clients (*Minnesota v. Murphy*, 1984) and that the *Miranda* warning is not required during the issuance of traffic citations (*Berkemer v. McCarty*, 1984). The following year, in *Oregon v. Elstad* (1985), a court decided that even though a confession was obtained before the *Miranda* warning was given, confessions obtained after it are admissible. In

STATEMENT OF RIGHTS AND WAIVER	CITY POLICE DEPARTMENT	DATE
PLACE		
NAME	CASE NO. *(If applicable)*	

Before we ask you any questions, you must understand your rights. You have the right to remain silent. Anything you say can be used against you in court or other proceedings. You have the right to talk to a lawyer for advice before we ask you questions, and to have him with you during questioning. You have this right to the advice and presence of a lawyer even if you cannot afford to hire one. In such a case you have a right to have a court-appointed attorney present at the interrogation. If you wish to answer questions now without a lawyer present, you have the right to stop answering questions at any time. You also have the right to stop answering at any time until you talk to a lawyer.

You may waive the right to advice of counsel and your right to remain silent and answer questions or make a statement without consulting a lawyer if you so desire.

WAIVER

I ☐ have read ☐ had read to me the statement of my rights shown above. I understand what my rights are and I elect to waive them. I am willing to answer questions and make a statement. I do not want a lawyer. I understand and know what I am doing. No promises or threats have been made to me and no pressure of any kind has been used against me. I was taken into custody at *(time)* __________ ☐ A.M. ☐ P.M., on *(date)* ________________,
and have signed this document at *(time)* __________ ☐ A.M. ☐ P.M., on *(date)* ________

WITNESS	SIGNATURE OF PERSON WAIVING RIGHTS
WITNESS	

Figure 8.1 Statement of Rights and Waiver form.

1994, however, in the case of *Davis v. United States,* the court put the burden on custodial suspects to make unequivocal invocations of the right to counsel. In the Davis case, a man being interrogated in the death of a sailor waived his *Miranda* rights, but later said "Maybe I should talk to a lawyer." Investigators asked the defendant clarifying questions and he responded, "No, I don't want a lawyer." Upon conviction he appealed, claiming that interrogation should have ceased when he mentioned a lawyer. The court, in affirming the conviction, stated that "It will often be a good police practice for the interviewing officers to clarify whether or not (the defendant) actually wants an attorney."

The Public Safety Exception to *Miranda*

The public safety exception to *Miranda* was ruled on in *New York v. Quarles* (1984). This decision found that police officers who are reasonably concerned for public safety may question people who are not in custody and who have not been read the *Miranda* warning. The court also found that subsequent statements are admissible in court. In this case, a woman complained to two officers that an armed man had just raped her. After giving the officers a description of the man, they proceeded to a nearby supermarket, where Benjamin Quarles was located. After a brief chase, the officers frisked Quarles and discovered an empty shoulder holster. Once the suspect was in handcuffs, the officer asked Quarles where the gun was, and he nodded in the direction of some empty cartons and said, "It's over there." The gun was retrieved and Quarles was arrested and read the *Miranda* warning.

When the case went to trial, the court ruled that under the requirements of *Miranda*, the statement "It's over there" and subsequent seizing of the weapon were inadmissible at the defendant's trial. On review, the Supreme Court acknowledged that Quarles should have been given the *Miranda* warnings. However, the court recognized that the need to have the suspect talk was more important than reading of the *Miranda* warning. The court also ruled that if *Miranda* warnings had deterred the suspect from giving such information, the cost to society would have been much greater than the simple loss of evidence. As long as the gun remained in the pile of cartons, it posed a public safety hazard.

Defining Custody

Miranda applies only when testimonial evidence is being sought. In addition, it applies only to *custodial interrogations*, not to circumstances in which the suspect is free to leave. The custodial interrogation rule applies not only when the suspect has been arrested before questioning, but also when his or her liberty has been restricted to a degree that is associated with arrest.

So the interview itself can also be considered custodial even though no arrest has been made. It depends on the circumstances. For example, if the suspect is being questioned in a relaxed atmosphere at his or her own residence, the *Miranda* warning need not be given. Conversely, if the suspect is approached in his or her own home by officers possessing an arrest warrant, the *Miranda* warning must be given before questioning. In brief, the test is whether the interview is custodial, not whether the investigation has focused on a particular person being interviewed.

Why Suspects Cooperate and Confess

When we consider that self-destruction and self-condemnation are not normal human behavioral characteristics, it is puzzling why someone would openly confess to a crime. In addition, one would assume that when a person is arrested and taken to a police station for questioning, he or she will not readily admit (and even choose to lie about) his or her part in a crime. Many criminals, in particular career criminals, have developed a keen sense of observation over the years. It is likely that this sense has aided them in the past in avoiding detection by police. Such criminals can easily see the direction in which an interrogation is going. Logically, then, one would think that the dialogue between the suspect and investigator would be brief. Strangely, because of complex psychological factors, this is not always the case.

Searching for Information

Depending on the crime in question and the particular suspect, it is logical to assume that many criminals follow the progress of the police through media accounts of the investigation. Still, they really don't have a good sense of exactly what the investigator knows and doesn't know about the suspect. It is the desire of the criminal to want to know exactly what the investigator knows about the crime. This "paranoia" frequently drives the suspect to accompany the investigator willingly to the police station for an interview. Once at the station, however, the suspect not only tries to learn what the investigator knows about the investigation but attempts to lead him or her away from the focus of the investigation.

Closing the Communication Gap

Research indicates that most guilty persons who confess are, from the outset, looking for the proper opening during the interrogation to communicate their guilt to investigators.[4] Suspects also make confessions when they believe that cooperation is the best course of action. Before they talk, they need to be convinced that investigators are willing to listen to all the circumstances surrounding the crimes. Finally, suspects confess when interrogators are able to speculate correctly on why the crimes were committed.[1] They want to know ahead of time that interrogators will believe what they have to say and will be understanding about what motivated them to commit the crime.

Admissions and Confessions

Although seemingly alike, there is a notable difference between admission of a criminal act and confession of complicity in a crime. An *admission* is a self-incriminating statement made by the suspect that falls short of an acknowledgment of guilt. It is, however, an acknowledgment of a certain fact or circumstance from which his or her guilt can be inferred. Conversely, a *confession* is direct acknowledgment by the suspect of his or her guilt in the commission of a specific crime or as being an integral part of a specific crime. For the confession to be lawful, the investigator must be mindful of the constitutional checks governing its admissibility.

The Written Statement

Because the interrogation will generally produce much more information than needed for the written statement, the investigator will have to decide what information he or she needs for preparation of the statement. A confession from the suspect should substantiate the elements of the charge or at least contain information related to the investigation. In addition, the statement of the confession should contain any details of extenuating circumstances or explanations offered by the suspect that might be grounds for additional inquiry (See Figure 8.2.)

Several variables determine what methods are used to take the statement. These include the intelligence level of the suspect, the amount and nature of information to be recorded, and the availability of stenographic services. In many cases the suspect will be willing to give a verbal statement about his or her involvement in a crime but might be unwilling to have it written down at the time. If this occurs, the investigator should not interrupt the remarks being made by the suspect just to ask for a signed statement. Instead, after the suspect is finished giving his or her account of what happened, the investigator should ask if the suspect would be willing to sign (or write) a statement to that effect. The suspect should be assured that only the information given to the investigator will be included in the statement and that he or she will have the prerogative of not signing it if it is not accurate. The following techniques can be used if the suspect decides to sign the written statement:

1. The suspect may respond orally to the investigator or a stenographer in response to questions. Responses are then written verbatim.
2. The suspect may give a statement orally without direction from the investigator. This technique is the most desirable provided that the end result is a clear and concise statement.
3. The investigator could give the suspect a list of the important points to cover during the statement and suggest that he or she include these.
4. The investigator may choose to write the statement according to the information given by the suspect in his or her oral statement. If this

CITY POLICE DEPARTMENT
VOLUNTARY STATEMENT

____
Case #

____
Date

I _______________________________ am _____ years of age and currently reside at ____________________________ which is located in the city of ____________________________.

Statement:

____
____
____
____
____
____
____
____
____
____
____

I have read this statement which consists of _____ page(s) and I affirm that it was given voluntarily and that all facts are truthful and accurate.

This statement was given at ____________________________ (location) on the ______ day of __________, 19__, at _______ (am) (pm).

____
Signed

____
Witness

____
Witness

Figure 8.2 Voluntary Statement form.

technique is adopted, the investigator must use the same phrases that were used by the suspect.

The completed statement should then be shown to the suspect so that any changes can be made. Once corrections are made, the statement is signed. The investigator should be careful to have the written statement reflect only one crime, because in a criminal trial the court will ordinarily not permit the introduction of evidence of additional crimes. Exceptions to this are when additional crimes tend to show (1) intent, (2) the identity of the defendant, or (3) the scheme used in the commission of the crime in question. Therefore, the best policy is to obtain a separate written statement for each crime committed.

Structuring the Written Statement

The statement should begin with the place, date, and identification of the maker and the name of the person who is giving the statement. It is acceptable for the body of the statement to be in narrative or expository form. In addition, it should include all the elements of the crime as well as any facts that connect the suspect with the crime. If the investigator or stenographer prepares the statement, the suspect should be asked to read and sign each page at the bottom. To ensure that the suspect actually reads the statement, he or she should be asked to correct any typographical errors, and to initial any corrections in ink. Finally, each page should be labeled "page ___ of ___ pages." The concluding paragraph should state that the suspect has read the statement consisting of so many pages and that the statement is "true and correct." After the suspect signs the statement in the space provided, two witnesses should sign it under the suspect's signature. Normally, the interrogators are the witnesses. Any more than two witnesses could give the court the impression that the suspect was intimidated by a large number of police at the time of the statement.

Tape-Recorded Statements

Frequently, the investigator will choose to record a suspect's statement. This can be especially advantageous when the suspect cannot read or write or when he or she is not fluent in English. One important point to remember is that when the investigator chooses to record the statement, the interrogation should still be conducted first. When it is time to record the statement, the investigator uses his or her notes from the first interrogation to develop the taped statement. When the recording is complete, the recorded statement is then played back for the suspect to hear so he or she can verify that it is a true and accurate representation of what was said during the interrogation.

Steps for Recording

The recording should begin with the investigator identifying himself or herself, the suspect, and any other investigators in the room (people entering and leaving the room during the interrogation should also be identified with corresponding times, but at the end of the tape). In addition, the opening remarks should include the location of the statement or interrogation, the time and date of the statement, and a statement by the investigator to the suspect explaining why the statement is being recorded. Once the important points of the statement are given, the investigator should ask the suspect if there are any additional comments that he or she would like to make.

Afterward, the investigator should state that the recorder is now going to be shut off and that the suspect can listen and verify its contents. Once the suspect listens and verifies the recording, it is then turned back on, and he or she should verbally acknowledge that (1) the contents accurately represent the statement, and (2) the recorder was not turned off or stopped at any time during the interrogation, except for the time when the suspect reviewed the tape. Finally, the investigator states that the session is concluded and repeats the names of the persons in the room and the time and date of the statement. The tape should then be entered into evidence and processed appropriately.

Use of the Polygraph

Of the mechanical devices that have been designed to aid investigators in obtaining information, the *polygraph*, or "lie detector," has proved to be of extreme value. Proper use of this tool can help an investigator determine a suspect's guilt or innocence. However, because of recent court rulings restricting the use of the polygraph in certain settings, the investigator should view this device as an aid only. The polygraph is designed simply to measure whether the person being tested is being deceptive. As the subject is asked different questions, the graphs observed by the operator will, it is hoped, indicate a truthful or a deceptive response. Indeed, the device does not actually do what its name indicates — it does not detect lies. What it does is measure the physiological responses from the subject, including fear, anxiety, excitation, and other emotions. So the critical consideration in the use of a polygraph is not the machine itself but the operator's skill in interpreting its results.

Accuracy and the Polygraph

The criminal justice field is divided as to its acceptance of polygraph results. In fact, most courts will not accept the findings of a polygraph exam as absolute evidence, except when stipulated to by all parties. Problems with the use of the polygraph have been in its application. Specifically, the machine should be used to identify statements as being false, not for the purpose of actually detecting a lie. The value of an examination can be looked at in two ways: reliability and validity. *Reliability* refers to the consistency of the examination's results. This can be shown by reproducing the examination repeatedly and obtaining the same results. When properly administered, the polygraph can produce very reliable results.

Validity refers to the accuracy of the examination. Validity can be affected by two considerations. First is the ability of the polygraph examiner to interpret the results of the examination accurately. Second, if the measurements recorded by the instrument fail to indicate lying directly, the test lacks validity.

Administration of the Exam

Before the exam, the examiner will request certain information from the investigator. Such information includes the specific offense in question, a copy of the case file, a list of the different types of evidence, specific personal information about the subject, and any physical or psychological data about the subject, if known. Next, questions are structured, usually in a "yes" and "no" format. These questions are reviewed with the subject before giving the test. This is to relax the person taking the test and, it is hoped, to elicit an admission of additional details of the alleged crime. When the test is completed, the subject is generally advised of the results in writing. If deception was detected, the subject might be interviewed about the weak points of the test. Frequently, this part of the process results in the subject admitting to additional complicity in the crime.

Although the polygraph should not be considered a definitive effort to attain a suspect's confession, it can save money for the investigating agency. For example, it can weed out suspects in an investigation and let the focus fall on specific persons.

Admissibility of Polygraph Results

Over the years, the courts have addressed various aspects of the issue of polygraph results and their admissibility in court. The machine can only detect certain changes in the human body, and it is estimated that such changes can be detected up to 95% of the time. Despite arguments in favor of use of the polygraph, its results are not currently admissible as absolute evidence in court. One early court case upheld a ruling of a trial court that refused acceptance of polygraph results (*Frye v. United States,* 1923). The 1933 *State v. Bohner* case also failed to accept the results of the polygraph but acknowledged its usefulness. Later that same year the court in *People v. Forts* considered the results of the polygraph inadmissible based on doubts about the instrument's reliability. Exceptions occur, however, when all parties stipulate to acceptance of the results before administration of the exam.

The Voice Stress Analyzer

An investigative tool gaining considerable popularity with law enforcement agencies is the voice stress analyzer (VSA). Unlike the computer polygraph, the VSA requires no wires be attached to the subject being tested. The VSA uses only a microphone plugged into a computer to analyze the subject's responses. As the subject speaks, the computer displays each voice pattern, numbers it, and saves each chart to file. Unlike the polygraph, drugs do not affect the results of the exam and there are no known counter-measures that will cause the ubiquitous "inconclusive" results associated with the polygraph.

Rapidly supplanting the polygraph, the VSA has been used in many investigative situations such as homicide, sex crimes, robbery, white collar crimes, and internal affairs investigations, as well as pre-employment examinations for background investigators. The system has been used as an investigative tool for verifying statements of witnesses, denials of suspects, and for determining the validity of allegations made against police officers.

Microtremors are tiny frequency modulations in the human voice. When a test subject is lying, the automatic or involuntary nervous system causes an inaudible increase in the microtremor's frequency. The VSA detects, measures, and displays changes in the voice print frequency. A laptop computer processes these voice frequencies and graphically displays a picture of the voice patterns. The VSA is not restricted to "yes" and "no" answers and is able to accurately analyze tape recordings of unstructured conversations

Summary

To any law enforcement officer, information is a powerful resource. One of the regular duties of the drug investigator is to interview those persons who are thought to have information about drug violations. Of course, one of the most likely individuals for this task would be the arrested defendant. But case law is full of judicial opinion on this subject, and law enforcement officers must be very careful during interviews or interrogations. This chapter begins with a brief discussion of the distinction between interview and interrogation, because this is important to the criminal investigator and may have legal implications. A step-by-step description of how to conduct an interrogation is discussed next. While many of these considerations may seem elementary in nature, it is critical that the drug investigator bear all of them in mind.

The U.S. Supreme Court has handed down many rulings regarding interview and interrogation over the years. Many of these rulings deal with police misconduct relating to coercement by the police. Law enforcement officers must safeguard against this possibility because failure to do so will most assuredly result in a criminal case being dismissed in court. One of the legal safeguards identified by the court in interviews and interrogations is the reading of the *Miranda* warning prior to questioning the suspect. Once that has been accomplished, the investigator must consider the location of the interrogation. The next section of the chapter provides some direction in that regard.

The chapter concludes with a brief discussion of the different approaches to interrogation and why suspects confess. It is here that a distinction is made between an admission and a confession. Making this distinction is another important legal observation to be made by the drug enforcement investigator.

Suggested Readings

Zulawski, D.E. and Wicklander, D.E., *Practical Aspects of Interview and Interrogation*, CRC Press, Boca Raton, FL, 1993.

Walters, S.B., *Principles of Kinesic Interview and Interrogation*, CRC Press, Boca Raton, FL, 1996.

Lyman, M. and Potter, G., *Organized Crime, 2nd ed.*, Prentice Hall, Upper Saddle River, NJ, 1999.

References

1. Tousignant, D.D., Why suspects confess, *FBI Law Enf. Bul.*, March, pp. 14–18, 1991.
2. U.S. Department of Justice, Drug Enforcement Administration, Drug Enforcement Handbook, U.S. Government Printing Office, Washington, D.C., 1988.
3. Evans, D.D., 10 ways to sharpen your interviewing skills, *Law Order,* Aug., pp. 90–95, 1990.
4. Coleman, R., Interrogation: The process, *FBI Law Enf. Bul.*, 1984.

Special Enforcement Problems

9

Because of the pervasiveness of drug trafficking, law enforcement agencies will commonly involve themselves in both street and high-level investigations. It is therefore essential that officers be adequately trained in both technical and tactical methods of investigation. These investigations will frequently focus on cultivated marijuana fields, illicit laboratories, smuggling operations, and pharmaceutical diversion investigations. Each represents a significant contribution to the country's illicit drug supply, which is why investigations into these areas should be undertaken regularly. This chapter will examine each of these areas of criminal investigation and identify problems and investigative methods used in each.

Marijuana Cultivation

Marijuana has consistently remained one of the economic staples in the illegal drug business. Because marijuana grows in almost all 50 states, domestic cultivation also contributes greatly to the nation's overall drug problem. Marijuana cultivation has proven to be a relatively easy-entry illicit market. All that is required for a simple growing operation is seeds, a water source, land, and a willingness to enter into a criminal enterprise, which in some states can result in a prison term as long as 25 years.

It is difficult to estimate the amount of marijuana actually produced in the United States. No single criminal organization is thought to control domestic marijuana production and trafficking, probably due to the easy-entry nature of the business and the difficulty criminal organizations would experience in attempting to monopolize it. Consequently, the domestic marijuana market has spawned the development of rural criminals who live and operate in scarcely populated agrarian areas. In addition to the protective rural environment, law enforcement in these areas is often diffuse. Growers can operate with impunity while their operations are cloaked by thick forests, lush vegetation, or inaccessible mountain slopes. These factors also help conceal marijuana-growing operations from rival growers or "pot poachers." Major outdoor cannabis cultivation takes place in Hawaii, Kentucky, Tennessee, California, and New York. Perhaps spurred on by successful efforts to curb outdoor cultivation, indoor cultivation flourishes, particularly in California, Florida, Oregon, Washington, and Kentucky.

To help hide their plants, outdoor growers frequently disperse them among corn and tomato plants, or along riverbeds and creeks. Over the years, police agents have discovered deadly booby traps in and around marijuana patches. Other safeguards have included hidden steel-jaw traps, guard dogs, and armed guards. These devices are designed not only to serve as a deterrent for police and poachers, but as a signal to nearby growers, who may be heavily armed and potentially violent. Growers have even resorted to indoor growing operations not only to conceal their operations, but to provide year-long harvesting opportunities.

Marijuana growers are a somewhat fragmented group of traffickers who rely on kinship or local ("good-old-boy") networks. Operations are typically financed by either previous transactions or by "jobbers" furnishing special lighting, fertilizer, or other equipment in exchange for a percentage of the harvest. Police have documented cases, however, in which large-scale cultivation operations were financed by business executives looking for alternate ways to invest their money. The packaging of marijuana remains universal. After harvest, it is usually placed in large trash bags for transportation. For smaller retail sales of one-quarter pound or less, smaller zipper-closing plastic bags are usually used.

Marijuana growers have learned that many police raids are products of so-called "search and destroy" missions based on information from informants. Therefore, many growing operations are now automated, allowing the grower to be absent in case of a police raid. This explains why search-and-destroy operations are often expensive and unproductive and rarely have a top enforcement priority for police.

Growing Marijuana

Three types of marijuana are commonly found in the United States: Indian hemp, commercial grade, and sinsemilla. The two cultivated grades are commercial and sinsemilla, which have significant growing differences.

Commercial Grade

Commercial grade marijuana is produced from cannabis plants that are cultivated in plots in which the male and female plants are allowed to grow together and the female plants are fertilized. The whole plant is harvested, stripped of its stems, and marketed. At maturity the plant will range from 7 to 15 feet high. Most of the leaves have 7 to 11 leaflets (almost always an odd number), with the center leaflet the longest.

Sinsemilla

The increased cultivation of sinsemilla reflects a growing trend to develop higher potency marijuana plants that result in greater profits. Many of these growers are horticulture specialists and they crossbreed different strains of marijuana to produce the highest potency plants possible. Some growers select high potency seeds from areas such as Mexico, Afghanistan, and Thailand; others attempt to produce their own high-quality seeds. In the latter case, a grower selects the largest female plant, impregnates a cotton swab with pollen, and places it on the largest bud of the plant. The cotton swab and bud are then covered with a plastic bag to protect the rest of the buds from the pollen. These fertilized buds will then produce seeds for the next growing season.

In 1996, the U.S. government estimated that 37% of the domestic marijuana crop was sinsemilla. Sinsemilla is produced from unfertilized female plants which are grown in plots from which all male cannabis plants have been removed prior to pollination. When grown in this fashion, the female plants flower more readily and produce more resin in an attempt to attract the male pollen. The resin contains THC (delta9-tetrahydracannabinol), which is the active agent in marijuana. The THC content in sinsemilla plants may be twice that of the commercial grade plants.

On average, a cultivated marijuana plant will produce one pound of marketable product. A plant that has had its flower tops removed, however, may be harvested two to three times in a growing season, thereby producing two to three pounds of marketable product. Prices of cultivated marijuana vary greatly from region to region, but range from $800 to $2000 per pound, and up to $200 per ounce for the higher grades.

Most cultivated marijuana plots are discovered as a result of search-and-destroy missions by police officers. Such activities have proven fruitful, but they frequently require four-wheel drive vehicles, spotter aircraft, and substantial training in guerrilla-warfare-type tactics in order to combat the snipers, guard dogs, and booby traps commonly associated with these operations.

Indoor Growing Operations

Many criminals are resorting to indoor growing methods, which (a) make police detection more difficult, and (b) enable growers to produce marijuana year-round. Growing structures such as greenhouses, converted residences, barns, basements, and chicken houses have been uncovered by drug enforcement officials. According to the Drug Enforcement Administration, two methods are commonly used for indoor cultivation:

Cloning: Cloning originated on the West Coast. Hybrid marijuana is cultivated and superior plants are selected for new cultivation. A cutting from a plant is obtained underwater, which prevents air from affecting the exposed ends. The cutting is wrapped in a paper towel that has been soaked in a root stimulant and then placed in a pot to grow. The cutting then develops roots. Growth is sometimes accelerated by the use of halide lights. Cloning permits a grower to produce hundreds of plants from a select few, and avoids the time-consuming process of waiting for the seeds to germinate.

Hydroponics: This popular cultivation process was originally perfected for plants such as tomatoes and cucumbers. Plants are grown in a soil-free, mineral-rich solution. Marijuana seedlings are taken to the hydroponic greenhouse and placed in 4-inch pipes, which contain the solution. In this environment, a sinsemilla plant measuring 8 to 10 feet high can be grown in 4 to 6 weeks. Cultivated marijuana plants grown hydroponically will contain up to twice the THC content found in even the highest commercial grades. One benefit of producing plants in this fashion is that greenhouses may be as small as 400 square feet: only one square foot is required to grow a mature plant. Such operations may operate year round and one such operation can possibly produce up to $5 million worth of marijuana annually. One way to investigate a possible greenhouse operation is to compare the suspect's utility bills with those of neighboring residences to check for excessive use of electricity and water.

Evidence of Marijuana Cultivation

Once cultivated, the packaged marijuana is transported by pick-up trucks with camper shells, vans, rental trailers, passenger vehicles, and (in some cases) general aviation aircraft. Commercial airlines are used more frequently to transport smaller quantities of drugs to various destinations within the United States. In addition, common carriers — even the U.S. Postal Service — have been discreetly used by traffickers to ship small quantities of marijuana. Because cultivation is mostly a rural operation, a lot of activities take place undetected by police or inquisitive neighbors. Certain types of behavior, however, might indicate the existence of a cultivation operation:

1. Individuals who purchase wooded lands, erecting high fences with heavy chains and locks on gates, and displaying "Keep Out" signs.
2. Individuals who buy land that could be used for farming or ranching, an do not use it for those purposes.

3. Out-of-state individuals who make large cash payments for tracts of land, or pay for the land in cash.
4. Buyers who purchase property through third parties and do not want to leave their addresses or telephone numbers with the seller.
5. People with no knowledge of ranching or farming who buy farms or ranch lands, and then show no visible means of support.
6. An unusual amount of vehicular traffic by which unknown individuals are transported on and off the property and the entrance gates are always locked after each entry or exit.
7. The erection of large greenhouses or tin buildings on property where these structures would not normally be utilized (for example, on very heavily wooded land where there are no animals to feed).
8. The use of guard dogs, alarms, and surveillance systems on property in the country (for example, dogs around a tin barn in an isolated area of the property).
9. A house in the country where men are constantly coming and going, but women and children are seldom seen.
10. Large purchases of fertilizer, garden hose, plastic PVC pipe, chicken wire, long 2" × 2" lumber, different sizes of pots, machetes, camouflage netting, camouflage clothing, or many sizes of stepladders.
11. The erection of tents or the use of camper trailers or other recreational vehicles on wooded property with no evidence of recreational activities.
12. An unusual pattern of vehicular traffic or appearance of a particular vehicle in the same isolated area.
13. Large purchases of green plastic sheet material, green spray paint, large trash bags, lanterns, portable heaters (e.g., large kerosene heaters), extension cords, heat lamps, and fans.
14. New owners of property who refuse to talk to neighboring property owners about how they use their property.
15. The purchase of large amounts of heavy plastic materials; the buyer is evasive about their use.
16. Unexplained and unreasonably high utility bills.
17. The purchase of properties formerly used as chicken or turkey farms by buyers whose use of the property would be suspicious.

Domestic Eradication

Domestically cultivated marijuana constituted approximately 19% of the total U.S. supply in 1985 and 18% in 1986. It is thought that these figures, which have increased since 1984, are a result of not only domestic interdiction programs but also eradication efforts in foreign source countries. In 1987, the Drug Enforcement Administration reported that more than one-third of the cultivated cannabis plants eradicated in 1985 and 1986 were sinsemilla, which is preferred over the commercial grades for its high THC content.

Marijuana eradication involves locating and seizing both cultivated plots and wild-growing patches. This is a difficult and expensive undertaking for law enforcement agencies and usually requires a joint effort on the part of several agencies. The U.S. Drug Enforcement Administration first provided financial aid for marijuana eradication in Hawaii in 1979. Since then, this federal program, which offers funding and investigative and aircraft resources, has been expanded to all 50 states. The program is considered successful: in 1984, for example, an estimated 3.8 million marijuana plants were eradicated in 48 states. In most states, a National Guard unit assists local drug enforcement officers in eradication maneuvers. This means that equipment such as trucks, helicopters, and additional manpower can be placed at the disposal of the local law enforcement agencies, thereby making such operations easier to complete.

Even with federal assistance, however, marijuana eradication is one of the most tedious and exhausting tasks in drug enforcement. Officers must be prepared to encounter cultivators who have military experience, police criminal records, and weapons. In addition, officers must also face long, hot days, with the risks of heat exhaustion, hornet and wasp stings, snakebites, poison ivy, sunstroke, and spider bites.

The enforcement unit should properly document each eradication effort. All pertinent information should be catalogued and indexed: type of field (cultivated or wild growing); the names and identifiers of suspects; the items seized (weapons, vehicles, cultivation equipment, etc.); and other information (booby traps, type of marijuana, number of plants, etc.).

Such documentation may be required under local or state law. In many cases, a state investigative police agency may collect the data from local law enforcement agencies throughout the state and maintain a master file of all plots and violators.

Smuggling Investigations

Typically, smuggling calls to mind national and international organizations, with far-reaching implications. We are aware, for example, that a considerable amount of heroin originates in Mexico and Southeast and Southwest Asia. Cocaine, for the most part, originates in South American countries such as Colombia, Peru, and Bolivia. Marijuana, aside from its domestic sources, is smuggled in from Mexico, Colombia, Panama, and Jamaica.

It should be obvious that once drugs arrive in the United States, there must be a domestic smuggling network, which then transports the drugs to places of distribution throughout the country. This is where local law enforcement must have sufficient expertise to deal with the problem of interstate and intrastate smuggling. This text will not address the task of international drug interdiction, but will focus on the role of domestic law enforcement in detection and investigation of the various modes of domestic smuggling.

Air Smuggling

Traditionally, the investigation of air smuggling had been the province of the federal government. During the last 10 years or so, however, it is increasingly common for state and local law enforcement agencies to conduct full-scale investigations into drug trafficking by air. Moreover, the recent federal task force concentrations in coastal cities and traditional ports of entry have caused many smugglers to transport their payloads further inland to areas considered safer by traffickers.

The U.S. Customs Service estimates that there are between 3 and 10 successful smuggling flights each day in the United States. Evidence of this is found in the number of aircraft (large and small) seized by authorities during the off-loading process. Moreover, some planes are occasionally discovered abandoned — full of drugs and out of fuel.

The Federal Aviation Administration (FAA) requires all flights by private aircraft originating in other countries to file flight plans 24 hours in advance and to land at airports nearest to their points of entry that have customs offices. By coordinating flight plan information with radar surveillance, any aircraft crossing a U.S. southern border without a flight plan can be identified as suspicious. Unfortunately, many areas of the border do not have low-altitude radar coverage, allowing many small aircraft to go undetected.

Air smuggling investigations are tedious and difficult to conduct, since pilots often change their destinations, making detection difficult. To help combat this problem, law enforcement officers may "wire" a suspected aircraft to track it. A law enforcement transponder is placed in the suspect aircraft, which emits a signal that can be received by FAA control towers. These transponders look exactly like standard aircraft transponders, thus leaving little clue as to their true function. These devices must be surreptitiously installed by investigators, and pursuant to a lawful court order. In investigations requiring the installation of a transponder, the U.S. Customs Service is usually contacted — which usually gives assistance in preparing the court order and technical assistance in installing the transponder.

Another way of detecting air smuggling is by locating and conducting surveillance on a suspected "ground crew." The ground crew consists of individuals employed by smugglers to meet the aircraft at a designated time and location, and to off-load the drugs for transport to various distribution points. These players may be hired to conduct only this particular task, or they might be involved in the overall planning of the operation. The ground crew usually employs vans or pick-up trucks with camper shells (which are sometimes rented for the operation). The ground crew will usually be equipped with two-way, ground-to-air radios to communicate with the pilot as he or she approaches the landing site. The landing site will vary in each air smuggling operation; typical sites include small, out-of-the-way airports, or even sections of highways that are seldom traveled.

The capture of a smuggling aircraft should be accomplished with caution: pilots and ground crew are often heavily armed to prevent possible ambushes by poachers. In addition, state and local agencies should always contact the U.S. Customs Air Branch, which will offer support and expertise in the pursuit and capture of suspect aircraft. The Customs Service currently has planes equipped with forward-looking infrared sensors for tracking smugglers at night without making visual contact. Dealing with an air operation can be complicated and requires interagency cooperation.

Smuggling Aircraft

To properly investigate a suspected air smuggling operation, officers should have a basic knowledge of the various types of aircraft that smugglers use, and which planes are best suited for different smuggling operations. Marijuana is usually packed in bails (50 or 100 pounds each), and smuggling normally requires larger aircraft, such as a C-132 or DC-3. Many other types of aircraft are commonly used, but regardless of type, most traffickers prefer older aircraft that can be abandoned (ditched) if necessary; older aircraft represent less potential financial loss than newer, more expensive planes.

Cocaine, however, is usually brought in on smaller planes (see Figure 9.1). The payload is smaller, and smaller aircraft normally fly much faster than larger planes. Popular planes for cocaine smuggling are single- and twin-engine aircraft such as the Cessna 400 series; other preferred models are the Aerocommander 680 and 690, Piper Aztec, and Piper Navajo twin-engine models. One of these planes can generally transport about a ton of cocaine over a range of about 1800 miles, and can stay airborne for about 11 hours with a standard fuel system — even longer with a bladder tank.

To maximize range and capability, smuggling aircraft are frequently "plumbed" or outfitted with auxiliary fuel systems. These systems, called "bladder tanks," are sometimes installed on the outside of the aircraft or on a wing. Some smugglers prefer to conceal the bladder by using a collapsible tank inside the aircraft; this may consist of nothing more than a waterbed, which is used for a one-way trip and thrown away after the flight. The space formerly occupied by the bladder can be used for storing cocaine on the return journey.

Figure 9.1 A small general aviation aircraft seized in rural Oklahoma after it ran out of fuel and was forced to make an emergency landing. It contained a payload of illicit drugs. (Photo courtesy of the Oklahoma Bureau of Narcotics and Dangerous Drugs Control.)

Air smuggling via general aviation aircraft is the most common method of importing cocaine from South America (Figure 9.2). Nearly two-thirds of the cocaine smuggled into the United States is transported in this fashion, though some use of commercial aircraft is also fairly common. (An estimated 64% of the marijuana consumed by American users is smuggled from foreign sources.) Planes that do not contain bladder tanks must refuel at predetermined transshipment points between the country of origin and the U.S. These points are critical in the smuggling phase and can be found throughout South America, Cuba, the Bahamas, and Puerto Rico. Transshipment stations may simply be refueling stops, or they may be areas where the drugs are off-loaded and repackaged.

Smugglers land at airports of every size and in large and small cities throughout the country. Although the planes may appear entirely "normal," there are telltale signs for profiling aircraft used in smuggling. These signs might not only be indicators of smuggling activity, but they could give investigators other leads to follow up and verify. Some physical characteristics of smuggling aircraft are:

1. Passenger seats missing from the aircraft
2. Strong, unusual odors, such as perfume (used to cover the scent of marijuana)
3. Numerous cardboard boxes, duffel bags, plastic bags, or other containers inside the aircraft

Figure 9.2 A twin-engine aircraft and a bulldozer seized on a makeshift clandestine airstrip in South America. (Photo courtesy of the U.S. Drug Enforcement Administration.)

4. Aircraft registration numbers are altered or otherwise falsified
5. Landings wherein aircraft meet ground vehicles and depart after only a brief period on the ground
6. Aircraft flying or landing after dark without lights
7. Trucks, campers, or vans waiting at or near areas suitable for aircraft landings; these are often equipped with radios for use in communications with aircraft
8. Pilots or passengers displaying large amounts of cash, and making cash payments for fuel and services
9. Windows of aircraft are covered by curtains or temporarily taped over
10. Pilots or passengers reluctant to leave the aircraft unattended during ground servicing
11. Aircraft parked a long distance from the line shack, or at the far end of a ramp

Aircraft Data Plates. When investigating suspect aircraft, it is often necessary to check the data plate of the aircraft to verify the authenticity of its externally displayed registration and to determine the true ownership. Occasionally, a plane's external registration will also show signs of being altered,

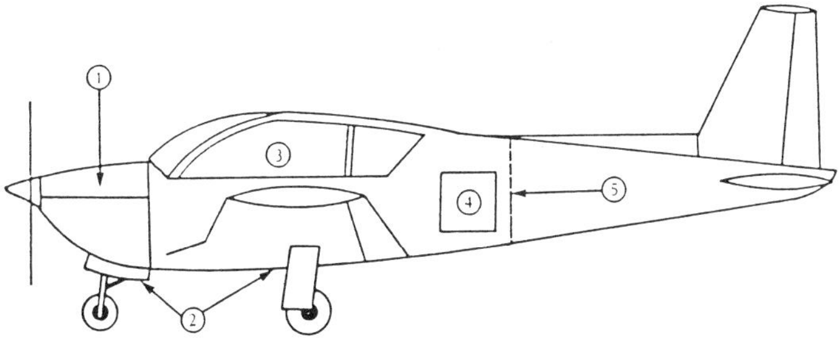

Figure 9.3 Areas searched in light aircraft.

or the aircraft may be devoid of any registration markings. The latter is usually true when a plane crashes and burns.

Search of a Typical Light Plane

In the event a suspected smuggler aircraft can be documented entering the country, U.S. Customs officers may search the aircraft without a warrant (a customs search). Absent any exigent circumstances, a search warrant or consent must be obtained.

Searching an airplane is quite different from searching an automobile or marine vessel (see Figure 9.3). Certain tools should be kept on hand for the task: a flashlight, an aircraft reference book, an inspection mirror, and a screwdriver (used as a probe). In addition, it may be necessary for officers to seek assistance of a certified mechanic in order to ensure the future airworthiness of the aircraft. Listed below are the main areas to search when concealed contraband is suspected:

1. *Engine compartment*: Have the pilot open the engine cowling on both sides. With the aid of a flashlight and inspection mirror, check for small packages that might be attached to the engine mount structure and other parts of the powerplant.
2. *Wheel wells*: With the aid of a floor creeper, inspection mirror, and flashlight, check the surrounding structure for small concealed packages.

In most light planes, a large area of the internal wing structure may be viewed from the main landing gear wheel wells because of access holes.

3. *Cabin area*: With the aid of an inspection mirror and flashlight, check under and behind the instrument panel; the glove compartment; under seat cushions; seat pockets; in the headliner if it has a zipper for inspection access; ashtrays; any open compartments; under the floor and above ceiling panes; ventilation ducts; baggage, map cases, and flight kits.
4. *The baggage compartment behind the rear bulkhead cover*: In most light planes, the rear bulkhead cover is a canvas or plastic sheet that is easily removed (it is usually held in place by snap fasteners, thumb disconnects, or Velcro® tape). With the aid of an inspection mirror and flashlight, examine the aft portion of the fuselage.
5. *The baggage compartment*: Examine all baggage and the interior of the compartment. Do not place baggage on top of the wing. The wing skin is light and may be easily damaged. Most light twin-engine aircraft also have baggage compartments in the noses of the plane.
6. *The exterior of the plane*: Examine the following areas for improper condition or operation, which may indicate the concealment of contraband: the nose cone, the prop spinner, light assemblies and bulbs, exhaust pipes, recessed areas in the landing gear, fuel cells, wing flaps, aileron tab, elevators, wheels and hubs, luggage compartments; wingtip fuel tanks, and filler caps.

Search of Commercial Aircraft

Commercial aircraft are frequently used to hide and transport drugs. A search of a commercial aircraft should include the baggage and storage compartments, the restrooms, life-raft compartments, trash containers, wheel wells, liquor locker, area under the floor of the cockpit.

The Pilots

It is somewhat difficult to profile a smuggler pilot: they do not seem to fit stereotypes. Pilots may be of any nationality, age, or sex. In addition, they may be licensed commercial pilots, unlicensed pilots, or even former military flight personnel. Because the drug business is so lucrative, most smuggler pilots usually operate with extremely sophisticated equipment. In many instances, this equipment is more sophisticated than that used by police agencies including:

1. Sophisticated electronic equipment to maintain communications within their organization: air-to-air radios, ground-to-air radios, and advanced radar
2. Equipment to monitor law enforcement radio transmissions

3. State-of-the-art communication scramblers; these are used to "garble" ordinary transmissions to anyone listening without a receiver having a scrambler with the same code
4. Pocket pagers
5. Digital inscription devices; these are used to send messages in code, and they can be accessed only after a security code is entered directly into the device
6. Radar altimeters
7. Beacon-interrogating digital radar
8. Position-tracking equipment
9. Long-range navigational instruments
10. Night-vision goggles; these are used to intensify any available light by a factor of 50,000, thereby reducing the smuggler's risk of detection by being able to fly "dark," or without lights

Ground Smuggling

Authorities are discovering an upsurge in ground-smuggling operations. Vehicles are used to transport drugs from aircraft and vessels to destinations within the United States, and transport drugs directly across the borders of the United States. The Border Patrol now uses a variety of sophisticated equipment to detect illegal intrusions: buried ground sensors, infrared heat sensors, night-vision goggles, and pocket-sized starlight scopes.

Search of a Typical Automobile

The legality for searching an automobile is discussed in Chapter 6 and should be considered before any search is conducted. Given legal grounds for a search, it should be determined whether the case involves smuggling or if the vehicle was used as a temporary hiding place for drugs. Normally, a smuggling operation will reveal a more extensive effort on the part of the driver to conceal drugs; the drugs will, therefore be more difficult to locate.

In either case, the search must be conducted thoroughly, with officers knowing specifically what areas to search (see Figure 9.4). Officers should begin at one end of the vehicle and slowly work toward the other. It is a good idea for more than one officer to be present for the search; both officers should search the vehicle, so that evidence will not be overlooked. In most cases, drugs will usually be concealed in a few standard areas:

1. *Radiator, grill, and bumpers*: Drug packages may be attached with duct tape to the rear of a license plate or inside a locking gas cap.
2. *Fenders and front wheels*: Look inside hubcaps and behind headlights.
3. *Powerplant area*: Search inside the air filter, and look for packages affixed to electrical wiring, hoses, or under the hood.

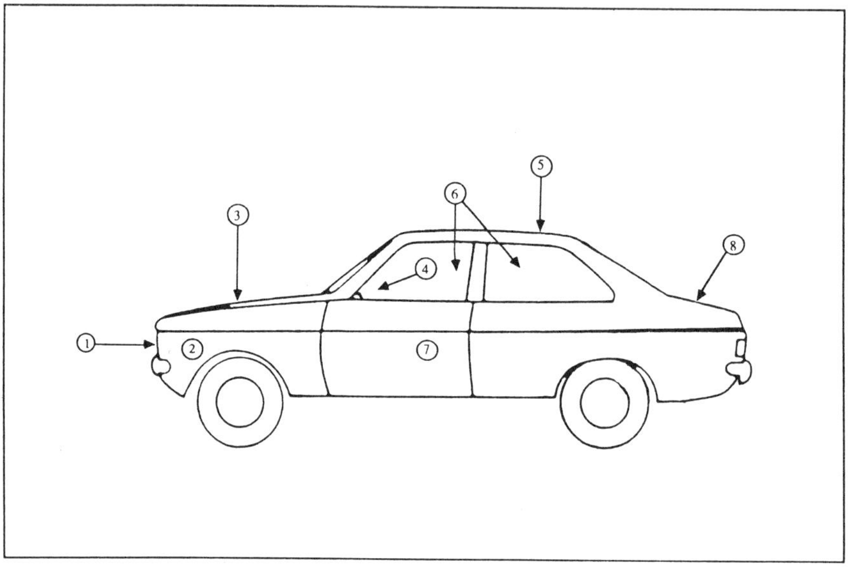

Figure 9.4 Areas searched in typical automobile.

4. *Dashboard area*: The driver could install removable panels, and these should be checked by operating all knobs. Search for packages affixed behind the foot pedals or in ventilation ducts.
5. *Header area*: It is common to discover concealed drugs within the cloth area of the headboard lining or within the sun visors.
6. *Front and back seat areas*: Drugs may be concealed between the seats, within the seats and spring assemblies, or within hidden compartments in the seat.
7. *Door panels*: Door panels are removable and offer the smuggler areas to hide drugs, which might go undetected by unobservant police officers.
8. *Trunk area*: Look within the trunk lid frame and beneath the insulation. Drugs are also commonly hidden within hollow tools, inside the spare tire assembly, under carpeting, or within clothing in the trunk.

Water-Borne Vessels

Jurisdictions bordering ocean coasts, lakes, or rivers experience unique problems with regard to drug smuggling. Bodies of water are often excellent conduits between points of entry and destinations for drugs. Smuggling through these arteries may be difficult to detect. The vessel used in each instance will vary with the size and type of the body of water, and according to the financial resources of the trafficker (see Figure 9.5). International deliveries by vessel are initially transported by a "mother ship," which is

Figure 9.5 A small speedboat used by smugglers to transport quantities of cocaine and marijuana from the mother ship to a coastal region of Florida. (Photo courtesy of the Florida Department of Law Enforcement.)

normally a large vessel traveling from its source country. These ships usually remain in international waters (12 miles or more off the coast of the U.S.), and commission smaller and faster ("go-fast") boats to transport small amounts of their cargo to shore. Once inland, the drugs are off-loaded and placed in aircraft or ground vehicles for transportation to their ultimate destinations.

Search of a Vessel

A captured vessel must be properly searched. Officers should be aware of prescribed searching methods because concealment aboard vessels can be quite tricky. The drugs might be located virtually anywhere within the vessel: between the deck and hull; within hollowed-out guardrails; under floor joints; inside fuel and oxygen tanks (and all other containers). Weighted objects at the bottoms of tanks and articles floating inside tanks should be inspected. Searchers should be suspicious if the crew claims to have been at sea for a long time and the fuel tanks are full. False decks, removable paneling, or blanked-off spaces in the bow should also be anticipated. In the case of large boats, once below the deck, searchers should locate and inspect heads, sinks, and basins as soon as possible in case smugglers attempt to flush the drugs. If flushing is suspected, the water surrounding the vessel should be

Figure 9.6 A small vessel transporting cocaine, being approached by a U.S. Coast Guard interdiction ship for arrest. (Photo courtesy of the Florida Department of Law Enforcement.)

inspected for evidence of the contraband. The investigator's imagination is his or her only limitation when searching vessels, and a thorough job will most likely prove productive (Figure 9.6).

Smuggling and Prisons

Another growing area of concern is illicit drug smuggling into federal, state, and county prisons. Prison smuggling poses a tremendous challenge for law enforcement officials.

Generally, inmates may possess only items issued by the institution; any other items are considered contraband: drugs, weapons, money, cigarettes, etc. Drugs are among the most sought-after forms of contraband because of their recreational and profit potential within the prison. The methods of smuggling vary from case to case. Drugs may be thrown over the walls by associates, transported into the institution via service trucks and their civilian personnel, carried into the institution in the body cavities of inmates, brought in by visitors, shipped through the postal service, or carried into institutions by corrupt employees.

In many cases, penal drug smuggling is conducted by an organized gang that operates within the institution. These gangs are widespread and exert great influence over their members. Many gangs have chapters operating in several institutions at the same time and frequently operate in the free society, as well. Among the gangs are the Aryan Brotherhood (ABs), the Texas Syndicate, the Mexican Mafia (EME), Black Guerilla Family (BGF), and Nuestra Familia (NF).

Figure 9.7 A state drug detection dog, commonly used for searching prisons and self-storage lockers for illicit drugs. (Photo courtesy of the Oklahoma Bureau of Narcotics and Dangerous Drugs Control.)

Many of these groups seek to monopolize drug trafficking in their particular institutions. Moreover, because of conflicting goals and philosophies, these gangs are constantly at war with each other, which poses additional enforcement problems for officials.

Drug Detection Dogs

The use of drug dogs has increased during the last decade for obvious reasons. A dog is trained to locate or "alert" on the scent of certain drugs such as heroin, cocaine, marijuana, methaqualone, and methamphetamine. A dog's sense of smell is difficult to fool (Figure 9.7).

Training is a lengthy process, which requires detailed documentation of the dog's successes in locating drugs. A certificate is issued to the dog handler, who will use it as evidence of training and competency if the alert is later questioned by defense attorneys. Any "false-alerts" must be documented. This detracts from the dog's credibility, and in many cases a false alert will require a dog to be recertified for continued service.

Drug detection dogs may be effective in searching storage lockers, vehicles, schools, correctional facilities, and airports. The use of drug detection dogs also makes search warrants easy to acquire because the alert (along with the dog's certification) is usually considered probable cause for the warrant.

Pharmaceutical Diversion

Diversion of pharmaceutical drugs is considered an expanding problem within the drug enforcement community. More and more criminal investigations are revealing the widespread involvement of health care professionals in the diversion of controlled substances from hospitals, clinics, pharmacies, and doctors' offices. The involvement of street criminals (or "professional patients") in this lucrative business is also on the increase, and will be discussed later in this section.

It is estimated that diverted pharmaceutical drugs account for an estimated 32% of the illegitimately consumed drugs in the U.S. The Drug Enforcement Administration estimates that 2% or 13,000 practicing physicians and pharmacists are involved in some form of illegal diversion activities.

The Law

Under the Controlled Substances Act of 1970, "Any person who handles or intends to handle controlled substances must obtain a registration issued by the Drug Enforcement Administration." In addition to federal law requiring registration of those who handle controlled substances, about 25 states also require that a firm or individual obtain a state controlled-substances registration. In some states, registration is necessary as a prerequisite before one is eligible for federal DEA registration.

Because of the differences in regulation of registrants, police officers should be familiar with their own state law regarding registration of controlled-substance handlers. They should also know which state agency is responsible for registration so that they are able to verify quickly whether a particular person or firm involved in dispensing drugs is lawfully registered.

The registration consists of a unique number assigned to each legitimate handler of controlled drugs: importers, exporters, manufacturers, wholesalers, hospitals, pharmacies, physicians, and researchers. The number must be made available to the supplier prior to any purchases of controlled substances, thus reducing the opportunity for unauthorized transactions.

Combatting the problem of pharmaceutical diversion is a difficult task. Many law enforcement officers and prosecutors are unfamiliar with the problem and how to deal with it. The violator in a drug diversion case may be a properly licensed registrant who abuses his or her authority, or a street criminal who might be running numerous scams aimed at deceiving unsuspecting physicians. We will now examine those who most commonly divert controlled substances and their preferred methods.

Medical Practitioners as Suspects

One necessary task of drug enforcement officials is the investigation of registered legal handlers of drugs such as physicians, pharmacists, and nurses.

Doctors in Diversion

Generally, four types of doctors are involved in the diversion of pharmaceutical drugs.

1. *Dishonest*: A dishonest doctor makes a profit from the illegal sale of pharmaceutical drugs, or may be involved in cases where prescriptions are given to suspects for the purpose of unlawfully distributing illicit drugs.
2. *Impaired*: Many physicians use drugs both on and off the job. Drug dependency may develop for a number of reasons: marital problems, stress on the job, and recreational use. The recidivism rate, however, is generally low for those who are treated properly and on a timely basis.
3. *Dated*: A doctor who has been in practice for a number of years. He may be willing to indiscriminately hand out drugs to anyone who has an apparent legitimate need for medication. Doctors who fall into this category are not necessarily criminals, but more likely are set in their ways and unwilling to conform to new rules and regulations.
4. *Gullible*: This physician is not cautious enough to recognize a scam. Although possibly an otherwise competent doctor, he or she will easily fall victim to professional patients.

Listed below are some of the specific methods physicians have commonly used to divert drugs.

1. A physician writes a prescription in a patient's name, picks up the drugs personally, and tells the pharmacist he or she will take it to the patient.
2. A physician sends a patient to the pharmacy to have a prescription filled, but requires the patient to bring the drugs back to his or her office. Only part of the drug is administered and the physician keeps the rest.
3. A physician writes a prescription in the name of a family member, then picks up and uses the drugs.

4. A physician writes a prescription in his or her own name at various pharmacies at the same time.
5. A physician self-administers injectable drugs taken from nurse stations, hospital emergency rooms, or hospital pharmacies.
6. A physician orders drugs from several pharmacies at the same time, using DEA official order forms, while at the same time orders the same drug from a mail-order drug company.
7. A physician obtains drug samples and self-administers them.

Although medical-care institutions bear legal and moral obligations to their employees, many shun their obligation to report a suspected diversion problem, or simply look the other way rather than acknowledge the situation. Hospitals, through their boards of directors, should adequately regulate personnel and establish formal policy regarding impairment (with strict enforcement provisions). In the case of addicted registrants, many state hospital boards have a system whereby a physician or nurse can voluntarily submit to treatment (employee assistance program) and remedy the problem before it results in criminal prosecution.

Nurses in Diversion

Diversion problems also involve nurses. A distinction needs to be made between diversion drugs for resale and diversion because of personal addiction. Both present unique problems, and may require different solutions. Studies have shown that of those nurses who are diverting drugs, more are physically addicted than are selling drugs for profit. This distinction may affect the manner in which an investigation is approached and how the suspect is dealt with.

Drug Theft

Most health-care institutions experience some degree of diversion, and generally the employees are the culprits. Those employees most likely involved with drugs are those who have access — physicians, nurses, pharmacists, and other employees. The most commonly diverted drugs are Valium, morphine, Demerol, Tylenol III with codeine, Percodan, Percocet, and Ritalin. The type of user and the opportunities available will have a bearing on whether tablets, capsules, or injectable substances are preferred. Diversion may occur in many different areas of the health-care facility, but it will most commonly take place at the hospital pharmacy, the nursing station, or the recovery floor.

Substituting Drugs

If outright theft is not considered safe by the violator, he or she may substitute a noncontrolled drug for a controlled drug. Drug substitution may be accomplished, for instance, by appearing to inject a patient with a prescribed medication while in fact a worthless substance may be used in its place. This may cause the patient to suffer and could result in medical setbacks.

Substitutions are commonly carried our through "charting" (backdating patients' charts to show that drugs were administered, which were in fact stolen), or forging other nurses' names. To avoid the possibility of substitution, two nurses should be required to obtain drugs needed on the floor. This would add a check-and-balance to prevent one of them diverting the drugs.

Diversion and Punishment

The problem of diversion is growing because many facilities fail to address the problem, and also because the violators have methods of avoiding punishment.

Suspected users often quit and join other hospitals. Other employees might suspect an on-the-job user, and to avoid being confronted with a diversion charge, he or she simply changes jobs. When the new hospital calls for a reference, information regarding any possible involvement in drug use or diversion is not shared. The user is therefore allowed continue his or her unlawful activities.

Employees who have been caught are often simply transferred. It has become evident that some hospitals are more willing to transfer employees caught in diversion activities to different units within the hospital rather than terminate their employment or seek prosecution. Medical care professionals are somewhat clannish and reluctant to "snitch" on fellow workers. Transferring suspected employees eliminates stigmatization by co-workers and embarrassing publicity for the institution. Unfortunately, this practice offers no incentive for violators to discontinue their involvement in diversion activity.

Finally, there is the problem of outright denial. One mistake investigators frequently make is to approach a suspect before any concrete evidence has been documented. If the suspect denies his or her involvement in the diversion, the investigator's bluff is called and he or she has no immediate recourse. Having a sound case prepared when approaching a suspected violator also maximizes the deterrent effects of diversion investigations within the medical facility.

The Professional Patient (The Scammer)

To understand the problem of drug diversion, investigators should also look at the various scams used by street criminals to obtain pharmaceutical drugs. The word "scam" is defined by Webster as "to cheat or swindle, as in a confidence game." This is precisely what is happening within the medical-care community. Street criminals are acquiring drugs through deceit and selling those drugs on the street for profit.

The most likely target of the scammer is the physician. Once the scammer is successful in conning a prescription out of a physician, he or she will usually experience little trouble in having it filled by a pharmacist.

Pharmacists are the second-most likely targets of the scammer, especially one who is trying to pass forged or altered prescriptions. In addition to forgery and alterations of prescriptions, a pharmacist can be an unwitting partner in a scam when he or she (a) fills prescriptions for the same patient from different physicians; (b) fills prescriptions for the same patient too frequently, or (c) accepts refill orders for prescriptions when the scammer calls in the prescription and pretends to be a physician.

Investigators have uncovered hundreds of diversion schemes over the years. Some of the more common scams experienced by many different jurisdictions are offered in brief below.

The Fat Lady Scam

This is a common deception, usually perpetrated by several women who are severely overweight. The women move into a new community and develop a schedule in which each member visits a maximum number of physicians each day for a week or so. Each woman tells each physician she visits that she is chronically unhappy with her life because of being overweight. She tells the doctor her husband is going to leave her and fight for custody of the children and she is considering having her stomach stapled, etc.

At this point the "patient" begins hinting about a particular drug (e.g., Preludin, amphetamines, or another Schedule II drug). The physician will usually refuse to prescribe Schedule II drugs for weight reduction, but might be willing to prescribe Didrex. After the patient is issued a prescription for Didrex, she might then request a prescription for Valium to keep from "getting too edgy."

The Breast Cancer Scam

This scam involves individuals who are actually experiencing legitimate medical problems. The scam was documented in the St. Louis area, and it involved a woman who had a form of breast cancer. She would simply show up at a physician's office and present her case for treatment. In this case, Dilaudid was the only drug that gave her relief, and the physicians would usually give her a prescription. The woman was seeing seven doctors on a regular basis in different surrounding towns. Physicians should be cautious about treating patients who are unknown to them, who have insufficient identification, or who otherwise behave suspiciously.

The Toothache Scam

This scam is popular among narcotics addicts who are also experiencing a tooth-decay problem. The addicts will try to obtain Schedule II narcotics from dentists and physicians at the same time. Addicts have attempted to obtain telephone prescriptions for the desired drug without even seeing a dentist. If the addict chooses to see the dentist, he or she will present a legitimate "reason" for having to be somewhere else so that the dentist will issue a prescription for a drug such as Demerol or Dilaudid. Dentists, in cases like this, should be suspicious of new patients showing up all in a brief period of time. This might indicate the existence of an organized diversion ring operating in the area.

The Altered Scrip Scam

Prescribers who short-cut proper prescription-writing practices — especially those who use Arabic numerals for the dose amounts and do not write out the numbers — are easy targets for professional patients. By simply matching the ink color of the prescriber's pen, a 10 can be altered to a 40, 5 can become 25, and so on. A reasonable prescription becomes excessive, and certainly more profitable to the professional patient.

The Phantom Refill Scam

Investigations are revealing an increasing number of prescriptions with refill numbers that have been altered by the patient without the knowledge of the physician or dentist. Professional patients — especially those who are addicted to or selling codeine-containing drugs, Schedule II drugs, Schedule IV tranquilizers, or sleep medications — commonly add refills to prescriptions which are not authorized by the physician or dentist.

Drugs obtained in this fashion provide the violator with a considerable profit margin, which in turn acts as an incentive for the commission of the act. For example, one Dilaudid tablet may bring as much as $50 to $60 on the street. A 10-mg Valium tablet (diazepam) may sell for $5 to $20. Some of the most popular drugs obtained by these scams are Dilaudid, Dolophine, Ritalin, Tuinal, Talwin, Preludin, Percodan, Valium, Seconal, Tylenol III and IV, and amphetamines. Officials in many cities are now reporting increased demands for Ritalin and Talwin tablets, which are usually ground up, dissolved in water, and injected by the user. The Ritalin–Talwin combination is cheaper than the traditional speedball, which is a combination of heroin and methamphetamine (or cocaine) powder.

Many other scams are facilitated by con artists who are elderly, handicapped, or simply clever or brazen enough to attempt such frauds. All professionals within the medical community are duty bound to report any such attempts to illegally obtain drugs as soon as they are detected.

The Drug Audit

In addition to the nine control mechanisms in the 1970 Controlled Substances Act (see Appendix), all registrants must keep full records of every controlled substance they manufacture, purchase, sell, or keep in inventory, regardless of which schedule the drugs fall under. (Limited exceptions to this requirement are only available to researchers and physicians.) Audits can be performed from these records to trace the flow of any drug from the time of manufacture, through the wholesale level, on to its destination at a pharmacy, hospital, or physician's office, and then on to the patient. The mere existence of this requirement is often enough to discourage many types of diversion.

One record-keeping distinction is made. All records for all Schedule I and II drugs must be maintained separately from all other records of the registrant. The purpose for this requirement is to allow investigators the ability to audit the most abused drugs more expeditiously.

Problems in Diversion Investigations

Even though pharmacists are required by law to account for every dose of dangerous drugs they order, suspicious fires, robberies, and break-ins can destroy prescription files and cover shortages of pills. For these and many other reasons, evidence of diversion is difficult to acquire. For example, undercover agents investigating this type of criminal behavior may find that the suspect doctors claim that they were just "practicing medicine" and attempting to cure a patient by prescribing drugs for an illness. Other violations are more blatant, such as when physicians sell drugs to friends and associates or barter prescriptions for merchandise.

Other problems arise in the prosecution of diversion cases. Prosecutors are usually eager to file charges against drug dealers from the street, but when a drug dealer happens to be a physician in the community, charges are sometimes difficult to bring, and prosecutors are often reluctant to try "respectable" citizens who have the resources to mount an active defense against the charges. In addition, there are other pressures on prosecutors. They may have a social or political relationship with the registrant. If they are in a rural county that has few doctors' offices, they know that any doctor forced out of business could leave some families without easy access to medical care.

Furthermore, inconvenienced voters often have good memories when the prosecutor has to stand for re-election, creating a situation in which the prosecutor may actually be punished by the very public he or she serves for attempting to apply diversion laws to physicians. Even when charges are brought against physicians, prosecutors may have a difficult time convincing juries of the seriousness of the violation, or it may be difficult to explain the complexities of the diversion case to the jury. Because of these considerations, a conviction may not be forthcoming.

Clandestine Laboratories

Of the many different drugs that have become popular over the years, some are organic in nature and some are synthesized by chemists in illicit drug laboratories. Even though some drugs may be of an organic origin, a degree of chemical synthesis is necessary for the completion of the finished product. This is true, for example, with heroin and cocaine.

Many popular drugs that have emerged over the years are synthetic and originate in the clandestine laboratory. These include:

- Hallucinogens (LSD, PCP, MDMA)
- Stimulants (methamphetamine and amphetamine)
- Controlled substance analogs (designer drugs)

Drugs such as LSD seem to be available almost everywhere in the country, but their production appears to be regional. LSD and PCP laboratories have been abundant in California, while much of the methamphetamine is produced in illegal laboratories in the West and Southwest. The size of most clandestine labs is relatively modest, since they generally produce one specific drug. Expertise needed to operate a lab is usually minimal, and the equipment and chemicals are readily available and inexpensive.

One of the most commonly produced illicit drugs in the United States is methamphetamine. One of its immediate precursors, phenyl-2-propanone, is easily synthesized into methamphetamine. Like many other drugs, the production of methamphetamine is fairly cheap and effortless. Setting up a lab can cost as little as $2,000 and can be enormously profitable, since one day's production can generate as much as $50,000.

The spreading popularity of illicit labs is partly due to successes in federal drug interdiction efforts. Many traffickers feel safer making their own drugs domestically than they do risking detection and arrest as a result of dealing with foreign suppliers. As with the marijuana cultivator, the clandestine lab operator commonly seeks isolation in rural settings where his or her activities will go unnoticed. One of the largest illicit methamphetamine laboratories ever discovered in the United States was located in the mountains of rural McCreary County, Kentucky, and involved participants from Kentucky, Florida, Illinois, and Tennessee. Often this desire for rural isolation is because of the distinctive odors emitted by "meth" and PCP labs. In an urban setting, these odors can reveal the existence of a lab.

The operators of these laboratories may be highly educated chemists or low-level street criminals. In many cases, when suspects without knowledge of chemistry decide to set up a clandestine laboratory, qualified and experienced chemists ("cookers") from outside the area are hired to set up the lab for a fee or a percentage of the anticipated profit. Once paid, the chemists return to their originating areas.

Types of Labs

Although many different types of drugs are produced by clandestine laboratories, there are three basic types of lab operations:

1. Extraction labs produce illicit substances by removing certain elements from one substance and creating another. Examples are:
   a. *Hashish*: This is an extraction of the marijuana plant made from boiling marijuana in a solvent and alcohol solution. The precipitant is then filtered through a strainer and the resulting material is allowed to dry.
   b. *Methamphetamine*: One somewhat primitive method of making a crude brand of methamphetamine is by collecting a large number of benezedrine inhalers and removing the cotton parts of the inhalers. This material is then placed in a vat filled with muriatic acid and heated until a film forms on the top of the solution.
2. Conversion labs convert existing controlled substances into different forms for street sales. A typical example:
   a. *Crack*. This free-base form of cocaine is made by mixing powdered cocaine with baking soda, ammonia, and water and heating the solution until residue is formed, which is then dried.
3. Synthesis labs convert one chemical to another. PCP and methamphetamine laboratories are typical examples. Such labs use controlled chemicals such as "P2P" to create yet a different product.

PCP

In the late 1970s, PCP was most commonly found in powder form and was called "angel dust" on the street. The powder was usually sprinkled on marijuana cigarettes by users, and smoked to achieve the desired high. The popularity of the powdered form of the drug, however, has gradually faded and is being replaced by the current liquid form. Moreover, liquid PCP is relatively easy to manufacture once the necessary materials have been acquired (the profit margin is still high). Because of relative ease in setting it up, the PCP lab can also be taken apart and moved with little effort, which presents investigative problems for law enforcement.

Methamphetamine

As discussed in Chapter 3, methamphetamine is a popular illicit drug with strong stimulant qualities. A tremendous market exists for this drug because

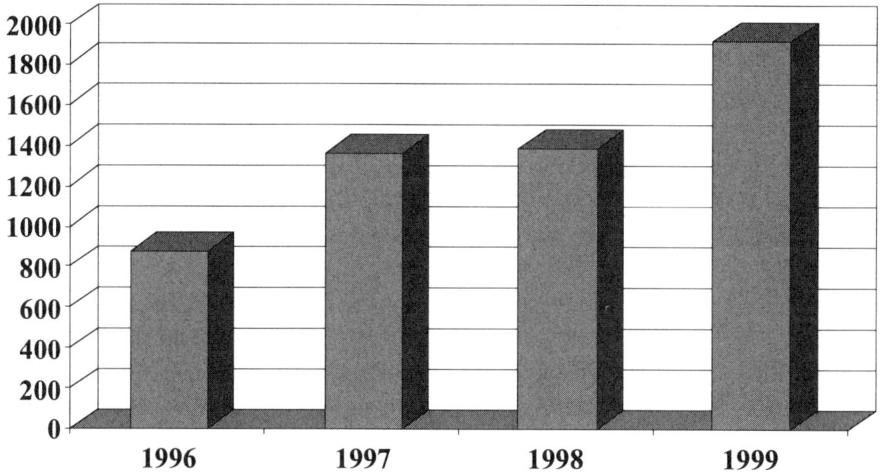

Figure 9.8 Methamphetamine clandestine lab seizures by the DEA between 1996 and 1998. Source: Office of National Drug Control Policy, May 2000.

of its effects, which are similar to those of cocaine, thereby creating significant profit margins for traffickers.

Recent statistics by the DEA illustrate a drastic and ongoing upsurge in illicit methamphetamine laboratories throughout the country (see Figure 9.8). Concern is so great that police investigators who once raided labs wearing street clothes are now wearing specially designed protective clothing and using oxygen tanks to breathe.

Clandestine labs constructed to make methamphetamine are often set up in houses, apartments, and motel rooms (see Figure 9.9). People who unknowingly come into contact with chemicals used to make the drug have become ill. Exposure can result in liver, lung, nerve, and kidney damage. Prolonged exposure can lead to cancer. Even months after a lab has been shut down, the chemical residue that has seeped into the carpet or wood can be dangerous.

Methamphetamine is commonly made from chemicals such as mercury chloride, hydrogen cyanide, and hydrochloric acid. The fumes are deadly and explosive. In one case, a DEA agent heading a task force in San Bernardino and Riverside Counties in California was not wearing protective gear during a 1984 raid and passed out after inhaling chemical fumes. The following month, tests showed that his liver was not functioning properly and that he had spots on his lungs. Officials suspected the damage was the result of the fumes he inhaled.

Methamphetamine, also called speed or crank, has now become one of the nation's primary drugs of choice among abusers. It is also becoming one of the nation's most dangerous drugs. In 1997, the DEA reported a 169%

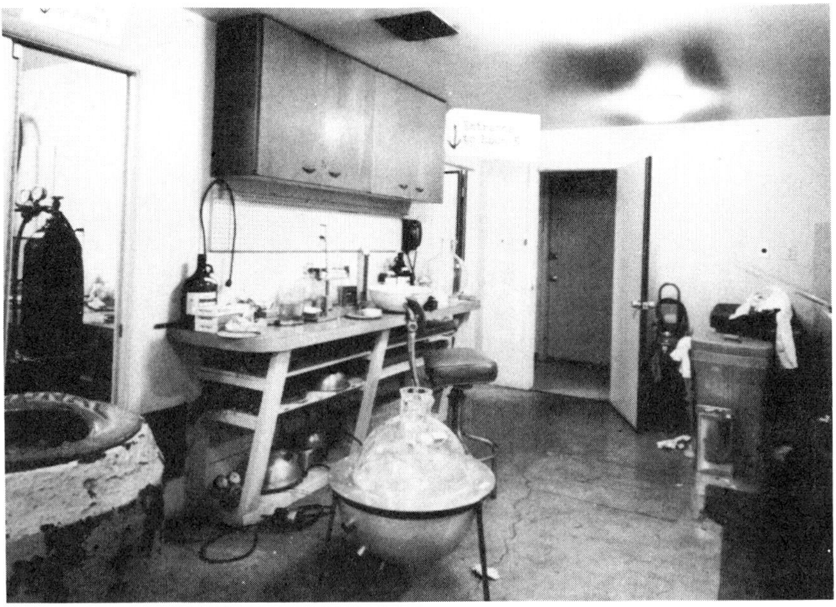

Figure 9.9 A seized illicit methamphetamine laboratory. (Photo courtesy of the U.S. Drug Enforcement Administration.)

increase in methamphetamine lab seizures, up from 327% in 1995 to 881% in 1996, and that figure represents only seizures by federal agents. In 1995, reports from a government survey revealed that the nation's medical examiners reported a 144% increase in methamphetamine-related deaths from 1992 to 1994. One of the reasons for meth's popularity is the widespread availability of the formula by which the drug is made, as well as the relative ease of making it. Today, almost anyone with a few beakers and some chemicals can make it.

In the 1960s, doctors in San Francisco began prescribing methamphetamine injections for treatment of heroin addiction. Widespread use by students and others followed, and while the drug became more tightly controlled, illegal meth labs began springing up around the country. San Francisco's Haight–Ashbury district became the heart of the worst abuse in the country toward the end of the 1960s. By the 1980s, methamphetamine was thought of as a cheap alternative to cocaine.

Methamphetamine is smoked, snorted, or injected mostly by white, 18- to 34-year-old, working-class abusers. Users crave the appetite suppression, euphoria, self-confidence, and burst of energy that the drug initially provides. To many, methamphetamine (also called "go-fast") is considered a better deal than cocaine; a gram costs $80 to $100 compared to $75 for the same amount of cocaine, but the high lasts almost five times longer. As meth users develop a tolerance for the drug, depression and then intense paranoia replace euphoria.

This is often made worse by the insomnia that soon sets in. In time, users become nervous and agitated, a condition known as "tweaking," and they become prone to violence.

In the United States, meth use occurs across the country. One of the hardest hit regions is California, where 799 meth labs were seized in 1996. While popular on both coasts, the drug has permeated mid-America as well. In Iowa, meth accounted for 47% of drug arrests in 1995, compared with less than 5% five years earlier. In February 1997, Nebraska authorities seized 34 pounds of the drug, worth an estimated $1.5 million. Furthermore, the DEA reports that meth arrests in a five-state area in the Midwest soared from 47 to 424% between 1992 and 1996. In 1996, DEA seized 303 meth labs in the Midwest compared with 187 only 4 years earlier. The bulk of them (250) were in Missouri.

Police files are filled with horror stories of meth labs that have exploded, severely injuring or even killing the meth "cooks." Many such labs could be characterized as "mom and pop" operations — modern-day versions of the moonshine still. The drug can be made with a skillet and stove, in a bathtub or even in a car trunk with a plastic drinking cup. Moreover, the formula is readily available in the public library and on the Internet. Compounding the problem is the fact that methamphetamine is profitable. A $1,000 investment can easily reap a $20,000 tax-free, cash return.

Investigation Techniques

Investigating a clandestine lab is especially dangerous for police because of the explosive, corrosive, and hazardous materials usually associated with the drug manufacturing process and because many labs are fortified with deadly booby traps. In many cases, even a slight spark can create a chain reaction resulting in a massive explosion of the laboratory. Agents have fainted from fumes emitted from the laboratories. Because of this, investigators who raid the labs now wear protective plastic jumpsuits, rubber gloves, respirators, and air tanks. Portable showers in vans are sometimes used to allow agents to wash off contaminants.

Not only do criminal drug lab operators mix deadly toxic chemicals, but they also have been found to dump toxic waste down bathroom drains or in holes dug in the ground. These actions make some lab locations akin to hazardous waste sites.

Clandestine laboratories are often operated by nonprofessional individuals with limited knowledge of chemistry. Some labs are run by people who have learned various processing techniques through their peers in the criminal underworld. The methamphetamine market, for example, was dominated for many years by the Pagans motorcycle club. The skills utilized in drug processing and the safety procedures used by a group like the Pagans are highly suspect.

The strongest weapon in fighting illicit laboratories is sound criminal intelligence. This can be acquired from other law enforcement agencies, informants, or surveillance activities. Before moving against a laboratory, investigating officers should learn:

1. Number of inhabitants of the lab
2. Identities of inhabitants
   a. Names and other personal identifiers
   b. Criminal histories
3. Any weapons located in the residence
4. Information on guard dogs, booby traps, and any exterior fortification
5. The progression of the cooking process (is there any finished product available for seizure?)

Additional intelligence can sometimes be acquired through a close working relationship with the chemical and laboratory equipment suppliers. Although some of these manufacturers may be involved with criminals, those who are not can be valuable sources of intelligence. Employees of these companies should watch for customers who:

1. Use names of unknown companies for orders
2. Pay cash for items purchased
3. Order unusually large amounts of chemicals commonly used in laboratory operations
4. Request shipments of chemicals or equipment sent to residences or post office box numbers
5. Phone in orders representing themselves as employees of companies

In some cases, law enforcement agencies have attempted to establish chemical "store-fronts," which are "sting" type operations consisting of undercover agents operating a contrived chemical distribution company. Officers provide needed chemicals to suspected lab operators and follow the suspects to their destination. Subsequent surveillance results in acquiring search warrants and raiding the location of the suspected lab. Although generally considered a successful strategy, problems are created when officers fail to maintain surveillance and thereby lose track of the perpetrators, who have possession of valuable chemicals.

The presence of illicit laboratories may be detected by an abundance of methamphetamine or PCP in the area at an unusually low price, indicating a fresh "cook-off." If a laboratory is suspected in an area, the following points should be considered:

1. A check with local utility companies may show an excessive use of electricity or water.
2. Postal officials may render information regarding residents' receiving mail at the suspected address, including any large deliveries.
3. Once identified, all of the residents' criminal backgrounds must be checked to determine previous involvement in drug violations. This information can be used later in establishing probable cause for a search warrant.
4. When the suspected residence is under surveillance, officers should look for ventilation systems such as window fans.
5. Investigators should be aware of any unusual odors in the area that might indicate the presence of an operating laboratory.
6. A trashing of the suspects' residence should be considered if the location provides an opportunity (see Chapter 1).
7. A list of the suspects' long-distance telephone tolls (a subpoena will be required) will provide a readout of all direct-dial long-distance calls made from the residence, thereby identifying possible associates or chemical supply companies used.

Controlling Precursor Chemicals

Legally obtained substances known as precursors are typically used by illicit lab operators to make their final product. Essential chemicals called solvents are also needed to produce the final drug product but they do not become part of the drug. In 1988, the Chemical Diversion and Trafficking Act was passed, requiring detailed record keeping and reporting of all purchases over a designated quantity of each chemical and reporting of all suspicious purchases to the DEA. In turn, the DEA has power to deny the sale of chemicals to any person or company it deems likely to use them for the making of an illegal drug.

In addition to the federal government, the Bureau of Justice Statistics reports that 37 state governments have passed legislation regulating the sale of precursor chemicals. Several require companies that manufacture these chemicals to obtain licenses from a state agency and to maintain records that are regularly supplied to that agency. Essentially, the controlling of precursors is yet another way in which manufacturers of illicit drugs can be identified for arrest or possibly deterred from drug trafficking activity.

Chemicals Found in Laboratories

Officers need to be aware of three distinct categories of chemicals found in illicit laboratories: precursors, reagents, and solvents.

Precursors

Precursors are raw materials used for manufacturing a controlled substance, and which later become part of the finished product. The law requires that these chemicals be reported when anyone sells, transfers, or furnishes them.

Reagents

Reagents chemically react with one or more precursors, but are not part of the finished product.

Solvents

Solvents do not react chemically with precursors or reagents, but become part of the finished product. These are used to dissolve solid precursors or reagents and to purify other chemicals. Solvents are explosive and should be considered extremely volatile and dangerous.

Hazardous Chemicals

Most laboratories will contain extremely volatile chemicals. Officers should be familiar with hazardous compounds.

Ether

Ether is a common ingredient used by lab operators. It is an extremely flammable liquid that tends to form explosive peroxides when evaporated to dryness. Empty or near-empty cans of ether should be handled with extreme care.

Mercuric Chloride (Bromide)

Mercuric halogen compounds are extremely violent poisons. Officers should avoid breathing the dust from these chemicals.

Lithium Aluminum Hydride

Lithium aluminum hydride (LAH) is commonly used in the manufacture of methamphetamine and amphetamine. It is a highly unstable compound that reacts violently to moisture or heat. *Keep moisture away from this reagent!* A chemical called Vitride has, in some instances, replaced LAH, and it should be handled with the same precautions.

Sodium or Potassium Cyanide

Sodium is a soft, shiny metal becomes dull gray when exposed to air. Sodium also reacts explosively with water. It should be stored in liquids containing no oxygen, such as kerosene.

Summary

This chapter deals with special enforcement problems encountered by the drug investigator. While no investigator can be completely prepared for all circumstances he or she will encounter on the street, it helps to have some basic exposure to many of the most common problems.

First, we discuss marijuana cultivation indoor and outdoor. Investigators must have a good grasp of the various hazards and types of evidence involved with this complex type of investigation. Next, smuggling operations are discussed. Drug smugglers know no boundaries and may be operating in your jurisdiction. This section informs you what to look for.

Next, pharmaceutical diversion is discussed. This section tells how pharmaceutical drugs end up on the street and who is typically responsible. Understanding how the drugs get there will help you in this unusual genre of drug investigation.

Finally, the clandestine laboratory investigation is examined. Investigating the illegal drug labs requires considerable expertise and caution. Such laboratories often explode during seizure so investigators must exercise considerable caution. Additionally, handling the hardware (glassware, chemicals, etc.) required to operate many of these labs requires considerable training. All such materials are evidence and require special training for their handling.

Suggested Readings

Inciardi, J. A., Lockwood, D., and Pottinger, A. E., *Women and Crack Cocaine*. McMillan Publishers, New York, 1993.

Gugliotta, G. and Leen, J., *Kings of Cocaine*. Simon and Schuster, New York, 1989.

Shannon, E., *Desperados*. Viking Press, New York, 1988.

Drug Raids

10

While working undercover and making arrests represent two very hazardous duties of undercover officers, it is the drug raid that poses imminent danger. Drug investigators have been shot and killed during drug raids where planning was insufficient. Tactical precision, timing, and accurate intelligence information all come into play at the time of the drug raid, for if there is a time when the stakes are highest, it is now!

The Laboratory Raid

Laboratory raids usually require a search warrant; probable cause will be established through surveillance, informant information, or other information accumulated during the investigation. Because large quantities of ether and other volatile and corrosive chemicals are normally used in laboratory setups, standard raid procedures must be followed to minimize casualties, and should be coordinated with both the prosecutor and the police chemist experienced in dealing with clandestine laboratories.

Caution should always be practiced in lab raids. Carelessness during the raid and search could result in a fire or explosion, resulting in personal injury, death, and/or destruction of evidence. During the search, the equipment and chemicals (primary and secondary precursors) to be seized should be pointed out to officers by the police chemist. In addition, officers should search for finished product (e.g., methamphetamine powder or PCP liquid). These items, along with formulas and any in-process material, will be used as evidence. At the conclusion of the raid, all items seized must be inventoried.

Precautions for the Raid

The following precautions are recommended during laboratory raids:

1. The fire department should be placed on stand-by alert.
2. A chemist should accompany officers during the raid.
3. There must be no smoking in or near the laboratory site.
4. No combustible items, such as flashbulbs, should be used on the lab site.

5. Neighborhood or area evacuation plans should be prearranged if needed.
6. Gas masks should be available for assault and search team officers.

All officers, chemists, or other personnel working in the laboratory should wear safety glasses and protective clothing. When spills do occur, a convenient, commercial available method of cleanup is chemical absorbent pillows. Another method is to throw sand or baking soda on the spill, creating a mixture that can then be scooped into a bucket for disposal.

Other dangerous chemicals found in the lab are concentrated inorganic acids such as hydrochloric, sulfuric, and nitric acids. Any skin contact with these chemicals will result in burns; inhalation of their toxic vapors will cause irritations of the mucus membranes and respiratory tract. The chemicals are, however, water soluble and can be washed away with large amounts of water, followed by the application of baking soda to the burned area to neutralize the action of the acid.

Packaging Laboratory Evidence

If an informer is not available to furnish information about the progress of production in the laboratory, officers may have difficulty determining whether any finished product is present to be seized as evidence. In this case, the investigators should consider filing conspiracy charges against suspects involved in the laboratory.

Much care must be taken in packaging and transportation of materials, mixtures, and chemicals seized during the lab raid. Reaction mixtures should be placed in sturdy, leak-proof containers. Highly volatile chemicals should be placed in nonglass containers because the pressure buildup in glass containers could create a safety problem. Strong acids, such as sulfuric acid and hydrochloric acid, should never be placed in the same containers with strong bases such as sodium hydroxide (lye) methylamine.

The Crack House Problem

With the crack cocaine boom of the late 1980s came the popularity of "crack house" operations. The crack house is a residence where crack dealings take place in volume, and because of the way in which it is managed, many unique investigative and tactical problems arise.

The crack house is a retail outlet for rock cocaine sales (Figure 10.1). There is usually only a small amount of drugs present at the location and they can easily be destroyed in the event of a raid by police. The amount of drugs on hand is usually limited to 50–100 rocks, selling from $10 to $50

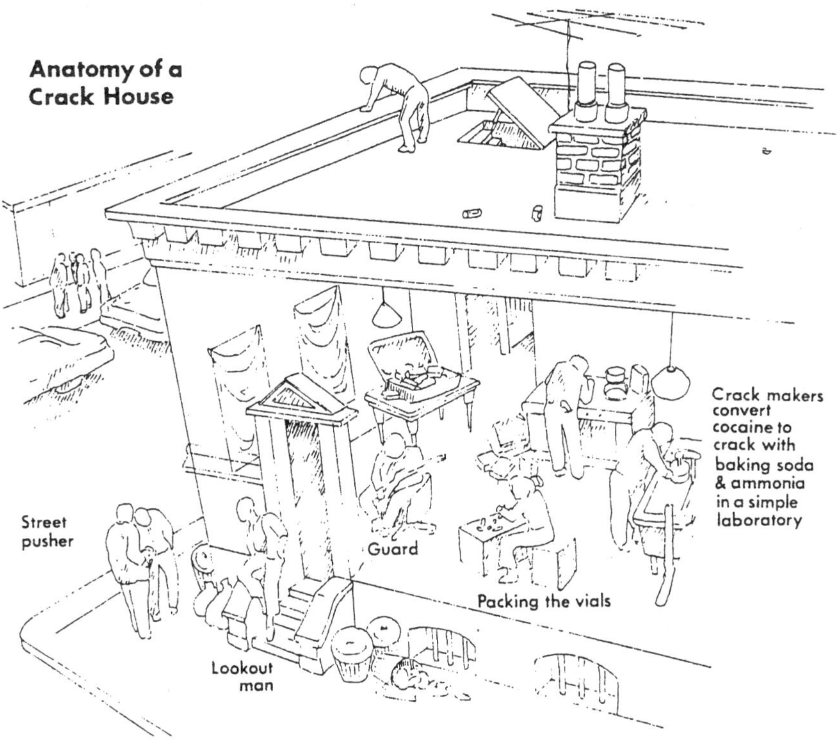

Figure 10.1 Anatomy of a crack house.

each. As buyers deplete the on-hand stock, it is rapidly replenished. The house is commonly fortified with steel bars on the windows, steel doors and door jams, 3–4 foot iron posts around the front door to stop ramming vehicles, and in many cases an entry "buffer" to delay entry by police officers attempting to serve search warrants. This gives the dealers time to dispose of the drug evidence by flushing or hiding it before police have a chance to seize any evidence.

In many cases the crack house is a residential house or apartment, but in some cases private clubs are used as fronts for crack distribution. In recent cases, otherwise law-abiding citizens have been approached by crack dealers offering a percentage of drug profits in exchange for letting their houses be used as a base for drug deals. In other cases vacant houses are commandeered by enterprising dealers looking for low-cost retail outlets for their drugs. In most cases, however, there are usually three to four persons present at the location to distribute the drugs, to maintain records of drug sales, and to safeguard money.

It should be understood that even though they are relatively easy targets, it is probably fruitless to concentrate on only crack "street dealers," because crack dealers are many in number and generally are replaced quickly after being arrested or removed from the operation. It is therefore essential for law enforcement officers to target those who are responsible for establishing and financing the crack house itself.

It is common for a crack house operator to control several houses at once and keep couriers busy by dropping off crack and picking up money during the day. Operations such as this create large distribution networks with many members (called "cells"), and due to the volume of sales at crack houses, profits are great and may easily range from $10,000 to $20,000 per house daily.

Although law enforcement agencies use many methods to deal with this problem, it is typical for the crack house, once raided, to be back in business in a short time. Because arresting crack house operators usually is not sufficient, additional incentives are offered to crack dealers to leave the area. This is where useful forfeiture sanctions under state and federal laws are beneficial.

Enforcement initiatives include the use of undercover drug buyers to verify the presence of drugs at the house, and the subsequent use of search warrants for raiding the location. Forced entry into the residence is a common tactical problem for police. Typical devices used in forced entry include battering rams, sledgehammers, or other similar devices for entry through doors and windows, as well as armored vehicles or even tractors to enter through doors or walls.

Short of initiating a full-scale investigation, the local police department can implement several preventive-policing strategies that may prove effective in deterring crack dealers in a given neighborhood. The patrol division can consider using the following initiatives:

1. Implement higher visibility patrol policy in the affected neighborhood.
2. Individuals suspected of criminal activity in the vicinity of the crack house should be stopped and questioned (using field interview techniques) by patrol officers.
3. If the crack house is rental property, the lawful owner should be contacted by investigators and advised that continued criminal activity will result in the property being seized by police.
4. If the crack house is located in an abandoned house, the local Public Works Department and/or the Fire Marshal's Office can cite the lawful owner for the code violations, which could include abandoned, unoccupied, structurally unsound, or dangerous premises. Such violations could result in fines as high as $1200 in some cases.

5. If the crack house is located in a restaurant or liquor-serving establishment, the Health Department can conduct code inspections 24 hours a day (in most jurisdictions).

The methods of control discussed above are nontraditional ways to attack the crack house problem. Such methods are only minimally effective with large crack operations, in which the loss of one or two houses is only a temporary inconvenience for the dealers. Again, this illustrates the necessity for attacking the operators of the crack house rather than just the street dealers.

Controlling the crack house requires cooperative law enforcement efforts among several divisions within the police department, including the drug enforcement unit, the patrol division, the street gang unit (if applicable), and the tactical division. Additionally, as with most other areas of drug enforcement, police agencies should properly communicate with one another by sharing intelligence information on crack house locations and their operators.

Booby Traps

Complicating enforcement efforts in marijuana eradication operations, raids on clandestine laboratories, and numerous other drug enforcement operations is the risk of encountering deadly booby traps. Indeed, booby traps are becoming an ever-increasing hazard for drug agents. Like technology in drug manufacturing, knowledge of how to manufacture new and ingenious traps is also spreading among traffickers. Much of this knowledge was originally acquired in Vietnam, where traps of this nature were common.

Traffickers plant booby traps in and around their operations because (a) the parts for the traps cost virtually nothing, and (b) the effectiveness of the devices is substantial. Traffickers use booby traps for three basic reasons:

1. To warn suspects of intruders (by the sound of explosions or by floodlights)
2. To deny intruders (police) access to the inhabited area by injuring or killing them
3. To slow down police pursuit during a raid by injuring or killing officers

When considering a laboratory raid, officers must realize that in the event that even one officer is injured, a minimum of one additional officer will most likely be needed to render assistance. If there is already a shortage of officers in the assault, the raid team will be even more undermanned and that much more vulnerable to attack. Therefore, just as a police chemist is recommended for the raid of a clandestine laboratory, officers who suspect booby traps should be accompanied by a qualified emergency ordinance disposal (EOD) specialist to help identify traps or bombs and otherwise assist the officers in the drug raid. In the absence of an EOD expert, however, officers should be aware of the clues that might indicate booby traps have been used:

1. Handbooks in the residence that give instructions on how to assemble traps: *The Anarchist's Cookbook,* by William Powell; *The Poor Man's James Bond,* by Kurt Saxon; *The OSS Special Weapons Devices and Equipment*, published by Paladin Press. These publications are manuals for bomb and booby-trap assembly; if the books are present, officers should assume that booby traps will also be present.
2. If the profile of any suspect includes either a criminal history involving prosecution for weapons offenses or past military services in Vietnam, booby traps should be expected.

Most booby traps fall into two categories: explosive and impaling. They can be activated by remote control, manual control, or by the victim (usually via trip wire). They may be located either outside or inside a structure. Traps may be used to scare the intruder, or to injure or kill. In all cases, however, they are to be considered extremely hazardous to investigating officers.

Officers who are not trained in dismantling or disarming bombs or booby traps should *not* attempt to disarm the devices. They should, however, be capable of identifying them. Normally, the trap will be located along an entrance to a location (a doorway, entry path, or stairway). It would therefore be advisable for officers to approach the target area off the main path, with a lead man looking for hard-to-spot signs of traps (such as trip wires) by using a probing rod, or a belt or strip of cloth dangling from a stick.

The types of traps officers may encounter will depend on only the perpetrators' imagination and cunning. Officers should always remember the cardinal rule, "Notice the unobvious and expect the unexpected."

Exterior Booby Traps

Regardless of the specific rank or assigned duties of each officer on the raid team, all officers should look out for the obvious or telltale signs of booby traps in the area and be aware that they could be installed anywhere. This is a difficult task, as traffickers usually succeed in hiding traps. Investigators should be alert for seemingly insignificant signs that might indicate the existence of a trap.

Officers should look for booby traps in the following areas:

1. Any cleared trail or pathway
2. Near any object that arouses curiosity (e.g., a dead animal used as a decoy for intruder observation)
3. Along escape routes
4. Affixed to any innocent looking, movable objects, such as doors, windows, and gates

The following signs may indicate the presence of traps:

1. Any disturbance in the terrain that looks unusual (like a cover-up)
2. Dead leaves in one area, surrounded by green leaves or any vegetation in a pile, which does not fit the area (possibly a punji-pit cover)
3. Any depressions in the soil caused by settling of the earth (possibly covering up a pit)
4. Any wires strung across walkways (possibly linked to explosive devices)
5. Items such as ropes, nails, or other fasteners that serve no obvious purpose (possibly used to activate explosive devices or anchor tripwires)

When a booby trap is encountered, officers should immediately notify fellow officers either vocally or via radio, and then identify it with a noticeable marker (e.g., an orange ribbon) to alert other officers entering or leaving the area. Again, nonspecialist officers should refrain from attempting to disarm booby traps and should simply bypass the area.

Safety Precautions

An explosives expert is recommended for each raid where traps are anticipated, and certain precautions should be practiced:

1. Only one officer should approach a trap. Other officers should be in nearby covered positions.
2. When a trip-wire is located, *both* ends of the wire should be checked.
3. All devices should be checked for more than one trip wire.
4. Trip wires should be cut only after any safeties are replaced.
5. Electric-looking wires should *not* be cut.
6. If twisted-type wires are present, only one wire at a time should be cut.
7. A mercury fuse may also be present in a device that has an obvious means of detonation (e.g., conspicuous fuse).
8. Before wires are traced, all suspect devices should be checked for a human operator, who might attempt to detonate the device from a hand-held controller.

9. If a suspect is apprehended in a raid, he or she should then be required to lead the search team through the site.
10. All officers in the raid team should move in pairs. In addition to having two sets of eyes on the alert, it also enables each officer to have first aid nearby in case of a casualty.
11. If one team member is injured as result of a trap, remaining officers must approach the injured officer with caution so that no additional injuries will result.

Types of Traps

The Punji Pit. A standard in guerilla warfare, the punji pit (Figure 10.2) was widely used in World War II and in Vietnam. The punji pit is a large, deep hole in the ground containing many bamboo spikes or rusty nails, which are coated commonly with feces, urine, antifreeze, and other substances designed to promote infection and cause discomfort for the victim. The punji pit is difficult to spot because it is covered with leaves and small tree branches. The intruder steps on the covering and his or her body weight breaks the branches, dumping the victim into the pit. Investigators should look for leaves and branches that are obviously not part of the surrounding greenery, or for anything in the road that does not seem to fit in the environment. Sometimes dead animals are nailed to or hung from trees to distract the intruder, or to lure him or her to the trap.

The Foot Breaker. This device can be manufactured by the perpetrator or purchased through mail order survivalist-type magazines. It consists of a metal pipe which is used to house a .22 or .25 caliber bullet. The bullet is placed inside with a spring-loaded firing pin at the base of the pipe. The pipe is then anchored in the ground (Figure 10.3). When it is stepped on, the weight of the victim activates the firing pin and shoots the bullet into the victim's foot. Although this device is not designed to kill the intruder, it will wound sufficiently to remove the officer from the assault team. Officers who wear boots with steel-shank soles may find these are sufficient to stop the bullet. This trap is difficult to detect, and it will most likely be located on the entry path to the target area.

The Trotline. This trap is inexpensive, easy to manufacture, and extremely effective. The trap consists of a monofilament fishing line strung between two trees at eye level. Anchored on the line are numerous fishing hooks, which injure the intruder. This trap is almost impossible to see, even under the best of lighting conditions. As with many of the other types of traps, it is not designed to kill, only to maim (Figures 10.4, 10.5).

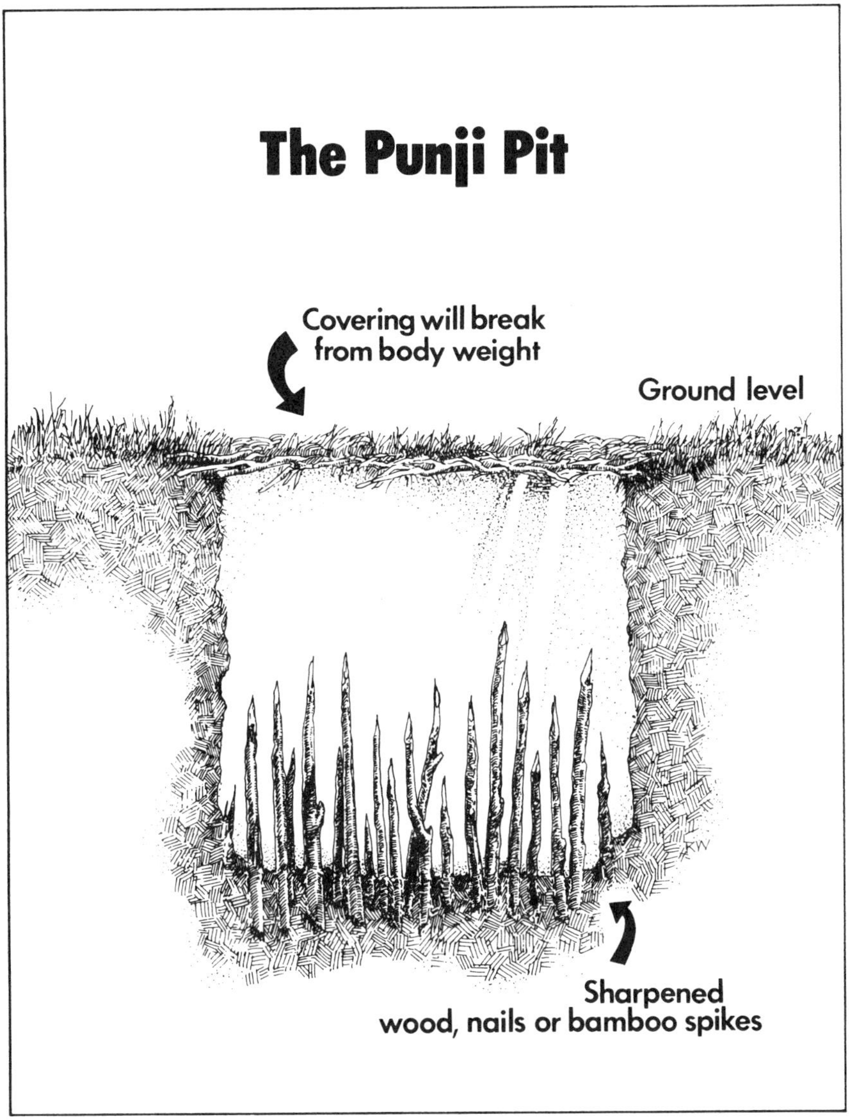

Figure 10.2 The punji pit.

The Mousetrap. The mousetrap is designed to kill and maim. It consists of a standard mousetrap, which is used as a firing pin for a shotgun shell that is attached to the trap. A trip wire activates the catch on the mousetrap, thereby detonating the shotgun shell. These traps are commonly attached to trees at both knee and head levels. Although the trap is usually fatal, sometimes it is used merely to warn suspects of intruders.

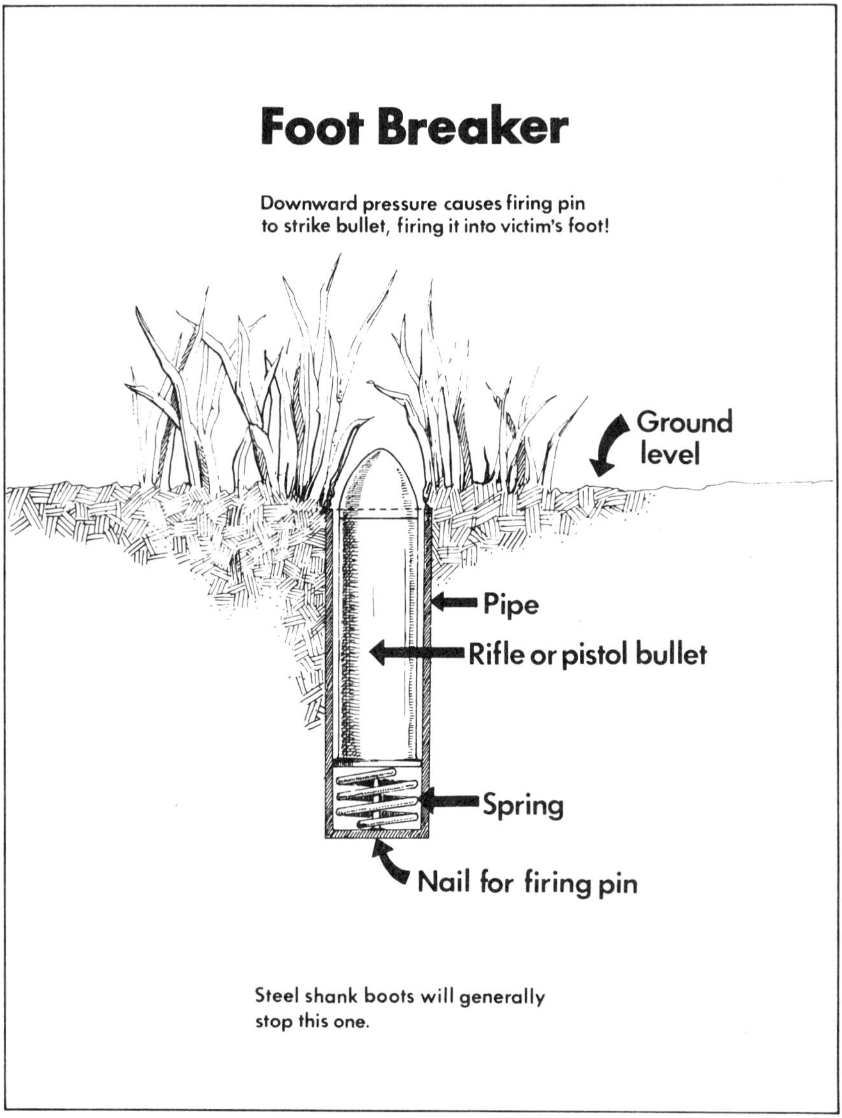

Figure 10.3 The foot breaker trap.

Interior Booby Traps

Once the outer perimeter has been cleared, the danger of encountering a trap is not yet over. Interior traps may be even more dangerous because they are usually contained in or wired to an object that appears to be perfectly normal; a lamp, a book, a door. All raid team members must practice caution at all times.

Figure 10.4 The trot line.

Trip-wires, electrical switches, or remote control can activate indoor traps. Typical indoor locations for traps are doors and windows, stairs and floorboards (pressure-type devices), gates, books or x-rated magazine (spring-release devices), refrigerators, drawers, packages, or furniture (pressure-type devices).

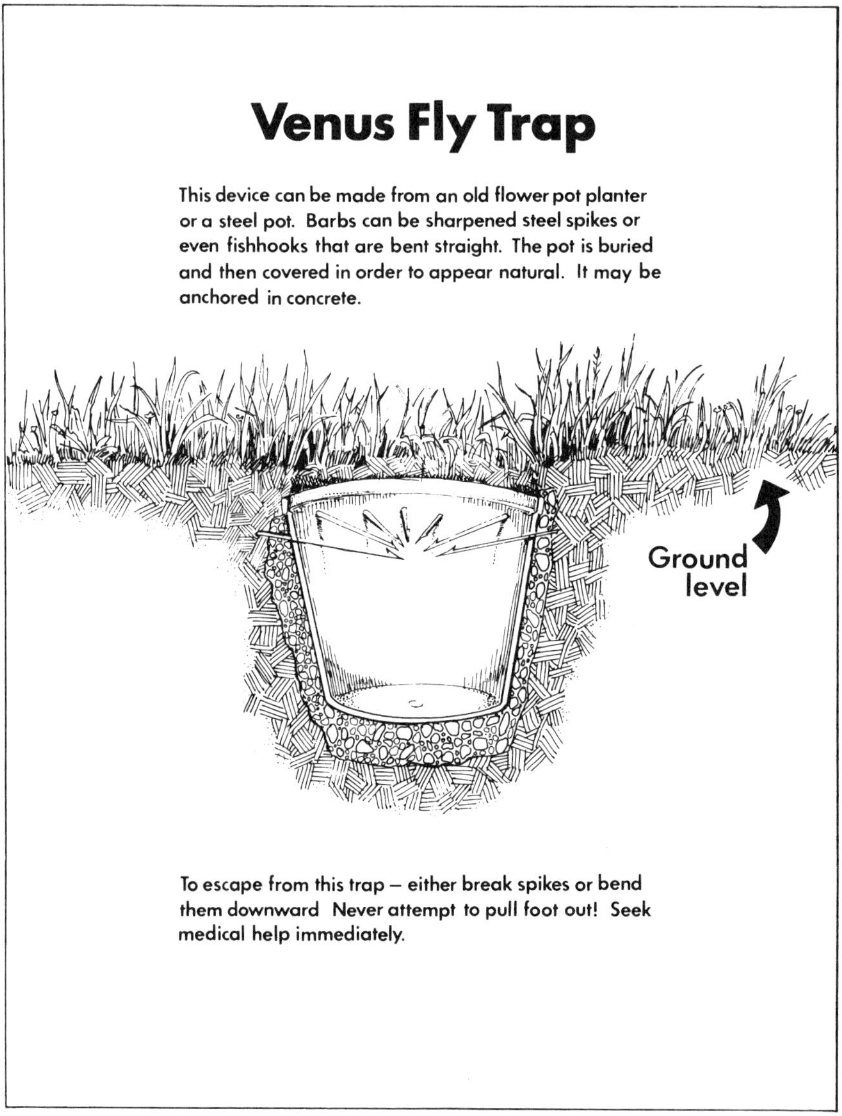

Figure 10.5 The venus fly trap.

Safety Precautions

As with outdoor traps, an explosives expert should be present. Other officers should observe the following precautions:

1. Do not attempt to open books or magazines.
2. No containers should be opened without a thorough examination.

3. Furniture should be closely examined.
4. Electrical switches should not be used if possible.
5. Officers should not consume food or beverages while at the raid site.
6. Anything that appears unusual should be regarded as suspect, and treated as such.
7. Booby traps that are located should be treated the same as outdoor traps: marked and avoided.

No single strategy can completely safeguard law enforcement officers in all raids in which booby traps are in place. Each raid is different and should be evaluated on an individual basis, with consideration given to the type of case, the number of possible suspects (and their backgrounds), and the location of the raid.

Types of Traps

Magazine Bomb. This device is a magazine that has had a portion of the inner pages removed so that a mousetrap will fit inside unobtrusively. The mousetrap is affixed to a blasting cap, which will detonate when the magazine is opened. X-rated magazines are normally used to lure the victim. Magazine bombs can cause injury to the face, loss of fingers, or even death.

Hot Light. This is an incendiary device consisting of a standard light bulb that has been filled with a combustible liquid such as ether, kerosene, or gasoline. When the light switch is turned on the device detonates, creating an explosion, and possibly igniting the victim's clothing. Variations of this trap include trap hand grenades that have been affixed to light sockets in place of light bulbs.

Armstrong's Mixture. Armstrong's mixture is a fairly new device, usually found in methamphetamine laboratories operated by outlaw motorcycle gangs. The device is made from a mixture of red phosphorous and potassium chlorate. After the chemicals are mixed together and rolled up in an aluminum foil ball, they are immersed in alcohol to render the material harmless. When the alcohol dries, the chemicals become volatile.

The devices are designed to look like packages of drugs wrapped in foil. When an officer attempts to open the package to check its contents, the tin foil activates the chemicals by rubbing against them, thereby triggering an explosion. The balls usually come in three sizes, and the extent of the injury will depend on the size of the ball: (a) marble-sized: loss of fingers or eyesight, facial damage; (b) egg-sized: loss of hand or part of arm, loss of eyesight, facial damage, possible fatality; (c) baseball-sized: always fatal (Figures 10.6, 10.7).

Figure 10.6 The flash fire bomb.

Other Weapons

Whether engaged in the search of a car or residence, the investigators should be aware of weapons other than traditional firearms (handguns, shotguns, rifles) that are commonly used by drug traffickers and may be cleverly hidden or otherwise unnoticed. One such weapon is the "bolt gun." This device appears to be an ordinary bolt and might even be used as an ordinary bolt in a motorcycle, car, or truck. The weapon is made from a standard ⅝"

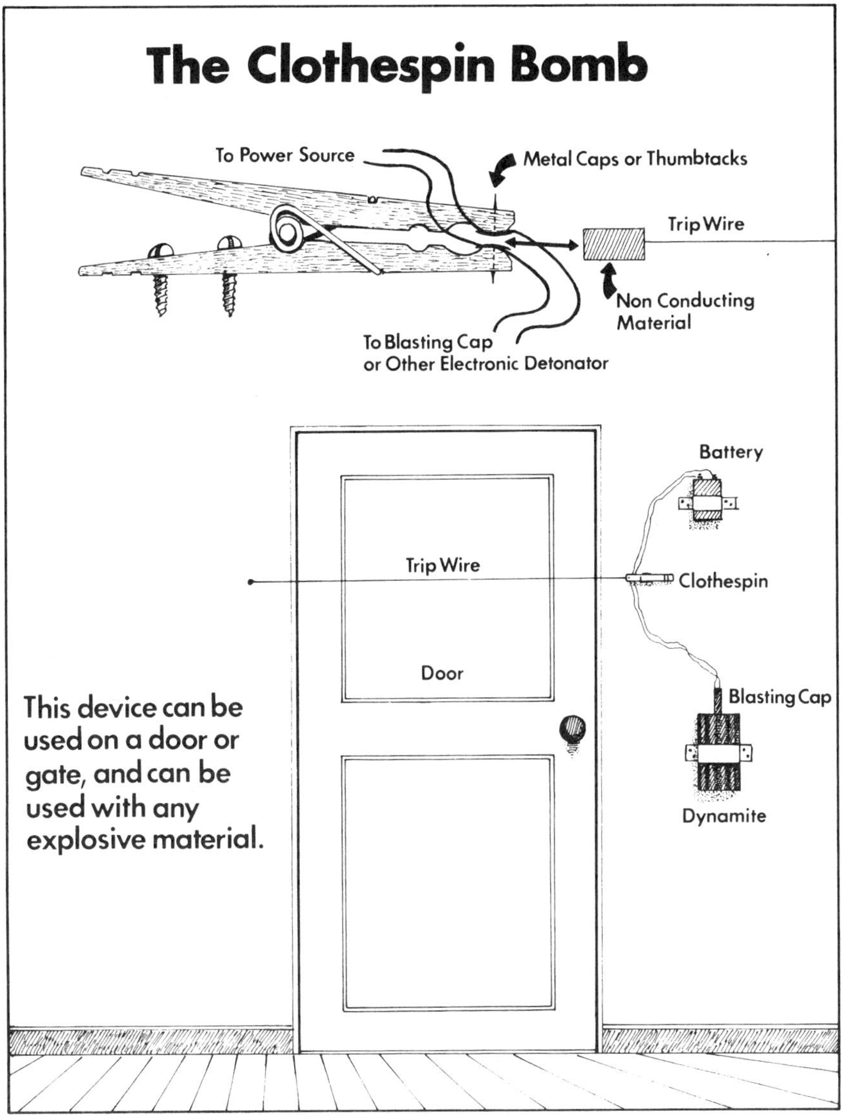

Figure 10.7 The clothespin bomb.

diameter (4½" long) machine bolt that is hollowed out to fire a .22 caliber long rifle or standard cartridge. To discharge the weapon, the hexagonal head is pulled back, and a spring-loaded firing pin comes into contact with the cartridge (Figure 10.8).

Knives can also be concealed in belts, gas tank caps, pens, and rulers. The officer should always remain cognizant of such devices when approaching suspects or their residences.

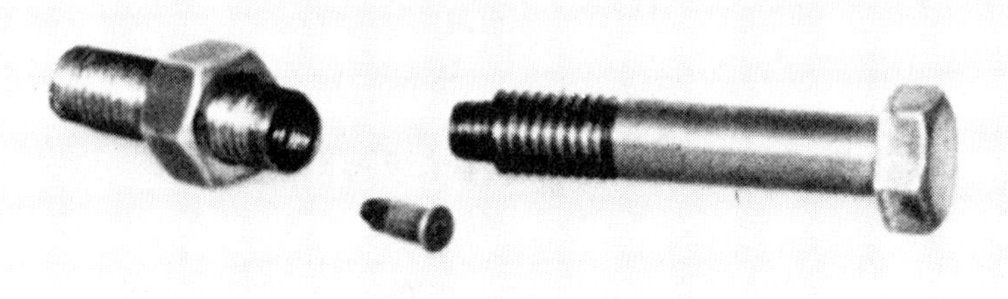

Figure 10.8 A bolt made into a gun that shoots a single small caliber bullet and is difficult to detect. (Photo courtesy of the U.S. Marshal Service.)

Drug Raid Procedures

Raids are some of the most life-threatening situations encountered by law enforcement officers. Because they are used so frequently in drug enforcement, it is essential that all drug enforcement personnel be aware of the procedures for planning and conducting a raid in order to minimize casualties and confusion. It is impossible to discuss every possible raid situation and how properly to plan for all unexpected predicaments. All raids hold surprises. But to best avoid unforeseen dangers, the drug agents' best weapon is quality intelligence. Good intelligence can reveal much-needed information about the circumstances officers will encounter: weapons or booby traps inside the residence; associates who might be present at the time of the raid; booby traps in or fortification of the residence; whether stolen goods are expected to be at the raid location. Raid planners must always prepare for the worst. When considering a drug raid, "Murphy's Law" should be remembered: "If anything can go wrong, it will!"

It is important to know the type and amount of drug being sought in the raid. This could make a difference in how the house is entered. If there is a suspected 100 pounds of marijuana in the residence it is unlikely that suspects will be able to dispose of if prior to entry by officers. If, however, there is one pound of cocaine suspected in the residence, then it is likely that it could be flushed or otherwise destroyed prior to entry; in this case, a "no-knock" warrant should be obtained.

In addition to the risk of encountering armed suspects during a raid, there is also the danger that officers may accidentally shoot each other in a crossfire situation, or through mistaken identity. This has happened on numerous occasions, and the possibility increases when all members of the raid team are not thoroughly acquainted with each other and with the raid plan. When casualties occur in raids, it is usually not as a result of poor planning but *over*planning. Raid plans should not be so complex as to create confusion and misunderstanding among officers. As most experienced officers will attest, there are enough unforeseen surprises in each raid without having an overly complex plan. The key to success with raids is simplicity.

Checklist for Raid Preparation

Although there are many considerations for the planning of a raid, basic planning should include the following:

1. Collect all intelligence regarding the suspects, associates, the structure to be raided, and the neighborhood (area) to be raided.
2. A thorough reconnaissance of the area should be conducted to identify all entrance and exit routes as well as any one-way or dead-end streets.
3. A sketch, drawing, or map should be made available to show team members where they are expected to be.
4. Organization of the raid team should be evaluated where the number of personnel and type of equipment needed are to be considered.
5. Communications are essential during a raid, in particular when multiple agencies are participating. Because most law enforcement agencies use different frequencies, a team leader from the host agency should be assigned to each team with reliable communications for unit to unit and unit to base.
6. Arrangements must be made for emergency response personnel, including SWAT officers, and fire and ambulance personnel.
7. If needed, a police chemist should be available to assist in the search and dismantling of any chemical laboratories.
8. The time of raid execution must be established. In addition, a briefing should be established at least one hour prior to the designated time of the raid.
9. A chain of command must be established and understood by all members.

The Raid Leader

The team leader is responsible for coordinating all aspects of the raid and should have sufficient authority within the unit to make field command decisions when necessary. Initially, all plans for manpower, equipment, and communications must be understood; the time to recognize deficiencies in planning is before the raid, not during it. Additional considerations such as food, water, and first aid must also be accounted for in the event of an extended operation, as should plans for the proper evacuation of neighbors in the area in the event of a possible shooting situation or explosive laboratory. The team leader has the responsibility of selecting team members for various tasks during the raid. These members must possess the necessary physical abilities, skills, and knowledge to conduct such an operation, and all team members must be properly outfitted with equipment (raid jackets, body armor, radios, shotguns/rifles, etc.) and have sufficient knowledge of the investigation, including information on suspects, weapons, vehicles, etc.

As it is common for multiple law enforcement agencies to participate in drug raids, the team leader must be sure every officer is familiar with the other officers involved in the raid (especially when undercover people are used). This is usually accomplished during the briefing where all parties are present. Second, raid/search teams must be established if there is more than one residence to raid. The teams will usually consist of five to seven officers. Again, the team leader for each team should be a member of the host agency for the raid and should possess communications between other team members.

To properly prepare a team for the raid, the following checklist should be considered:

1. Communications
   a. Electronic: radios (encoded), battery-powered headsets, flashlights
   b. Other: flares, whistles, vocal or hand signals
2. Equipment
   a. Weapons
   b. Uniforms (i.e., raid jackets)
   c. Camouflage
   d. Specialized equipment: night vision devices, bolt cutters, etc.
   e. Food and water
   f. Contingency plan for a shooting situation
   g. Prisoner transportation plan
   h. Transportation for team members
3. Investigative considerations
   a. Searching techniques
   b. Search warrant execution
   c. Arrangements for prisoner interviews
   d. Processing crime scene and prisoners: sketches and photographs
   e. Arrangements for proper press release
4. Search team members
   a. Recording officer (the search unit)
   b. Evidence-seizing officer (the search unit)
   c. Prisoner control officer (optional)

Tactical Considerations

Because many raid situations do not offer the luxury of a trained SWAT (special weapons and tactics) team, raid team members must be knowledgeable about basic assault tactics. The tactics discussed here are general and should be considered for each raid situation on an individual basis.

Raids will be conducted in both urban and rural environments, so the individual raid plan will vary in each case. For example, a raid in a rural area, such as a cultivated marijuana patch or illegal laboratory, may present different dangers than if it were conducted in the city. This is true because of the lack of sufficient cover for officers involved in the initial assault, as well as the possibility of hidden booby traps and snipers located in wooded areas of the property. For this reason, a raid conducted on a structure suspected of containing booby traps should be conducted in three phases: (a) the securing of suspects, (b) a sweep by an EOD expert for hidden booby traps to remove hazards, and (c) the search of the residence for contraband (if authorized by a search warrant).

All suspects must be controlled immediately upon the assault of the structure. Once under control, all suspects (whether under arrest or not) should initially be detained and turned over to the prisoner control officer for monitoring. It can later be determined who should be placed under arrest after the search of the residence is conducted and evidence is located. In this phase, the team leader must also maintain control of his or her own team members. Prior intelligence of the structure and area should assist officers in knowing which strategy of entry to use.

The initial assault of the raid location usually requires four unit functions:

1. *Perimeter unit*: This is the unit that seals off the raid site from intruders (curious bystanders) and may aid in apprehending individuals attempting to escape from the structure. The perimeter unit might also be used in the event neighbors need to be evacuated from the raid site prior to assault of the premises.
2. *Assault unit*: This is the initial entry unit whose primary responsibility is to control all suspects within the structure, thereby making it possible to safely conduct a search.
3. *Cover unit*: This unit supports the assault unit in case of an altercation or confrontation by suspects, and usually enters the structure immediately after the assault unit.
4. *Search unit*: This unit is assigned to conduct a thorough search of the structure once the suspects are accounted for and secured.

There are several assault and control maneuvers that should be considered and discussed with team members during the raid briefing. These tactics cover the approach to the structure as well as entry methods, and should remain flexible to adapt to any raid situation.

External Control Methods

If the suspect inhabiting a raid structure detects an approaching officer, he or she will be forewarned to either destroy any evidence, acquire weapons with which to attack officers, or escape. Organized methods of approach are essential in ensuring the officers greatest assistance in any raids: the element of surprise.

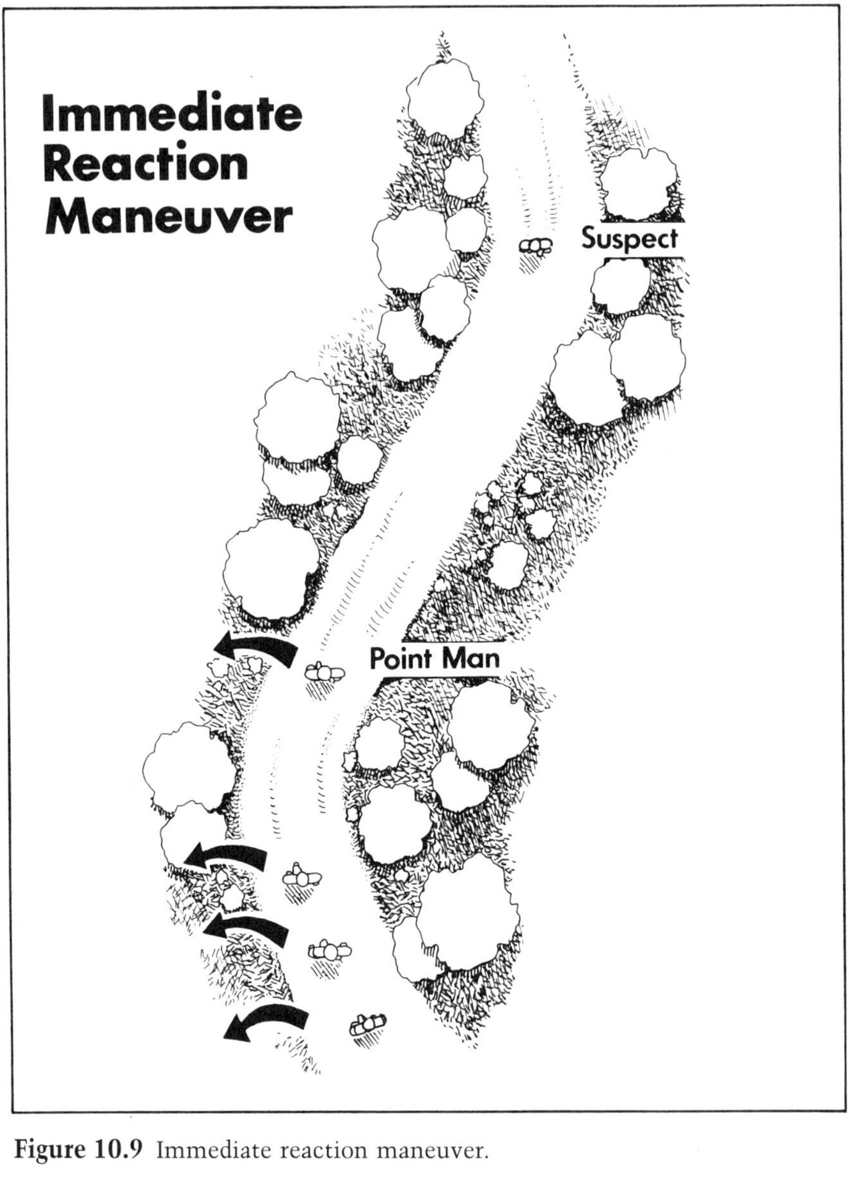

Figure 10.9 Immediate reaction maneuver.

Immediate Reaction Maneuver

This is an assault maneuver conducted primarily in rural areas while approaching marijuana patches or clandestine laboratories. A point man must lead the raid team and act as an initial scout for suspects, guard dogs, or booby traps. If the suspect is sighted, the point man should immediately move off the path quietly toward the area with the most cover. The rest of the team moves off the path in the same direction, thus eliminating a crossfire situation (Figure 10.9).

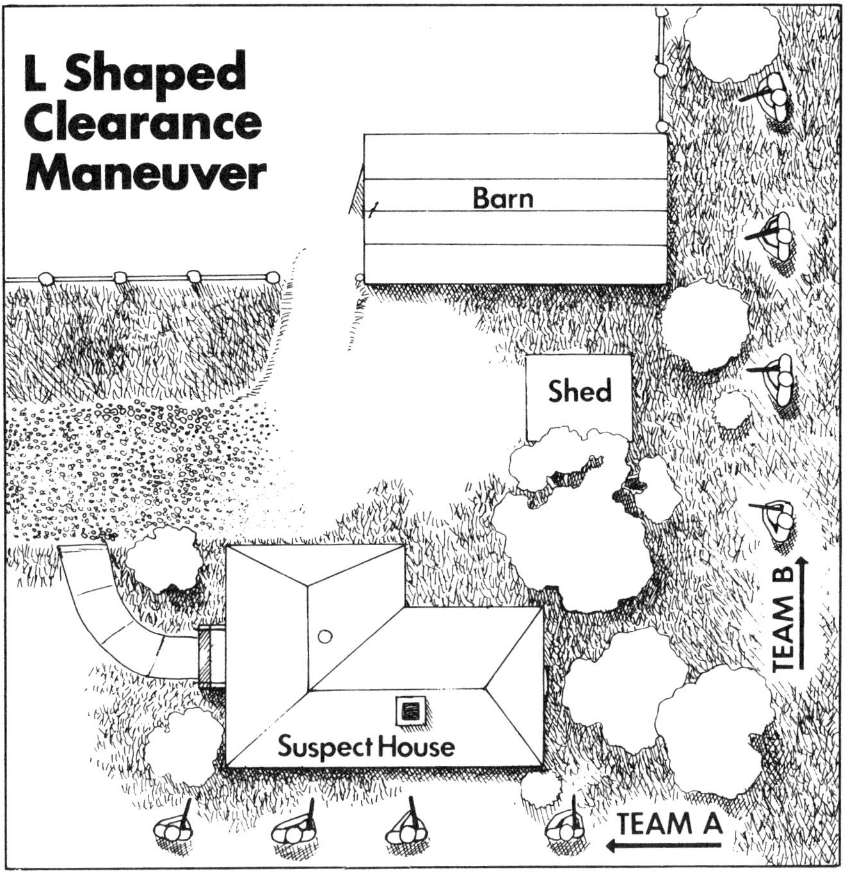

Figure 10.10 L-Shaped clearance maneuver.

L-Shaped Clearance Maneuver

In the event there are several structures on the property of a raid site, the use of the L-shaped clearance maneuver should be considered. This will help to prevent a possible crossfire situation and most effectively contain any suspects. In this scenario, team "B" must be in place before team "A" arrives. This plan also allows team "B" to converge on the out-buildings prior to moving in on the suspect's residence (Figure 10.10).

L-Shaped Sweep Maneuver

This is a maneuver most appropriate for marijuana operations, since it automatically flanks any opposing targets that are encountered and concurrently eliminates the possibility for escape. In this sequence, the team leader is positioned at the corner of the L formation so he or she can better direct all team members. In the event the suspect confronts either flank with gunfire,

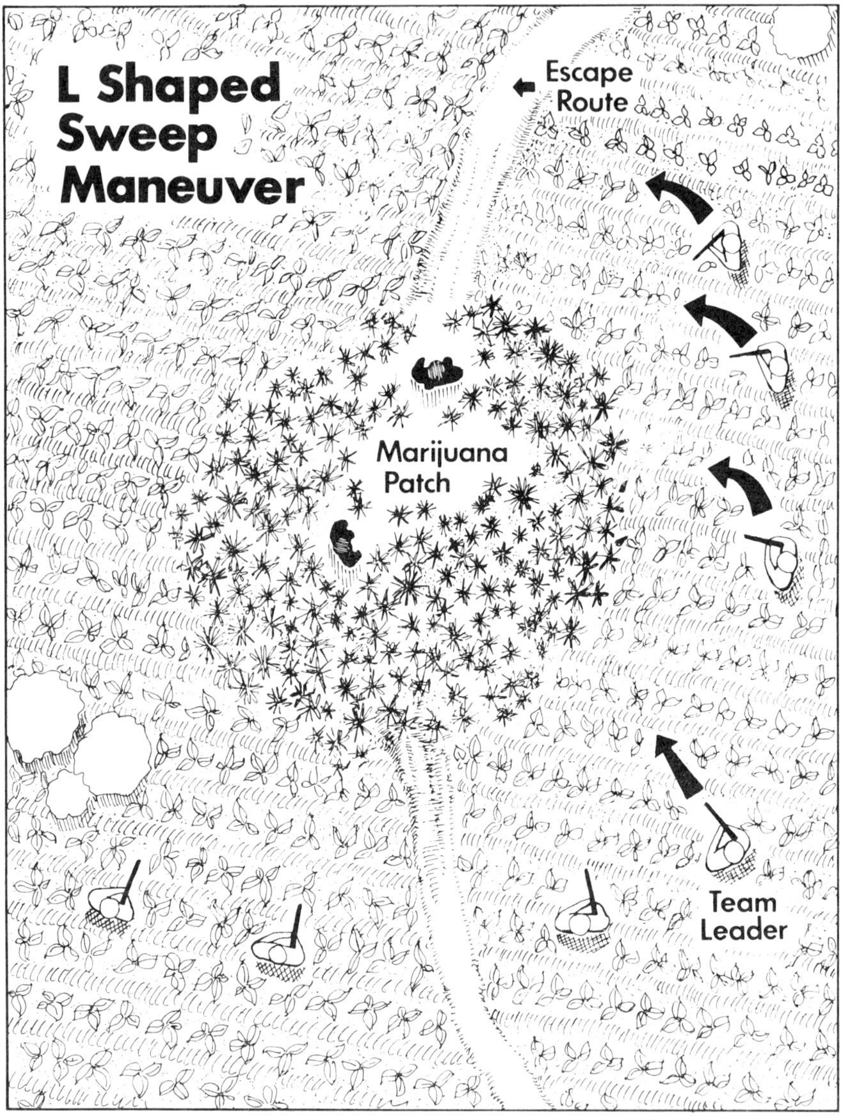

Figure 10.11 L-Shaped sweep maneuver.

the flank fired upon immediately halts and lays down the first base of fire. The remaining team then changes position and returns fire. Containment and control are the ultimate results of this paramilitary maneuver.

It should be noted that in many cases, the use of hand-held radios may give away the location of agents seeking cover; the raid team should develop hand signals (in advance) to use when radios must be turned off and silence is necessary for either a discreet approach or officer safety (Figure 10.11).

Internal Control Methods

One of the most dangerous duties in drug enforcement is when officers enter the residence during a raid. Most of the officers injured or killed make the same mistakes, usually while passing through the doorway into the residence. The most common mistake is that when the door is first opened, the first officer through the door will usually stand in the doorway and scout the layout of the room. The danger is that no matter where the suspects are located in the room, their chance of hitting a target standing in the doorway (the "fatal funnel") is almost 100%.

Given that there are only so many ways to enter a doorway in a raid situation, officers should practice accepted entry methods and remain in the doorway only long enough to enter the room: never linger in the doorway! There are three methods of entry during a raid, which can eliminate complications and maximize the control of suspects.

The Wrap-Around Entry Method

Although dangers may exist within the residence, officers are at much less risk using this approach. Two officers should be used when possible, thus enabling each officer to survey one-half of the room for possible suspects. As these officers maintain their posts, other officers enter the structure and practice the same method for each additional room (Figure 10.12).

The Crisscross Entry Method

This method of internal structure control is effective because it allows two officers to enter the structure and immediately position themselves inside the structure, providing mutual coverage of the control area. Once in position, the entry officers can maintain control of the room and permit support officers to enter and perform the same maneuver for each room within the structure until all occupants are accounted for and controlled (Figure 10.13).

The High-Risk Entry Method

When entry must be made into a structure where risk factors are usually high, the high-risk entry method should be considered (Figure 10.14). This method should be employed whenever a drug raid is planned or a search warrent is being served. It addresses one of the most important considerations in drug enforcement — officer safety.

The Final Raid Report

At the conclusion of each raid, the case agent should prepare a report summarizing all significant aspects of the raid. It is advisable for the case agent to prepare this report, as he or she will be most familiar with the suspects,

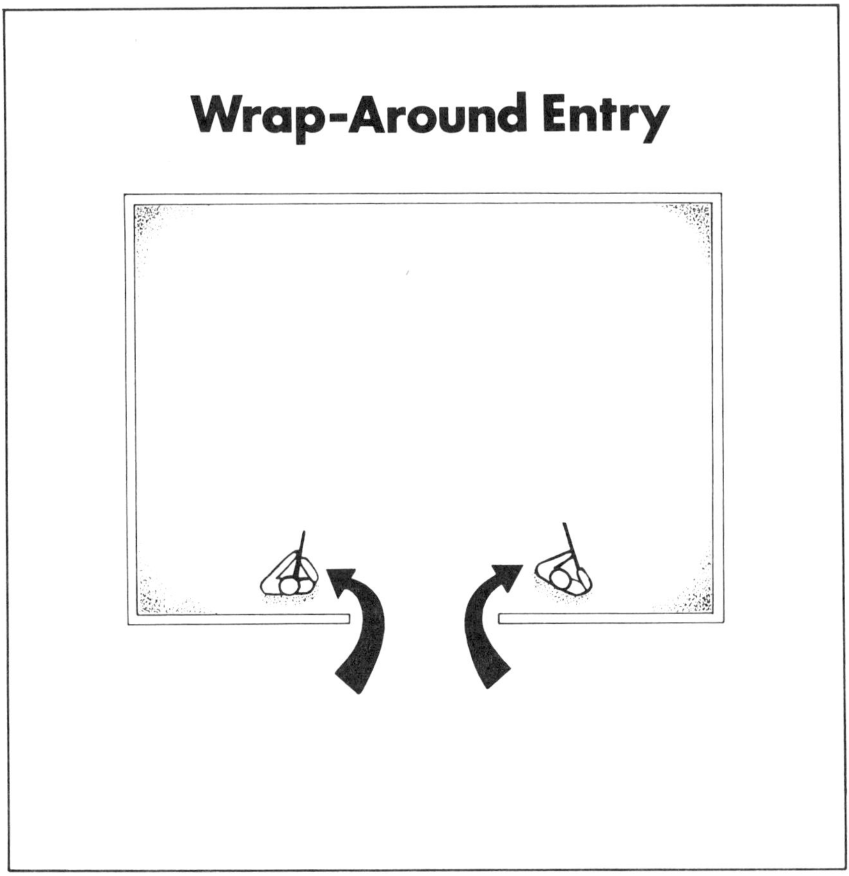

Figure 10.12 Wrap-around entry.

addresses, and other aspects of the case. The final raid report may be prepared at the office, but notes for the report should be taken at the scene of the raid to ensure accuracy of times, locations, suspects' names, officers present, and other details.

When structuring the report, certain fundamentals must be included:

1. Information on the raid team
   a. Size of the team
   b. Names of each team member (plus each jurisdiction, if applicable)
   c. The specific task of the team
   d. Times of arrival and departure
2. Information on the raided structure
   a. Entry and exit routes

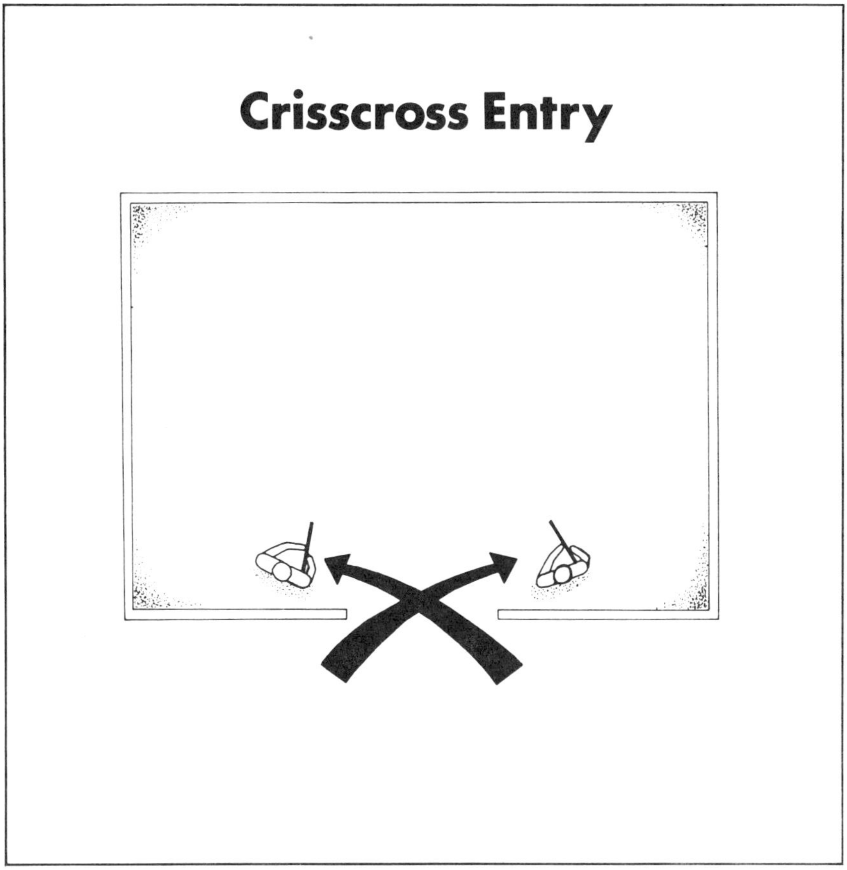

Figure 10.13 Crisscross entry.

   b. Environmental information (rain, snow, night, dawn, etc.)
   c. Terrain information, including sketches, photographs, and/or diagrams to depict the approach methods and the location of any important pieces of evidence
   d. Other locations of evidence inside structure
   e. Locations of weapons
3. Information on suspects
   a. Suspect information
   b. Confrontations with suspects
4. Other information
   a. Officer injuries
   b. Any other information that may later be important

Figure 10.14 High-risk entry.

Summary

Much is to be considered when addressing the many different situations encountered in drug enforcement. A technique that is effective in one investigation may not be successful in another. The investigator must be flexible in his or her approach in dealing with all types of investigations.

The marijuana cultivation operation is a drug enforcement problem that poses many unique hazards and investigative challenges. The recognition of such an operation is the first step in the investigation, which can be best accomplished by the receipt of credible informant information; in some cases, this may be difficult to obtain. Locating cultivators may also require investigators to profile the violators themselves by observing their actions, growing equipment or supplies, and the type of land most commonly chosen for such an endeavor.

Another significant source of drugs is through diversion scams practiced by drug registrants, medical care facility employees, and street criminals. This source of drugs is perpetuated by registrants through substitution scams, false charting, and outright theft. Careful observation of employees' actions and quality of work may indicate diversion. When investigating this type of violation, it should be remembered that violators divert drugs both for profit motives and for reasons of personal addiction.

Investigators must also be cognizant of the street criminals who will try to scam physicians by claiming false ailments or by attempting other inventive scams. When investigating these violations, a paper trail must be established to determine the origin of stolen or forged prescriptions. The problem of drug smuggling creates other unique challenges for the investigator. There are several types of smuggling operations: air, ground, marine vessel, and body packing. Each requires a degree of surveillance and the ability to search persons, places, and things effectively.

Like the marijuana cultivation operation, the clandestine laboratory operation is also largely a rural phenomenon, which makes detection both tedious and difficult. The operator will set up his or her laboratory after first accumulating chemicals and hardware from numerous sources. Investigators who identify such a violator should conduct extensive surveillance to determine the sources of supply for necessary equipment and precursors. Observing the suspect in possession of special equipment and chemicals may be sufficient probable cause for acquiring search warrants for those locations associated with the suspect. Lab operators commonly choose a rural environment because of the distinctive odor emitted from the lab while it is in operation. This odor would easily be noticed by passers-by if it were in a more populated environment. Again, the odor alone may be sufficient probable cause for a search warrant if detected and properly documented.

Compounding problems in cultivation and laboratory operations are deadly booby traps, which are commonly associated with these operations. When approaching a location suspected of being booby trapped, a qualified EOD expert should be present to help identify possible traps. If an EOD expert is not available, officers should be knowledgeable in how to recognize a trap. When raids are considered, precautions should be taken in the handling of prisoners, collection of evidence, and coordinating the raid while multiple jurisdictions are present. If the raid is kept simple, confusion and casualties will be minimized.

Suggested Readings

Geberth, V. J., *Narcotic Buy Operations,* Law and Order Magazine, March, 1979.

Shelden, R.G., Tracy, S.K., Brown, W.B., Youth Gangs in American Society, Wadsworth, Belmont, CA, 2001.

11 Preparation for Court

My experience as a drug enforcement agent has afforded me ample opportunity to testify in courts in every level of government. During that time I have testified in 150 jury trials in both federal and state courts. This is not unusual, since most drug investigators are involved in a considerable number of felony cases in the course of their careers — either as the case agent or support officer. I recall the first time I was subpoenaed to testify; I was a nervous wreck. Over the years, other agents have shared their stories about their first time on the stand as well.

Testifying in court does not have to be the nightmare that some officers make it out to be. Realizing that you, and all that you have written on the case in question, are now under scrutiny by judges, lawyers, and jurors can be stressful, but you must remember one thing: no one knows your case better than you do! You were there, and all you need to do is give an honest account of what happened: dates, times, names, places. What you did, what you saw. That's all. It is up the judge and jury to sort it out.

I have learned one valuable thing in my experience as a drug investigator: nothing makes you a better investigator than testifying in court. Any mistakes you make one day or any embarrassing moments you experience will most assuredly not be repeated next time. This makes you a better, more thorough, more reliable, and more professional investigator, and in time, it will be the defense attorneys who won't want to see you in the courtroom rather than the other way around.

Not all drug cases go to trial. In fact, most are settled outside the courtroom through the plea bargaining process. For those cases that make it to the trial stage, however, it is imperative that the evidence be well organized and that the drug investigator, who is essentially the "star witness," be prepared to give skilled courtroom testimony in the case. The admissibility of evidence in court is the compelling reason for investigators to follow closely the correct procedures in evidence collection. Once investigators are satisfied that the evidence has been collected appropriately, the question of how best to present the evidence to the judge and jurors is addressed. For such a critical task, investigators do not always understand their role in the courtroom. After all, most police officers spend most of their time on the street and not in the courtroom. In this chapter we will examine several critical aspects of the courtroom process and how this important criminal justice function interacts with the duties of the drug investigator.

Pretrial Procedures

By the time the case makes its way to court, several critical phases in processing the criminal case will already have occurred:

1. The prosecutor will have filed a complaint against the suspect.
2. The defendant will have been arrested for the charge.
3. The defendant will have pleaded "not guilty" to the charges.
4. Discovery proceedings will have been conducted.
5. The case will have gone to preliminary hearing, and the defendant will have been bound over for trial (if the state does not use a grand jury system).
6. The defense attorney and prosecutor will have presented any pretrial motions in the case. Some of the most common are a continuance of the case, a change of venue, suppression of the evidence, severance of trials, and severance of defendants.
7. Any efforts to plea-bargain the case out before going to trial will have been tried and failed.

Thorough case preparation is required as well as close cooperation between the investigator and the prosecutor. It makes little sense for an investigator to conduct a complicated investigation and have no intention of prosecuting the case. In working together, both parties can avoid wasting valuable time.

Pretrial Conference

When preparing for trial, the investigator should keep these suggestions in mind. First, it is important for the investigator to meet with the prosecutor a few days before the scheduled date of the trial. This meeting, known as the pretrial conference, is when the prosecutor and investigator discuss (1) the role that the investigator will play at the trial; (2) the roles of different articles of evidence that will be offered; and (3) the overall strategy of the case.

The second thing the investigator can do is make sure that he or she is familiar with the rules of evidence, courtroom demeanor, and the roles of the other players in the courtroom such as the judge, jury, and defense attorney. The prosecutor usually initiates the pretrial conference, but because they are often very busy with crowded dockets, this important aspect of the case may be put off until the last minute. Therefore, the officer should make periodic contact with the prosecutor to inquire about preferred times and locations for the conference. Simply put, the pretrial conference allows the officer and prosecutor to discuss the case in an informal setting where the strategy for the case can be jointly strengthened. The conference also gives the prosecutor an opportunity to clear up any questions that he or she may have regarding the officer's role in the case.

Going to Court

Before attending the criminal court procedure, officers should ready themselves for the situation. One of the first steps is for the officer to prepare him or herself psychologically, by strengthening feelings of confidence and self-assurance. Officers should also realize that as witnesses they are on display, as they are when on duty. It is a simple fact that the general public expects more stringent behavior from a law enforcement officer than from an average citizen. Vail suggests that the following steps be followed before entering a courtroom:[1]

- Know which courtroom you'll be testifying in. If you are unfamiliar with the particular courthouse or courtroom, check it out before the trial so that you will know your way around.
- Do not discuss anything about the case in public or where your conversation might be overheard. Anyone could be a juror or defense witness.
- Treat people with respect, as if they were the judges or jurors. Your professionalism, politeness, and courtesy will be noted and remembered especially by those who see you in court in an official capacity.
- Do not discuss your personal life, official business, biases, prejudices, likes and dislikes, or controversial subjects in public, for the same reasons as listed above. You might impress a judge, juror, or witness the wrong way.
- Judges and attorneys have little patience with officers appearing in court late, so be on time. Know when you will be expected to testify.
- Dress appropriately. Look businesslike and official. If in uniform, it should be neat, clean, and complete. If not in uniform, a sport coat and slacks are as appropriate as a business suit.
- Avoid contact with the defense counsel and any defense witnesses before the trial. Assume that they will try to get you to say something about the case, to their advantage.

These suggestions, in addition to the pretrial conference, will prepare the officer well for the courtroom experience. Above all, however, officers are expected to tell the truth.

The Criminal Trial Process

Many officers who regularly testify at trials are still not completely aware of the trial process because they seldom stay for the entire proceeding after their testimony is given. Additionally, in the event that the investigator is not the chief case officer, he or she will probably be sequestered from the courtroom. This is a process where witnesses are not permitted to remain in the courtroom and hear testimony of other witnesses, thereby reducing the likelihood that their testimony might be affected by what they hear others say on the witness stand. The trial process involves many critical stages in which the investigator is typically involved in some capacity.

Selection of the Jury

Defendants in criminal proceedings may often choose between a trial by judge and a trial by jury. Most decide on trial by jury. Jury selection is crucial because the jurors will be the deciders of fact (while the judge is the decider of law). Both the prosecutor and defense attorney are looking for jurors who will return a verdict in their behalf. The prosecutor wants a jury that will convict, whereas the defense wants one that will acquit the accused.

Understanding the psychology of a jury and being able to predict the outcome of a trial is a complicated and often impossible task. It is therefore important for the investigator and witness to understand that the determination of guilt or innocence may have little to do with the evidence presented at the trial. Indeed, it may have much to do with courtroom theatrics by the prosecutor and the defense attorney, the demeanor and appearance of the defendant or the prosecution witnesses, or the manner in which the witness reacts to cross-examination.

Opening Statements

Unlike closing statements, opening statements are not argumentative. They simply give both prosecutor and defense an opportunity to address the jury and discuss the testimony and evidence that they will use to support their arguments. Essentially, the opening statements set the stage for the remainder of the trial.

Direct Examination

Following opening statements, witnesses are called to the stand one by one to testify as to their knowledge of the crime. Before taking the stand, each witness is placed under oath: "Do you solemnly swear to tell the truth, the whole truth, and nothing but the truth, so help you God?" It is the prosecutor's responsibility to begin the direct examination process, which usually involves asking names of each witness, his or her address, the dates and times of the alleged offense, and a brief explanation of what the witness personally observed or knows about the incident. Prosecution witnesses are encouraged to make eye contact with the members of the jury when responding to questions during direct examination.

Cross-Examination

During cross-examination, the courtroom spotlight shifts from the witnesses to the attorneys. It is designed to weaken or discredit any testimony given during direct examination by attempting to show that previous testimony given under direct examination was untruthful or intentionally exaggerated or slanted. If this is accomplished successfully, statements given by witnesses will probably not be believed by members of the jury.

During cross-examination, short questions are usually asked of the witnesses. The rules also change during cross-examination. For example, leading questions can be asked provided that they are within the scope of direct examination. However, while under cross-examination, if the witness slips and discloses something outside the scope of direct examination, the door will have been opened, and the attorneys can then explore topics that would otherwise have been inadmissible. The two basic purposes of the cross-examination phase of a trial are:

1. To elicit favorable testimony from witnesses
2. To discredit testimony from witnesses

One way to discredit the witnesses' testimony is to try to show that they are being dishonest. This can be done by pointing out any of the following to the jury:

- Prior inconsistent statement
- Ulterior motives of witness
- Any prior convictions of crimes dealing with truthfulness (e.g., perjury or embezzlement)
- Reputation of being a liar
- Evidence that witness was "coached" to testify in a certain manner
- Any other evidence that disputes any of the witnesses' prior testimony

Objections

Either side can object to the line of questioning offered by the opposing side. Essentially, an objection refers to the form of the question asked of the witness. For example, one common objection by defense attorneys is that the prosecutor is leading the witness during direct examination. Another is to object that the examining attorney is being argumentative with the witness. After an objection, the judge rules that the objection is either sustained or overruled. If sustained, the question will be stricken from the court record and must be reworded. If overruled, the question stands, and the witness must respond.

Pre- and Post-Trial Motions

A motion is a written request (also called a petition) or an oral request made to the court any time before, during, or after court proceedings. Motions ask the court to make certain findings or decisions. Here are the most typical types of motions made by both sides of a criminal case.

Motion for Discovery

Typically filed by the defense, this motion requests that the court allow the defense to review any evidence that is to be used by the prosecution at the trial. Such evidence includes a witness list, physical evidence, photographs, documents, and similar material.

Motion to Suppress Evidence

Prior to the trial, the defense may move to suppress any evidence that is thought to have been obtained illegally by the prosecution. If granted, this motion will result in the evidence in question being excluded from consideration at the trial.

Motion to Dismiss

This motion, also made by the defense, asks the court to throw out the charges against the accused. It can be based on a number of violations of procedural due process.

Motion for Continuance

This motion seeks to delay the trial for a specified reason and is usually based on a need for more time either to locate witnesses or to allow for an illness by one of the parties in the case.

Motion for Change of Venue

Because of pretrial publicity, a defense attorney might wish for the case to be moved to another location where it might be easier to select an impartial jury.

Motion for Severance of Charges

Defendants charged with more than one crime might request that they be tried separately for each charge.

Motion for Severance of Defendants

As with the severance of charges motion, when there are multiple defendants, one might wish to be tried separately from the other because of damaging evidence that might pertain only to a codefendant.

Motion for a Mistrial

A mistrial can be declared at any time and is usually initiated by this motion. Either the defense or the prosecution may move for a mistrial when highly controversial remarks are made by either attorney or by the witnesses.

Motion for a New Trial

This motion is usually initiated after the jury has returned a guilty verdict and new evidence has been found to prove the defendant's innocence.

Closing Arguments

The closing arguments generally wind down the trial proceeding. Each attorney is permitted to conduct a closing argument. Typically, they begin with the attorney thanking the jurors for their time and service on the jury. The body of the argument is basically a summation of the evidence offered by that attorney, in which he or she draws a conclusion as to the guilt or innocence of the defendant. On conclusion, the attorney asks the jury to find their client either guilty or not guilty, depending on which side they represent.

Jury Instructions and the Verdict

After both sides are finished with their closing arguments, the judge will instruct or charge the jury as to the law that applies to the case in question. The jury instructions include a recitation of the elements of the crime and possibly elements of a similar but lesser offense. When completed, the jury retires to the jury room, where a jury foreperson is chosen from their ranks. The court bailiff keeps close security on the jurors, and no one is allowed to enter the jury room or speak to the jurors. When the jurors have reached a verdict, they return to the courtroom and the foreperson reads the verdict aloud to the court.

The Drug Investigator as a Professional Witness

The testimony given by the investigator is a crucial part of any criminal trial. An experienced and knowledgeable witness can make the job of the prosecutor and subsequent conviction of the defendant much easier. Conversely, a witness who is disorganized, unkempt, and unclear in thought can inadvertently sabotage even the best of criminal cases.

Witness Preparation

Although it is inappropriate for the prosecutor (or defense) attorney to coach a witness before testifying, it is also not a good idea to place someone on the stand "cold." A certain amount of preparation is called for regarding practical, legal, and ethical issues. Many officers have little experience testifying in court and therefore require some degree of orientation to the trial process. Things that should be emphasized to the potential witness include the following:

- Always tell the truth.
- Concentrate on the question being asked, not the person asking the question.
- Testify with confidence.
- Respond to all questions directly; don't elaborate unless asked to do so.
- Unless otherwise asked, remember to explain "what," not "why," something happened.
- When asked to give exact times and measurements, be careful to "approximate" your response.
- If you don't know the answer or don't remember, say so.
- If you need to refer to your notes, turn to the judge and request that you be permitted to refresh your memory with them.
- Remember to testify only to things you know, and avoid testifying to hearsay information.
- Always control your anger on the witness stand.
- If you are asked a leading question containing a half-truth, clarify your response by saying "That statement is only partly true," and then explain.
- If confronted with a prior inconsistent statement, be calm and cool headed and be truthful in your response.

Preparing for Court

The best way for an investigator to prepare for trial is not to wait for one or two days before trial to get organized, but to keep the rules of evidence in mind from the beginning of the investigation through its closure months (even years in some cases). In addition, the investigator should be sure to meet with the prosecutor sometime before trial for the pretrial conference.

The officer should check all personal reports and notes pertaining to the case and be sure that he or she has sufficient information to respond to the anticipated "who, what, when, where, why, and how" questions.

Investigator's Courtroom Checklist[2]

- Elements of offense
- Probable cause for arrest

- Defendant's story
- Confession of suspect
- Prior statements and testimony of witnesses
- Reliability of witnesses
- Warrants and affidavits
- Physical evidence
- Exhibits, sketches, and diagrams

Reviewing Evidence and Reports

Before the trial, the investigator should go back over his or her list of evidence and be sure that all is accounted for and easily identifiable. The chain of custody should also be reexamined to be sure that all persons who were involved with the evidence will be available if needed to testify in court. The investigator should also consider how the evidence will be transported to court and who will maintain possession of it once the court proceeding is under way. In the case of drug or forensic evidence, it is likely that the police chemist will already have custody and transport it to court. The investigator, however, might be required to locate and transport other items in evidence, such as written statements, cassette or videotapes of transactions and statements, or photographs. All such evidence should be closely reviewed by the officer before trial.

Because the investigator may not testify solely from his or her notes and reports, they should be reviewed before the trial. Although it is lawful and appropriate to use notes, the defense attorney may inquire of the officer on the witness stand whether this was done before trial, and may even attempt to take custody of the report to place into evidence under the past recollection recorded exception to the hearsay rule. If the defense attorney gains access to the official report of the investigator, the report can be used to attack the credibility of the investigator. One typical defense ploy is to attack the credibility of the officer by highlighting any inconsistencies between the testimony given by the officer and what is reflected in the official report. An inconsistency can be just about anything, but can include facts testified to that differ from the report, or a seemingly important fact in the report that the witness failed to mention in his or her testimony.

In the event that this occurs, it is usually a good idea to acknowledge the discrepancy and not become defensive about it. The prosecutor can then decide whether or not to "clean up" the problem through additional questioning if it appears to be of any consequence to the prosecution strategy.

Credibility

Defense attorneys will use many means to attack an officer's credibility. This is usually accomplished through attempting to demonstrate the officer's bias, or that he or she is lying. Bias can be raised in many different circumstances. For example, the defense attorney can try to convince the jury that the officer is just trying to protect his or her "conviction" record by embellishing his or her answers to make the suspect look guilty, thus resulting in a conviction. Racial bias can sometimes be argued if the defendant is a minority and from a different ethnic background from the officer. In this case, the officer must testify only to the facts of the case that indicate guilt of the defendant, not on stereotypic perceptions of the defendant's racial or ethnic group.

Credibility can also be attacked on the basis of the officer's reputation for truthfulness. This is most typically used against undercover officers, who are required to work proactively and assume a false identity (e.g., a cover story and an assumed name). It is common for the attorney to have the officer affirm that he or she was required to lie while working undercover, and then try to convince the jury that the officer is a liar by nature. If successful, the defense can argue that the investigator's testimony is not credible.

Courtroom Demeanor

The investigator should also remember that a certain amount of theatrics also plays a role in the trial. Both the judge and jury will be watching the investigator closely and listening to what he or she has to say. First impressions can make a difference. Juries expect a certain type of person as a police witness. They expect an organized, intelligent, serious, no-nonsense kind of person to represent the government. There are times, however, when witnesses may reveal a sense of humor, and the jury can be impressed. Such displays of humor in the courtroom should not be directed toward anyone in particular and should be made with caution to avoid offending any member of the jury.

Although the investigator may wear faded blue jeans when on duty, it is important for him or her to dress more formally for court. Some disagreement exists in this area, as some think that the witness's choice of clothing should coincide with the atmosphere of the community. Others believe that an otherwise uniformed officer should wear plain clothes in court to avoid the authoritarian appearance depicted by the uniform.

Giving a Positive Impression

Police witnesses must always be truthful while testifying in a criminal case. The investigator should follow these guidelines:

- Speak in a clear voice, loud enough to be heard anywhere in the courtroom. Face the jury when testifying. Speak slowly and distinctly, and avoid street slang and departmental jargon.

- Sit up straight in the witness chair. Don't slouch with your legs crossed or respond to questions in a nonchalant manner.
- Listen closely to the questions, and answer only the question asked. Don't venture opinions or conjecture about your observations, or what was implied by the occurrence of certain events, unless prompted accordingly. In short, don't volunteer information unless specifically asked to do so.
- Don't testify about unverified information; avoid hearsay.
- Avoid "formula" answers and the appearance of testifying about previously prepared answers.
- Don't "hedge" on your answers. If you don't know the answer to a question, simply say so. Otherwise, both the judge and jury will think you are hiding something.

The Expert Witness

Prosecutors may locate an officer with extensive experience in a given area and qualify him or her as an expert witness. This can strengthen the prosecution's case and pave the way for testimony by other witnesses. Once the officer is designated by the court as an expert, conclusions may be drawn and the officer may give his or her personal opinion as to the facts and circumstances surrounding the case.

The expert witness is one whose knowledge exceeds that of anyone with a moderate education or experience in the field. Qualifications for the expert witness to establish when on the witness stand include the following:

- Name
- Occupation (and how long)
- Department (and how long)
- Specialized experience (e.g., drug enforcement, and how long)
- Officer's training
- Number of training course hours
- Number of similar investigations in which the officer has participated
- Number of arrests made in this type of investigation
- Past experience as an expert witness (and how many court appearances)

At the end of the questioning, the judge will excuse the witness. Officers must remember that the the jury is still watching and making judgments; therefore, when exiting, the witness should refrain from staring, smiling, or showing any emotion toward anyone in the courtroom.

Summary

For the most part, drug cases result in successful prosecution. Such cases are the result of hard physical evidence, corroborative evidence, and expert testimony. But like all cases, the drug case can be complex, and sloppy police work can and usually will result in a dismissal of the case. Drug investigators are cautioned not to lose the case before it reaches the court. In other words, understand the laws of evidence, constitutional safeguards of search and seizure, arrest and interrogation, criminal law as it relates to various drug violations, and of course, your own agency's standard operating procedure.

This chapter explains the process of going to court with your case. Beginning with pretrial procedures and a walk-through of the criminal trial, the stage is set for what drug investigators must do and know in order to successfully prosecute a defendant. The best advice one can give the drug investigator is to be prepared. This is accomplished by knowing your case, understanding all items of evidence, properly documenting what happened on the date in question, and writing a sound investigative report. Cases are often lost in court due to credibility issues with witnesses — and remember, you are one of those witnesses. This chapter discusses some things that should be observed to protect your credibility on the stand.

The chapter concludes with a discussion of courtroom demeanor and its importance in winning your case. Remember, the judge's eyes are on you as are those of the jury, and even the press in some cases. How you present yourself and handle difficult questions is paramount.

Suggested Readings

Inciardi, J., McBride, D.C., and Rivers, J.E., *Drug Control and the Courts*, Sage, Thousand Oaks, CA, 1996.

References

1. Vail, Christopher, Presenting winning testimony in court, *Law Order*, June, 1992.
2. United States Department of Justice. The Investigator in the Courtroom. Research in Brief. National Institute of Justice, 1987.

APPENDIX: DEA's Drug Enforcement Programs

Aviation Program

The present Drug Enforcement Agency (DEA) aviation program represents an evolutionary process started in early 1971 when the Bureau of Narcotics and Dangerous Drugs acquired its first aircraft. Over the next few years, additional aircraft were acquired from the U.S. military, and the aviation program was made part of the Special Projects Division. Management of the aviation resources came under the direction of a chief pilot who utilized experienced special agents as pilots, which gave the program the expertise necessary to perform a wide range of enforcement missions that would be impossible with the use of civilian pilots.

Upon the creation of the DEA in 1973, the aviation program consisted of 24 aircraft and 41 special agents/pilots. The program continued to grow, and in 1994 the Aviation Section was granted field division status and renamed the Office of Aviation Operations (OA). The chief pilot was redesignated Special Agent in Charge and the two deputy chief pilots became Assistant Special Agents in Charge. Today, the OA consists of 95 aircrafts and 117 special agents/pilots.

Further evidence of the expansion and importance of the OA to the DEA's enforcement mission is the move to new facilities at Alliance Airport in Fort Worth, Texas in February 1994. The new facility, known as the Aviation Operations Center, is the primary maintenance facility for the Office of Aviation fleet of aircraft, and headquarters to the OA's supervisory and administrative personnel, as well as contractor personnel.

The OA provides aviation support to domestic offices throughout the United States, High Intensity Drug Trafficking Areas (HIDTA), Special Enforcement Operations, Mobile Enforcement Teams, the Southwest Border Initiative, and the National Marijuana Eradication Strategy. These operations consist of air-to-ground, air-to-water, air-to-air, and electronic surveillance, and photographic reconnaissance.

The OA has Posts of Duty located in Peru, Colombia, Bolivia, Mexico, Puerto Rico, and the Bahamas. These country offices, as well as other offices in Central and South America, are supported in operations involving enforcement and logistical missions to include air-to-ground surveillance, overflights, photographic reconnaissance, diplomatic missions, rapid deployment of personnel and equipment, expeditious removal of fugitives from foreign countries, over-water surveillance and search for suspect vessel activity, and medical evacuation.

DEA pilots are experienced special agents, as well as highly qualified aviators. Their dedication to law enforcement and the OA's internal network of support and cooperation provide numerous advantages to DEA. The OA has evolved into an international support entity upon which a high percentage of DEA initiatives have become dependent.

Diversion Program

Of all the major drugs of abuse, only marijuana is available as a natural, harvested product. All of the others, whether illicit drugs such as cocaine, heroin, methamphetamine, or legitimately produced pharmaceuticals, must be produced or manufactured. Many problems associated with drug abuse are the result of legitimately manufactured controlled substances being diverted from their lawful purposes into the illicit drug traffic. The DEA's Office of Diversion Control is responsible for two distinct problems: the diversion of controlled pharmaceuticals and the diversion of controlled chemicals.

Many of the narcotics, depressants, and stimulants manufactured for legitimate medical use are subject to abuse and have therefore been brought under legal control. The goal of controls is to ensure that these "controlled substances" are readily available for medical use, while preventing their distribution for illicit sale and abuse. Under federal law, all businesses which manufacture or distribute controlled drugs, all health professionals entitled to dispense, administer, or prescribe them, and all pharmacies entitled to fill prescriptions must register with the DEA. Registrants must comply with a series of regulatory requirements relating to drug security, records accountability, and adherence to standards.

The DEA is obligated under international treaties to monitor the movement of licit controlled substances across United States borders, and is responsible for issuing import and export permits for that movement. The DEA also devises ways to deal with problems of international drug diversion.

Diversion cases involve, but are not limited to, physicians who sell prescriptions to drug dealers or abusers; pharmacists who falsify records and subsequently sell the drugs, employees who steal from inventory, executives who falsify orders to cover illicit sales, prescription forgers, and individuals who commit armed robbery of pharmacies and drug distributors. At present, the largest problem results from the criminal activity of physicians and pharmacy personnel.

Most of the drugs in the illicit traffic are products of illicit processing or synthesis. Cocaine, for example, can only be extracted and converted to its preferred form by using a tremendous quantity of industrial chemicals. Heroin must be synthesized by using an acetylating agent after the morphine has been extracted from raw, harvested opium. Methamphetamine, PCP, LSD, MDMA, and methaqualone are purely synthetic drugs manufactured from chemical precursors.

Until recently, there were virtually no legal impediments to obtaining the chemicals necessary to manufacture drugs of abuse, no records required to be maintained for inspection, and no penalties for negligence or willful diversion. The Chemical Diversion and Trafficking Act of 1988 extended the concept of commodity control to those chemicals most often used for the manufacture and synthesis of drugs of abuse. With the support of the State Department, the DEA pursued the same goal on the international level. The result was the incorporation of Article 12 into the U.N. Convention Against Illicit Drug Traffic of 1988 (the Vienna Convention). This provision establishes similar controls over a list of 22 critical chemicals commonly diverted for the production of the major drugs of abuse. In February 1991, the Anabolic Steroid Control Act was passed by Congress. The act classified 27 named steroids as Schedule III substances under the Controlled Substances Act which DEA administers.

The Office of Diversion consists of diversion investigators, special agents, chemists, pharmacologists, program analysts, and others. The office's activities include: program priorities and field management oversight, coordination of major investigations, drafting and promulgating regulations, establishment of national drug production quotas, design and execution of diplomatic missions, U.S. obligations under drug control treaties, design and proposal of national legislation, advice and leadership on state legislation/regulation, legal control of drugs and chemicals not previously under federal control, control of imports and exports of drugs and chemicals, computerized monitoring and tracking the distribution of certain controlled drugs, providing distribution intelligence to the states, industry liaison, and program resource planning and allocation.

El Paso Intelligence Center

The El Paso Intelligence Center (EPIC) was established in 1974 in response to a Department of Justice study. The study, which detailed drug and border enforcement strategy and programs, proposed the establishment of a Southwest Border intelligence service center to be staffed by representatives of the Immigration and Naturalization Service, the U.S. Customs Service, and the

DEA. The original EPIC staff was comprised of 17 employees from the three founding agencies.

Initially, EPIC focused on the U.S.–Mexico border and its primary interest was drug movement and immigration violations. Today, EPIC still concentrates primarily on drug movement and immigration violations. Because these criminal activities are seldom limited to one geographic area, EPIC's focus has broadened to include all of the United States and the Western Hemisphere where drug and alien movements are directed toward the United States.

Staffing at the DEA-led center has increased to over 300 analysts, agents, and support personnel from 15 federal agencies, the Texas Department of Public Safety, and the Texas Air National Guard. Information-sharing agreements with other federal law enforcement agencies, the Royal Canadian Mounted Police, and each of the 50 states ensure that EPIC support is available to those who need it. A telephone call, fax, or teletype from any of these agencies provides the requestor real-time information from different federal databases, plus EPIC's own internal database.

In addition to these services, a number of EPIC programs are dedicated to post-seizure analysis and the establishment of links between recent enforcement actions and ongoing investigations. EPIC also coordinates training for state and local officers in the methods of highway drug and drug currency interdiction through its Operation Pipeline program. EPIC personnel coordinate and conduct training seminars throughout the United States, covering such topics as indicators of trafficking and concealment methods used by couriers.

In a continuing effort to stay abreast of changing trends, EPIC has developed the National Clandestine Laboratory Seizure Database. EPIC's future course will also be driven by the National General Counterdrug Intelligence Plan. As a major national center in the new drug intelligence architecture, EPIC will serve as a clearinghouse for the HIDTA Intelligence Centers, gathering state and local law enforcement drug information and providing drug intelligence back to the HIDTA Intelligence Centers.

National Drug Pointer Index

For many years, state and local law enforcement envisioned a drug pointer system that would allow them to determine if other law enforcement organizations were investigating the same drug suspect. The DEA was designated by the Office of National Drug Control Policy in 1992 to take the lead in developing a national drug pointer system to assist federal, state, and local law enforcement agencies investigating drug trafficking organizations and to enhance officer safety by preventing duplicate investigations. The DEA recognized that the development of this system would require a truly cooperative effort among state, local, and federal law enforcement agencies. The DEA drew from the experience of state and local agencies to make certain that their concerns were addressed and that they had extensive input and involvement in the development of the system. The nominees from 19 states and 24 law enforcement organizations formed a Project Steering Committee and six working groups.

The National Drug Pointer Index (NDPIX) became operational throughout the United States in October 1997. The National Law Enforcement Telecommunications System (NLETS) — a fast and effective network that reaches into almost every police entity in the United States — is the backbone for the NDPIX. Participating agencies are required to submit active case-targeting information to NDPIX in order to receive pointer information from the NDPIX.

The greater the number of data elements entered, the greater the likelihood of identifying possible matches. Designed to be a true pointer system rather than an intelligence system, the NDPIX merely serves as a "switchboard" that provides a vehicle for timely notification of common investigative targets. The actual case information is shared only when telephonic contact is made between the officers/agents who have been linked by their entries into the NDPIX.

The DEA is a full participant in the NDPIX and has entered 86,000 drug investigative targets into the system as of June 2000. As more and more law enforcement agencies participate in the NDPIX, it will have far-reaching implications in the effort to dismantle the drug organizations that are causing most of the violence in the United States.

Organized Crime Drug Enforcement Task Forces

In 1982, the Organized Crime Drug Enforcement Task Forces (OCDETF) program was initiated to combine federal, state, and local law enforcement efforts into a comprehensive attack against organized crime and drug traffickers. Aspects of the program have served as models for every major law enforcement initiative in recent years, such as HIDTA, Weed and Seed, and the Anti-Violence Initiative.

The success of OCDETF has been highly attributed to fostering collaboration among federal, state, and local law enforcement and effectively using prosecution attorneys at the early stages of investigations. Since the inception of OCDETF, the DEA has played a leading role and now has 1000 positions, including 775 special agents, dedicated to the program.

Mobile Enforcement Teams

The Mobile Enforcement Team (MET) program was created by the DEA in early 1995 as a response to the overwhelming problem of drug-related violent crime that plagues neighborhoods and communities throughout the United States. The challenges facing law enforcement today are daunting. The increasing sophistication of drug-trafficking organizations and the availability of automatic weapons make drug law enforcement more difficult and dangerous than ever before. Unfortunately, police departments must face these challenges with smaller budgets and fewer police officers. The MET program helps local law enforcement entities attack the violent drug organizations in their neighborhoods and restores a safer environment for the residents of these communities. MET agents assist local law enforcement officers in the following ways:

- Identifying major drug traffickers and organizations that commit homicide and other violent crimes
- Collecting, analyzing, and sharing intelligence with state and local counterparts
- Cultivating investigations against violent drug offenders and gangs
- Arresting drug traffickers and assisting in the arrests of violent offenders and gangs
- Seizing the assets of violent drug offenders and gangs
- Providing support to federal, state, and local prosecutors

MET Deployments: The Process

Local police chiefs, county sheriffs, and state and local prosecutors who feel that there is a need for MET assistance in their jurisdiction can submit a written request to the DEA Special Agent in Charge responsible for their particular area. Upon acceptance of a request, the MET in that jurisdiction sends a pre-deployment assessment team consisting of two to three agents to meet with the requesting official and other cooperating local law enforcement agencies in order to evaluate the problem. Upon approval, the entire MET is deployed to that city to begin investigative activity against the primary drug trafficking individuals and organizations identified in the pre-deployment assessment.

Following the closure of a MET-assisted operation, DEA officials meet with representatives of the requesting agency to evaluate the long-term success of the operation. Measures of operational effectiveness include: visible reduction of drug use and sales, the stability of the target area, community reaction and involvement, and an assessment by the requesting agency.

The tremendous success of MET deployments throughout the country, along with overwhelmingly positive responses from the law enforcement community and the public, have demonstrated the efficacy of the MET program.

As of August 2000, the DEA had received 378 requests for MET deployments nationwide. Pursuant to these requests, a total of 265 deployments have been completed. These deployments have made a significant impact in neighborhoods across the United States. In areas where the DEA has deployed the MET, assaults have been reduced by 15%, homicides by 16%, and robberies by 14%. METs have also contributed to the overall national decrease in violent crime; from 1993 to 1999 the number of violent crimes committed in the United States dropped by 26%.

Marijuana Eradication

Marijuana is the most widely used and readily available drug in the United States, and it is the only major drug of abuse grown within our borders. The DEA is aggressively striving to halt the spread of marijuana cultivation in the United States. To accomplish this, the DEA initiated the Domestic Cannabis Eradication and Suppression Program (DCE/SP), the only nationwide program that exclusively targets marijuana. The DCE/SP began funding eradication programs in Hawaii and California in 1979, and rapidly expanded to include programs in 25 states by 1982, and in all 50 states by 1985. In 2000, DEA continues to improve the effectiveness of its marijuana eradication efforts, spending $13 million to support the 96 state and local agencies that are now active DCE/SP participants. This funding allows the enhancement of already aggressive eradication enforcement activities. In 1999, the DCE/SP was responsible for the eradication of 3,413,083 cultivated outdoor plants and 208,027 indoor plants. In addition, the DEA secured 11,922 arrests and seized 3707 weapons and $26,911,262 in assets.

These DCE/SP successes can be directly attributed to the decision by participating agencies to share intelligence, technology, and manpower. These cooperative efforts have curbed the availability of domestically grown marijuana and have caused the outdoor cultivators to abandon larger outdoor plots for the safety and concealment of smaller, indoor cultivating areas. In addition, marijuana growers are now using sophisticated indoor growing techniques, such as computerized irrigation. Another technologically advanced technique employed by marijuana growers is hydroponic cultivation, which is the cultivation of plants in nutrient solution rather than soil. Hydroponic cultivation not only makes it easier for growers to clandestinely cultivate marijuana indoors, it also enables them to produce extremely potent marijuana.

Even though indoor cultivation is more difficult to detect, the DEA and cooperating agencies are adapting to this new challenge by employing equally advanced technologies to build effective cases against indoor violators. One such technique is thermal imaging, a process that identifies indoor marijuana grows by detecting the signature heat from lighting used to grow the plant.

Southwest Border Initiative

The Southwest Border Initiative (SWBI), in operation since 1994, is a cooperative effort by federal law enforcement agencies to combat the substantial threat posed by Mexico-based trafficking groups operating along the Southwest Border. These groups transport multi-ton shipments of heroin, methamphetamine, and marijuana. They are also hired by trafficking groups from Colombia to transport equally huge amounts of cocaine into the United States.

The SWBI attacks organizations by targeting the communication systems of their command and control centers. Working in concert, the DEA, the FBI, U.S. Customs Service, and U.S. Attorneys' offices around the country conduct wiretaps that ultimately identify all levels of the Mexico- or Colombia-based organizations. This strategy allows the DEA to track the seamless continuum of drug traffic as it gradually flows from Colombia or Mexico to the streets of the United States where it is distributed.

The initiative is anchored by the DEA's belief that the only way to successfully attack any organized crime syndicate is to build strong cases against its leadership and their command and control functions. With the assistance of foreign governments, the long-term incarceration of those in leadership positions typically leaves entire organizations in disarray and renders them unable to conduct business in the United States.

This initiative, along with bi-national task forces in Monterrey, Juarez, and Tijuana, has provided a solid base for effective law enforcement operations aimed at major international drug traffickers. Examples of the success of the SWBI can be found in several DEA operations. Specifically, Operation Zorro II, Operation Reciprocity, and Operation Limelight each relied extensively on numerous court-ordered wiretaps that were coordinated and monitored by law enforcement officers operating under the SWBI. Collectively, these three operations resulted in the arrest of 156 individuals and the seizure of over 22,000 kilograms of illegal drugs and $35 million. The SWBI has also helped to reduce corruption, violence, and alien smuggling associated with drug trafficking activities carried out along the border.

Operations Pipeline and Convoy

Beginning in the early 1980s, New Mexico state troopers grew suspicious following a sharp increase in the number of motor vehicle violations, particularly along Interstate-40, that resulted in drug seizures and arrests. Simultaneously, troopers in New Jersey began making similar seizures during highway stops along the Interstate-95 "drug corridor" from Florida to the Northeast. Troopers in New Mexico and New Jersey independently established their own highway drug-interdiction programs. Their drug and money seizures grew immediately.

Seizure and arrest increases signaled to law enforcement officers that the nation's highways had become major arteries for drug transportation. In addition, they found that tons of illicit drugs were flowing north and east from Florida and the nation's southwest border, while millions of dollars of drug profits returned south and west — as if traveling through a pipeline.

Over time, as seizures mounted, highway officers found that these drug couriers shared many characteristics, tendencies, and methods. Highway law enforcement officers began to ask key questions to help determine whether motorists they had stopped for traffic violations were carrying drugs. These interview techniques proved extremely effective. The road patrol officers also found it beneficial to share their observations and experiences in highway interdiction at conferences and other multi-agency gatherings.

The success of the highway interdiction programs in New Mexico and New Jersey eventually led to the creation of Operation Pipeline in 1984. Pipeline, a nationwide highway interdiction program that focuses on private motor vehicles, is one of the DEA's most effective operations and continues to provide essential cooperation between the DEA and state and local law enforcement agencies. The operation is composed of three elements: training, real-time communication, and analytic support.

Each year, state and local highway officers conduct dozens of training schools across the country, attended by other highway officers. These classes are intended to inform officers of interdiction laws and policies, to increase their knowledge of drug trafficking, and to sharpen their detection of highway couriers. Training classes focus on: (1) the law, policy, and ethics governing highway stops and drug prosecution, and (2) drug trafficking trends and key characteristics, or indicators, that are shared by drug traffickers. Also, through the El Paso Intelligence Center (EPIC), state and local agencies continue to share real-time information with other agencies and can immediately obtain the results of their record checks and receive detailed analysis of drug seizures to support their investigations.

Although Operation Pipeline relies in part on training officers to use certain characteristics to determine potential drug traffickers, the program does not advocate such profiling by race or ethnic background. The issue of suspect profiling has been reviewed extensively over the past decade in an effort to assure government officials that all the necessary precautions have been and will continue to be taken to ensure the fair, ethical, and impartial treatment of criminal suspects. Officers are trained to recognize a number of exceptional indicators that would lead law enforcement personnel to suspect criminal activity. During training, they are exposed to both the visual and audio indicators of deception and their potential links to criminal activity. Participants in this training learn concealment methods used by criminals based on prior interdiction efforts, and how particular indicators of deception have led officers to extend their roadside interviews during traffic stops.

In 1990, Operation Convoy, Pipeline's sister operation, was created to target drug transportation organizations that use commercial vehicles to traffic drugs. Operation Convoy conducts long-term surveillance undercover operations and other enforcement activities aimed at transportation organizations. Much of the investigative work conducted through Operation Convoy occurs at truck stops, cargo transshipment areas, and motels. In addition, Operation Convoy began training DEA special agents to drive large commercial motor vehicles during undercover investigations. The DEA also assists state agencies with investigations following seizures of commercial vehicles on the nation's highways.

Index

C

I

J

K

L

M

T

U

V

W

X

Z